T0157445

# DOUBLE DECEIT

Order this book online at www.trafford.com
or email orders@trafford.com

Most Trafford titles are also available at major online book retailers.

© Copyright 2013 Dr. Agnes Chambers-Glenn.
All rights reserved. No part of this publication may be reproduced, stored in a retrieval
system, or transmitted, in any form or by any means, electronic, mechanical, photocopying,
recording, or otherwise, without the written prior permission of the author.

Printed in the United States of America.

ISBN: 978-1-4669-9438-6 (sc)
ISBN: 978-1-4669-9437-9 (hc)
ISBN: 978-1-4669-9439-3 (e)

Library of Congress Control Number: 2013908812

*Trafford rev. 05/14/2013*

 www.trafford.com

**North America & international**
toll-free: 1 888 232 4444 (USA & Canada)
fax: 812 355 4082

*In Memory of Dr. Hassan Abdel-Hadi Mashaal*

# ACKNOWLEDGEMENTS

My gratitude goes to all the people that made this book possible. I am most grateful to the late Dr. Hassan Mashaal, my friend of twenty years, who asked me to write this book after giving me three binders containing nearly 400 pages of faxes, e-mails and notes recorded from telephone messages. It was his belief that others should not fall into the same trap that he had after receiving an e-mail from a desperate young lady living in Ghana.

# INTRODUCTION

## DR. HASSAN ABEL-HADI MASHAAL

In February 2012, a Canadian daily newspaper, the Globe and Mail, carried a short article saying that a person named Joshua Oyeniyi Aransiola, a sociologist at Obafemi Awolowo University in Ile-Ife, Nigeria, had prepared a profile of the so-called *Yahoo Boys*. After six months of infiltrating a group, Aransiola had gained their trust and was then able to form a profile after interviewing forty of them. This group was one of many Nigerian scam groups who attempt to out-smart one another. The article assumed that everyone has or will receive an e-mail from one of these clever deceitful persons.

The sender creates a story about the great amount of money he/she has inherited and the need to get it out of their country. All that is required is your bank account information. Having this will enable them to easily move their large sum of money to a bank account in a foreign country. Of course, you, the receiver of the e-mail, will receive a very large portion of the funds.

Aransiola's summary of their character included that these *Yahoo Boys* are usually undergraduates who are aware that what they are doing is not legal. To run their deceptive money-making business, they willingly pay bribes to the local police and to the organization whose mandate is to stop them from initiating their scam ideals.

The real-life story in this book is one of the many clever schemes devised by an African Yahoo group to outwit an elderly medical doctor of some of his life savings. This person was Dr. Hassan Abdel-Hadi Mashaal, a long-time retired medical doctor who worked most of his medical career with the World Health Organization out of Geneva, Switzerland. Having specialized in malaria and bilharzias within his tropical disease specialty, he was posted by WHO to tropical countries and to the Middle East during his near 50-year medical career which began in Alexandria, Egypt, in January 1950. Four pages of Dr. Mashaal's publications, his professional experience and contracts in retirement, are listed in author John L. Pellam's article, *500 Great Minds of the early 21*st *Century.* This article is found on http://www.epu-eg.com/ Biographies_by_HTML/Egyptian%20 Parasitologists%20Abroad/ Dr.%20 . . . . 09/11/2007

The reason for making reference to the 4-page Internet article was to reveal to the reader that those who get involved in money scams are often very intelligent people. As Dr. Mashaal's story proceeds in *Double Deceit,* he reveals to the reader his purpose for involvement and the good use that he intended for his share of the inheritance money to play. He is an example of the type of person these scammers love to engage with—elderly and trusting and one whom the scammer can easily convince with their trickery cat and mouse play.

*Double Deceit* is a story of trickery on the part of the Nigerian money scammers in Accra, Ghana, and deceitful play on the part of both parties involved—the Ghanaian scammers and the scammed elderly gentleman. It was a continuous frenzied attempt by the scammers to obtain money and later by the scammed doctor to attempt to recover that money. Dr. Mashaal used to often jokingly say in daily conversation *I want my money back!* Would he be able to do so from his involvement in this deceitful scam? The letter containing a fantastic offer of fortune that arrived by e-mail in April 2007 changed Dr. Mashaal's life forever. Not for richer, but for poorer, both in money and in health.

Following the story of the doctor's scam involvement is a section on a variety of scam types and examples from friends. These are mostly of Nigerian design but originated in a number of countries.

# CHAPTER 1

## Ms Linda Morgan & Dr Mashaal

*And why do you believe that you were the chosen one?* This was my response to Dr. Mashaal when he told me the story on July 4 about what he had eluded to in his e-mail of June 23. That message had arrived in my e-mail just prior to his leaving Europe for Canada having spent six months there. The major purpose of that e-mail was to ask me if I would phone his automobile insurance company and inform them of his arrival in Canada on July 2. I was to ask the company to re-instate his auto insurance commencing that day. However, it was the closing paragraph perhaps that his excitement showed through. It read: *An interesting story happened to me recently. No one will believe it. It is one of the extremely rare happening. I shall tell you details when I see you.* So I was left for a week to wonder what this unbelievable event could be. It sounded like this year's message would be much happier than last year's. The latter was about the accidental death of his 41-year old daughter, Monika.

On July 4, he came to my home for help to launch his newly purchased cordless mouse for his computer. Over a cup of coffee, he excitedly told me about *the extremely rare event* that was occurring in his life. I listened with amazement that anyone as intelligent as he could get caught in such a deceitful scam. After a moment of silence, I spoke up and gave him my response as I quoted above. Then, to his utter surprise, I suggested to him that this was a scam in which the other party was taking his money under false pretence with the excuse that the purpose was to pay for certain clearance certificates so he would gain much more money. His reply left me stunned! It appeared that my suggestion had not made any mark on him. He simply refused to believe me, showed annoyance at my suggestion of a scam, and repeated that these people were his friends ever since he had received Linda Morgan's first e-mail of April 24. In that, she had offered to transfer her family inheritance to him, US$10.5 million. He said that very recently Linda had inherited that money due to the tragic deaths of her parents and two sisters in an automobile accident in Africa. As she was expected to die soon, she wanted to transfer this money to him so he would do *good works;* that is, help the poor. And with that, he left my home.

Following is the *very urgent* letter that Dr. Mashaal received from Ms Linda Morgan in which she asked him to accept her inheritance and with it carry out good deeds to the poor in the world.

```
Subj:  VERY URGENT
Date:  4/24/2007 5:05:34 P.M. Pacific Daylight Time
From:  rosemkingw@excite.com
Reply-to:    lindamorgan200@yahoo.com

Dear Friend:

I apologize if the contents in this mail are contrary to
your moral ethics, which I feel may be of great disturbance
to your personal life, But please treat with absolute
secrecy and personal. I pray that this email reaches you in
the best of health.

I am Linda Morgan, I was hospitalize after I had a car
accident with my family, I lost my Father,Mother and my Two
Sisters who were also on board in the accident. After the
accident, I have been battling with some health problems
from the major injuries that I sustained in the cause of
accident. Recently, My doctor told me that I have some few
months to live due the surgery that was conducted, it was
discovered that I have a bone Cancer.

Though what disturbs is my inability to walk again, due to
the injuries that I sustained and damaged of my spinal cords
in the accident. Having known my condition, I decided to
transfer My father's fund to a reliable and trusted fellow
who can invest tyhis money in a profitable ventures.I want
to you use the money in all sincerity for its purpose. I
took this decision because I am the only surviving person
and nobody else that will inherit this money because they
are now dead. I don't want a situation whereby this deposit
will be confiscated and will be used in an Unholy manner by
the official of the finance company where it was deposited
```

by my later father. Hence the reasons for this bold
decision.

All I want you to do is to assist in safe-keep this fund
valued atUS$10.5 Million United States Dollars deposited at
the custody of the security firm before it gets confiscated
or declared unserviceable.I

seek your consent to present you as the Trustee/Foreign
Investor to my late father, so that the proceeds of
this account can be paid to you. I have all necessary
information, guidelines and document, all I require from
you is your honest co-operation to enable us see this
transaction through. Bit it is imminent I state to you
clearly now that this transaction should be executed through
normal proceedings. I guarantee that this will be executed
under an arrangement that will be highly protected by me
here. I hope to receive your positive response And your
co-operation in keeping this highly Confidential.

If your are interested in carrying out this task,iwant you
to contact me immediately, so that I can arrange all the
mordalities to effect the release of the fund to you. I know I
have never met you but my mind tells me to do this,and I hope
you act sincerely.I have also decided that 40% of this money
should be taken by you from the total sum upon the success
release of this fund,because I am now too weak and frigile to
do things myself because of my present health problems.

I have been given 21 working days by the finance company
for the collection of the deposited item before it will be
confiscated. I will appreciate your utmost confidentiality
in this matter until the task is accomplished,as I don't
want anything that will Jeopardize my last wish.Kindly reach
me on my alternative email:amazingrace4all@yahoo.com

for more information and explanation.

Kindly furnish me your full name and your telephone
number,so that I will prepare all relevant documents to
effect the release of the fund to you.

Yours Faithfully,

Linda Morgan

---

Join Excite! – http://www.excite.com
The most personalized portal on the Web!

NOTE: *Linda's message was NOT addressed to Dr. Mashaal.*

From e-mails that Dr. Mashaal turned over to me four months later, I became aware that his so-called *friendship* really began on May 8 when he opened Linda's *very urgent message* of April 24. Late that evening, he read Linda's fantastic offer and replied immediately. (See message below.) That was approximately two months before he told me of his pending good fortune. Note in the above message Linda had requested three times not to discuss her offer with anybody as *this must be kept with absolute secrecy and personal.*

```
Subj:  ref your e mail dated 24 April 2007
Date:  5/8/2007 11:58:11 P.M. Pacific Daylight Time
From:  Malara expert
To:    lindamorgan200@yahoo.com

Dear Linda Morgan

I was travelling and just returned.I read your letter today.
I am really very sad for this serious accident.Also it was
unfortunate your family died in such a sad accident.My
condolescence

I am working in different countries and I am helping many
projects to save life and control diseases.
The funds you wish to be transferred can be utelized in many
programs to help humanity but it should referred to your
name as the original supplier.

My name and address and Phone number etc. as follows

Dr.Hassan A.H.MASHAAL
United Nations WHO Malaria Experts Pen.
International Malaria Consultant
Address: 5A Brunearmel
         37431 Bad-Lautenberg.Harz
         Germany
Tel: (also fax)0049 5524 80907
E-mail:malaraexpert@aol.com
```

After reading Dr. Mashaal's reply to Linda's offer, probably you have formed some impressions. A believer? Very greedy? Naive? Very trusting? Or . . . ?

You will notice that Linda's reply shown below was dated May 14, but it made reference to *your e mail dated 24 April 2007*. This appears what might be the first indication that more than one African person was handling this money transaction. Some people used all capitals while others used mostly small letters, even for the pronoun *I*. You can observe from the e-mail above that the date was that of the first offer to the doctor from Linda, not his letter of acceptance which was sent on May 8. For something as urgent as Linda had stated, her reply was not returned until six days later. Perhaps it took the Ghanaian group near a week to get organized after receiving the doctor's positive reply.

In studying Linda's offer, it appears that Dr. Mashaal had misinterpreted her kind offer as his share to be $10.5 million. However, you will see that she actually offered him 40% of the total sum after the money had been successfully transferred to a safe country. Dr. Mashaal never mentioned the amount four million two hundred thousand US dollars ($4,200 thousand US). Once he did speak of 40% but otherwise he always spoke of the total amount, $10.5 million. After explaining her condition, Linda mentioned that she was *the only surviving person and nobody else that will inherit this money because they are now dead.*

Below is Linda Morgan's thankyou to Dr. Mashaal for agreeing to accept her inheritance—to be her beneficiary—and to dispose of the money as per her wishes.

```
Subj:  ref your e mail dated 24 April 2007
Date:  5/14/2007 2:41:50 P.M. Pacific Daylight Time
From:  lindamorgan200@yahoo.com
To:    malaraexpert@aol.com
```

```
DEAR SIR,
IT'S MY PLEASUER TO RECEIVE YOUR MAIL. I AM VERY GRATEFUL
AFTER GOING THROUGH YOU RE FOR ASSISTANCE TO SECURE THE
RELEASE OF THE FUND TO YOU AS THE BENEFIIARY, TRUSTEE
FOREIGN PARTNER. AND I PRAY YOU WILL BE GRANTED THE GRACE
AND WISDOM TO COMPLET THIS. I FULLY KNOW THAT YOU WILL
BE SURPRISED RECEIVING MY MAIL, SINCE WE HAVE NOT MET
EACHOTHER, "WHY ME"? YOU MIGHT HAVE BEING ASKING YOURSELF.
I WANT YOU TO KNOW THAT GOD WORKS IN A MIRACULOUS WAY
AND YOU MAY JUST FOUND OUT HOW CONTACT YOU. PLEASE KNOW
THAT THIS MAIL WAS MEANT FOR YOU, SINCE THE DEATH OF MY
PARENTSLIFE HAS TURNED AROUND, I CANT SAY TO THE WORSE, BUT
I HAVE TO THANK GOD FOR SPEARING ME FOR THIS MOMENT THAT
I AM WRITING TO YOU. BEFORE THE DEATH OF MY FATHER,WE HAD
```

TRAVEL TO GHANA BECAUSE OF DIAMON,BEFORE THE ACCIDENT THAT
KILLED MY PARENT AND 2 SISTRS,BEING THE FIRST CHILD I WAS
INFORMED AND WAS GIVEN ALL THE NECESSARY DOCUMENTS THAT
WAS ISSUED TO MY FATHER WHEN MADE. SINCE AFTER THE DEATH
OF MY FATHER, I HAVE BEING HAVING PROBLEM WITH OTHERS AND
ARE FIGHT WITH TOOTH AND JAIL TO INHERIT MY FATHER'S WEALTH
FOR THEIR PRESONAL BENEFIT. I HAVE DECIDED TO CONTACT YOU
IN FAR AWAY COUNTRY, BECAUSE I HAVE A STRONG CONVICTION
AND HELPING PEOPLE I HAVE NEVER KNOWN OR WILL EVER MEET IN
THIS LIFE GIVES ME GREAT HAPPINESS. SO I WANT YOU TO ACCEPT
THIS TASK AND HELP ME AND IF YOU HAVE GREATER GRACE YOU CAN
REACT. LIKE I HAVE REACHED OU TO YOU. AS REGARDS THE FUN,
IT IS DEPOSITED WITH A BANK, DUE TO MY STATE OF MY PRESENT
PROGNOSIS I HAVE INFORMED AN ATTORNEY IN GHANA, WHO HAS
INDICATED HIS WILLING/INTEREST TO ASSIST ME. I MIGHT NOT BE
ABLE TO BE RUNNING ROUND, GOING FROM THE COURT TO THE OFFICE
OF THE SAVINGS BANK WHO HAVE CONTACTED AN ATTORNEYHERE, HE
WILL BE WORKING WITH YOU, HANDLING ALL LEGAL ASP OF THE
FUND, TIL THE FUND GETS TO YOU.
I DECIDED TO TRANSFER MY LATE FATHER'S FUND TO A MORE
RELIAABLE FOREIGN PARTNER TO BE USED WELL. I MUST LET YOU
KNOW THAT THIS TRANSACTION IS FREE FROM ALL
RISK AS I HAVE SUBMITTED ALL THE NECESSARY DOCUMENTS TO
HIM.I HAVE ALSO TOLD HIM ABOUT YOUR WILLINGNESS TO ASSIST
ME, HE WILL GIVE YOUALL THE DETAILS ON WHAT IS TO BE DONE
AND FINALIZED ALL THE ARRANGEMENTS WITH THE SECURITY COMPANY
FOR THE RELEASE OF THE FUND TO YOU AFTER REACHING A WORKABLE
AGREEMENT WITH YOU.
I HAVE DECIDED TO GIVE YOU 40% OF THE TOTAL SUM FOR YOUR
ASSISTANCE AND AS WELL CHOOSE TO GO INTO A PARTNERSHIP FOR
THE PROPER INVESTMENT OF THE MONEY IN YOUR COUNTRY. PLEASE,
I WANT YOU TO KINDLY WORK HAND IN HAND WITH HIM, SO THAT HE
CAN GIVE YOU FUTTHER DETAILS AS WELL AS GUIDE YOU TO THE
FUND,BECAUSE HE PROMISED ME THAT HE WILL NOT TAKE A DINE
FROM ME,UNTIL THE SECURITY COMPANY HAS RELEASED THE MONEY
TO YOU BEING THE BENEFICIARY/TRUSTEE. ALSO I WILL LIKE YOU
TO KEEP THIS PROJECT AS CONFIDENTIAL AS POSSIBLE,BECAUSE OF
FATHER'S FAMILY MEMBERS ARE WAITING FOR ME TO DIE SO THAT
THEY CAN INHERIT MY FATHER'S WEALTH.
ALL THIS IS BECAUSE I DON'T' HAVE ANY BODY WHO CAN CLAIM
THIS FUND. MY ATTORNEY WILL BE SENDING YOU THE LEGAL
DOCUMENT OF THE FUND AS SOON AS POSSIBLE.
THANKS AND REMEMBER ME IN YOUR PRAYERS.
GOD BLESS YOU,
LINDA MORGAN

Although Mashaal had already supplied Linda Morgan with his
name, address and telephone and fax number in his first reply on May

8, as per her request, he repeated these and added his Swiss bank name and account number in his message of May 15. This information should ensure that the $10.5 million that he believed he was to inherit would be transferred to Switzerland soon. He also told her that he did not require this money for personal use as he has *a very high income from United Nations.* However, he would welcome the money so he could *help many organizations and people in other countries.*

In his reply, he offered Linda a cancer cure that he truly believed in. She had mentioned in her first communication that bone cancer had been discovered during surgery she underwent due to the automobile accident. That is the accident in which she had lost her parents and two sisters. In addition, he offered to send her a copy of a book that he had recently published.

```
Subj:  ref e mail 14 May 2007
Date:  5/15/2007 9:10:27 Pacific Daylight Time
From:  Malara expert
To:    lindamorgan200@yahoo.com
```

Dear Linda Morgan

Many thanks for your E mail letter.It is nice to hear from you Today I wish to present few subjects. These are:

1-TREATMENT OF CANCER
    From your first letter I undersood youhad bone cancer.Of course, many medical dotors all over the world they learned no final treatment (radical treatment).It is interesting a private organization in USA treate almost 100% cancer. My sister in law had very advvancd ovarian cancer.The specialists gave her about 6 months to live after X ray treatment drug treatment.She shawed the highly specialists the treatment of cancer by the organization in USA.All of them said this is noneense.However on my advise my sister in law applied the the treatment of this organization for three months.She was completely cured.Since 5 years she is in perfect health.All her collegues who were not so advanced like her were dead.

I sincerely advice you to get contact by your medical doctor to this organization and asked their advice and radical treatment Their detail address as follows
    S.R.BURZYNSKI
    ADAM COLLUNSKI
9432 OLD KATY TOAD,SUITE 200.HOUSTON,TEXAS 77055

Dr. Agnes Chambers-Glenn

(713)335-5601. FAX (713)335-5699
e-mail:golunski@burzynskiclinic.com
Website :http://www.cancermed.com

Please take action.You can be cured from cancer.Many top
specilists will not accept there is treatment of cancer but
it is true.You can live long

2-YOUR ADVISE 40% FOR ME
I have very high income from United Nations,It is far than
my requirements.That is why I am helping many families
No need to have additional money for me
All the money you will transfer will be utelizd for helping
many organizations and people in many countries.

3-RECENT BOOK I PUBLISHED
I published many technical books but recently I published
a book on countries I visited and many actual stories.The
first chapter detail of my life.The second book is under
printing,will be soon available
I can post to you the available first book.Pleae give me
your postal address to send the book

4-TRANSFER OF FUNDS
In future the safest way to transfer funds to me,the best
and safest to transfer to my US $ account in my Swiss Bank.
It is very safe & best
The address as follows:
          Name : Dr.Hassan A.H.MASHAAL
          Account No. (deleted by author)
          Bank : UBS AG
                 Chemin Louis Dunant 17
                 Box 2800
                 CH-1211 Geneve 2
                 Switzerland

Many thanks and best wishes

Dr.H.A.H.MASHAAL
5A Brunearmel
37431 Bad-Lauterberg- Harz
GERMANY

In the above reply, Mashaal did address the 40% of the funds for
his portion. However, after this he continually spoke of being the
beneficiary of $10.5 million.

# CHAPTER 2

## BARRISTER ADAMS SMITH

On May 16, there were two e-mails that were confusing. First, Dr. Mashaal e-mailed Barrister Adams Smith as Linda Morgan had asked him to do and supplied an extensive list of information wanting to hurry the transfer of the funds to him. Included were his name and a Swiss bank account number and the address where the money should be sent. Still later that day, the doctor received a message from Barrister Smith. His message appeared more like a reply to Linda's message that was e-mailed on May 14. In this message, Lawyer Smith introduced himself then asked for the same information that Dr. Mashaal had already sent to Linda. There appeared to be a mix-up here but Dr. Mashaal seemed not to have noticed the timing of events—answers to before requests from some of the parties involved. Smith thanked the doctor for being willing to take part in receiving and disposing of the US$10.5 million. In addition to the request for the bank information, Smith also wanted a copy of Mashaal's passport or driver's licence and his direct telephone number where he could be reached. Smith gave his private phone number and asked for a phone call as soon as this e-mail was received, and he said that he awaited the doctor's *urgent reply*. Dr. Mashaal told me later that he and Smith had established an excellent rapport and that he truly trusted him to act honestly on his behalf.

Dr. Agnes Chambers-Glenn

Subj:  Re: Hallo
Date:  5/16/2007 10:38:23 A.M. Pcific Daylight Time
From:  associate_lawfirm@yahoo.com
To:    malaraexpert@aol.com

Dear Sir,
     Many thanks for your email. I I have also received
instruction from her to represent her interest in release
and transfer of cash assets totalling US$10,500, 000.00
(TEN MILLION FIVE HUNDRED THOUSAND UNITED STATE DOLLARS)
deposited in a bank.

I wish to bring to your notice that I received an
instruction and re-commendation from my client Ms.Linda
Morgan about your willingness to assist her in lodging the
sum of US$10.5million that was deposited in a custody of
Gold Coast Security company which later was transfered to
the International Commercial Bank of Ghana.
On this note, I want to re-assure you that since you
have indicated your interest to act as the trustee of
the fund. You will never be regret involving yourself as
all n=modalities had been concluded with all the parties
involved to effect the transfer of the fund into your
nominated account in your country. Upon the successful
transfer of this fund into your account, I would need your
assurance that you shall assist with the procurement of all
traveling documents for my client,so that she can meet you
in your country for the sharing and onward investment of the
fun.

Again. Please provide me with the following bank details:
BANK NAME
BANK ADDRESS
SWIFT CODE
ACCOUNT HOLDER'S NAME
ACCOUNT HOLDER'S ADDRESS
ACCOUNT NUMBER

COPY OF YOUR INT PASSPORT OR DRIVER LICENSE
DIRECT TEL NUMBER

With the above details I can file for an application
claiming your name being the foreign partner,beneficiary and
trustee of the fund.
I have contracted the finance about our readiness to claim
the fund before the end of this month. I shall be working
with you to procure all the necessary documents as I stated
earlier until the transfer has being completed. I will
require the following details from you to enable me begin

```
with the process and submit an application to the finance
house for the release of the fund to you being the new
beneficiary.

Upon receipt of these details, all the relevant documents
will be sent to you for your perusal and Kindly do the
necessary things on your side to se to the actualization
of this God's given project. You are therefore required to
keep this transaction of utmost secrecy and condidentila, I
don't want you to be distracted by anybody in the cause of
actalizing this project.
Kindly call me on 00233 243 243 493 upon the receipt of my
mail.
I await your urgent reply.
Best Regards
Barr.Adams Smith
```

Notice in the second paragraph of the above letter that Barrister Smith said that he needed Mashaal's assistance in securing travel documents for his client, Ms Morgan, so she could meet him in his country. Would a terminally ill patient travel such a long distance as from Ghana to Germany or Switzerland? In that same paragraph Smith also said that Mashaal would never regret involving yourself. What an ironic statement Mashaal would later learn! Near the end of the e-mail, Dr. Mashaal was asked to *keep this transaction at utmost secrecy and confidential.* You will recall that Linda Morgan had requested the same in her response to Mashaal when he accepted her offer. Why would one keep such good news a secret? This large windfall was like winning a lottery. Also notice that Smith referred to Linda as Mashaal's client. Does that make sense?

Dr. Mashaal's reply to Linda Morgan's message is shown below. A copy was sent to Lawyer Smith's law firm as well. There is possibly an error in reference to the date of May 18 which is actually the day this e-mail was sent. Dr. Mashaal must have noticed the discrepancy in the date as he pencilled on the message the date that he actually received it. The doctor gave Linda Morgan the opportunity to learn of additional documents that Lawyer Smith had requested and of which he had spoken to his Swiss banker. Small observation here but it appeared that Mashaal had missed the 's' on Adams' name and he continued to call him Adam as did most of the other people in this drama from this point on. Also, it seemed that it was not important now to the Ghanaian crooks the fact that Mashaal had been assigned personally 40% of the total inheritance, as no further mention appeared from now on in any correspondence. He continued to speak about receiving $10.5 million and it appeared that most probably the opponents were willing to go along with him so as to keep him in their game of providing a source of income for them.

Next day, Dr. Mashaal sent to Smith the message below in which he offered his sincere hope that Linda would live through the operation, and then he suggested strategy to have the money transferred to his Swiss account. If the money was not transferred he would consider that *the administration is not correct*. This statement could indicate that the doctor was having some doubts of the authenticity of his fantastic inheritance. It seemed that Dr. Mashaal had learned, probably through telephone conversations with Adams Smith, that Linda Morgan was about to have an operation, as I was unable to find any previous e-mails in which any further operation was mentioned. As to his statement about an *incorrect administration*, this was probably due to the Swiss bank's employee of not wanting to get involved in his client's (Dr. Mashaal) fantastic inheritance transfer. Much later—in early September—Dr. Mashaal mentioned to me his Swiss bank's unwillingness to transfer any money for him to Ghana. In the message that follows, Mashaal also offered a strategy that would work for him, and he hoped Smith would accept it as he said he did not have the $8,400 at that time but would send it to Smith immediately after some money arrived from Ghana.

```
Subj:  ref your e mail dated 18 May 2007
Date:  5/16/2007 7:17:45 P.M. Pcific Daylight Time
From:  malaraexpert@aol.com
To:    lindamorgan200@yahoo.com
CC:    associate lawfirm@yahoo.com

Dear Linda Morgan

Many thanks for your E mail dated 18 May 2007
I gave to your excellent Lawyer Mr. Barrister Adam Smith
all the information he requested. Also I asked the Director
of my Swiss Bank to contact him by phone .The bank requires
```

certain documents before transfer.. Mr Adam Smith informed
me that these documents are the following
-MONEY LAUNDERING CERTIFICATE
-ANTI-TERRORIST CERTIFICATE
-DRUG FREE CERTIFICATE
-INSRANCE BOND CERTIFICATE

Mr.Adam Smith informed me to obtain these certificate It
will take about a week and cost not less than $ 8400 I feel
Mr Adam Smith is very good lawyer and very honest.He will do
his best to obtain the above certificaes as early as possible
and provide them to my Swiss Bank.Once this is doen he has no
prlblem to transthe money Swiss Band is highly efficient and
highly reliable.I am dealing with them all my life.

I wish you treat your cancer as I wrote to you details about
organization who really can treat cancer very efficiently.
This will help you greatly

Many thanks and best wishes

Dr.Hassan A.H.Mashaal
International Malaria Consultant

It appeared that Smith responded to the message that was copied
to him from Mashaal's message to Linda. Below is an additional
message that the doctor sent to Lawyer Smith a few days after
that cc'd one arrived. With a mix up in dates, the sequence of their
receiving was difficult to determine. Sometimes it was difficult to
determine order also as prior to passing all the correspondence on to
me, Mashaal had often not printed the date on the e-mail or he had
cut it off for his filing convenience.

Dear Mr.Smith

Many thanks for your E mail dated 18 May 2007 received today
I hope sincerely as well as I pray to save Linda Morgan and
to have successful operation.

As you said before the cost of the Certificates not less
than $ 8400 You kindly Ask Linda to pay this sum from the
10+ Millions Dollar in the bank

Regarding myself my money in the Swiss Bank in Geneve is
under investment.I cannot release it unless I made a request
which my require several months to release the sum required.

```
I understand if you request Linda or even you have the
authority to obtain the sum from the bank which has over
10 Million Dollar.If this is not done ,then I consider the
administration is not correct.

Other solution you get loan 8400 $ and as soon the money is
transferred to my account in Geneve Iwill request this to be
transferred to you

Thank you

Dr.Hassan A.H.Mashaal
International Malaria Consultant (UN-WHO)
```

Just at the time when negotiations were progressing well, very sad news arrived from Smith later in the day. He informed Mashaal that Linda had *KICK THE BUCKET' means DEAD*. It appeared that his prayer put her soul at peace and then on with the business! Smith continuously referred to Linda as *he* in this message. Mashaal needed Linda to help move the funds out of Ghana and now she was no longer living to give him that assistance. Smith even mentioned here that Y*ou also cannot have access to the funds except he arrive at your bank*. Mashaal should have read this message more carefully as it would seem that he would not be able to have these funds since Linda died before they were transferred to his bank in Switzerland. Perhaps, had he not kept this all a secret as advised by the Ghanaian gang but had shared his good fortune with somebody who might interpret for him the information more accurately, he would have dropped out of this extortion scheme at this point—before getting involved in sending money. As English was not Dr. Mashaal's first language, he really should have had assistance in interpreting these messages. However, he had his sights on the large inheritance and as such, business must go on. It seemed that Smith must have been in touch via telephone with Nicholas, an employee at the bank in Switzerland, and he had received instructions as to what was required to transfer the funds out of Ghana and to Dr. Mashaal's Swiss account. Lawyer Smith indicated that Linda's death had created a big problem in getting access to her inheritance and having the funds transferred to the Swiss bank. What would most people think of Barrister Smith announcing the death of a client in the manner he did? Perhaps Smith's announcement would be culturally acceptable in Ghana.

```
Subj:  SAD NEWS
Date:  5/19/2007 10:32:26 A.M. Pacific Daylight Time
From:  associate_lawfirm@yahoo.com
To:    Malaraexpert@aol.com
```

Dear Sir,
    Doctor just confirm to me that Linda has 'KICK THE BUCKET' means DEAD.
Infact this is terrible news because I still spoke to her yesterday night but I pray that her soul rest in perfect peace. Sir, regarding the document fees, Absolutely there is no way that I can take a penny from the account unless the late lady authorise the bank , the account does not belongs to me, I also talk to the bank manager to see if there is anything that could be done for me to have access to the funds but he reply that there is rukles and regulation within the banking system unless if am the next of kin and in the opening account form that the late linda fill, there is not next of kin except the letter that he wrote to the bank that he want the funds to be transfer to his partner account in swiss which is you , so this means you also cannot have access to the funds except he arrive at your bank.
Now, I want you to show your exceeding kindness for the late lady wishes to become true. You have toassist in anyway . I only want to know if you can be able to assist with partofthe $8400 then I will also be looking for way to get the remaining balance, we got to do this together , I know that apart from investment funds in swiss account kyou can still manover to assist with part of the document fees, is for the benefit of both of us because if your banker did not askmeto get the document I would have instruct the bank towire the funds but it will be difficult for Nicolas to credit according to him via our telephone conversation and I follow his advice that I should get the doiument as soon as possible.
I await your positive reply.
God bless you
REGARDS,
SMITH

Later that day, Mashaal replied to Smith offering his condolences in the death of *Lady Linda Morgan*. Notice that both men have given her the title of *Lady*. Mashaal's message continued with him suggesting a strategy for getting that money from the bank in Ghana to his bank in Switzerland, but first he must confer on Monday with his Swiss bank. If it refused to get involved in this money transfer, he would then send Smith the details of his German bank as that bank did not require documents like the Swiss bank did, he had previously mentioned.

That evening, Lawyer Smith sent a reply to Mashaal's earlier message of that day. He insisted that the doctor *must* acquire the correct documents and the cost was $8,400. (Note that all money involved in the transfer of the funds to Dr. Mashaal is in US funds.) Smith gave the reason that all funds would be transferred to the Swiss bank through *CITI BANK NEW YORK* from the bank in Ghana; and as the documents were necessary, Mashaal must pay for those documents. He continued telling Mashaal that the Swiss bank employee, Nicholas, and the manager at the International Commercial Bank, Accra, Ghana, insisted that all documents covering the movement of the funds were necessary because the US authority, without proof, might seize the money. Smith indicated that he had spoken not to one but to two Swiss bank employees. So there was pressure on Mashaal to come up with $8,400 if he expected to receive Linda Morgan's inheritance transferred to his European bank account. See the following message from Smith to Mashaal. But wait a minute! Those funds could not be transferred without Linda travelling to Switzerland to the bank he had been told earlier by Smith. Now Linda Morgan was dead, but did that make any difference? There is another *but* here. Did Dr. Mashaal ever have authority to give her an invitation letter for her to apply for a visa to visit Switzerland? He was neither a citizen nor a resident of Switzerland. To my knowledge he claimed part-time residency in Germany and the other part-time in Canada with several visits to other countries. Do you suppose he ever considered the fact of how he would procure an invitation letter for Linda to visit Switzerland?

```
Subj:  Re: ref e mail 19 May 2007
Date:  5/19/2007 1:05:44 P.M. Pacific Daylight Time
From:  associate_lawfirm@yahoo.com
To:    Malaraexpert@aol.com
```

Dear Sir,
    Already the bank is aware that the late lady has authorize them to transfer the said sum to your swiss

account but Nicolas made me to understand that without those document even thought you ask them to receive the funds in your account in swiss, they still have difficulty in crediting the funds in your account in swiss ,the bank manager here also stated the same issue that I should ensure that all document covering the funds are intact because their correspondence bank is CITIBANK NEW YOR and the funds has to pass through them before arriving in your account in swiss so they are afraid that the funds may be seize by US authority if no proof of funds paper is presented to them as well as other mention documents.

Sir, I guess you work at UN and you should be able to understand the fact that to transfer huge money out of Africa with getting proper documentation covering it may result in questioning the receiver on how he/she acquire the huge funds, you can check the patriot act attach to this email which the bank gave to me.

Even though you gave me your German account the same process must be done as confirm to me via phone by the bank manager of INTERNATIONAL COMMERCIAL BANK ,ACCRA-GHANA ,where the funds is been kept for safe-keeping.

Sir,am trying to ensure that the funds is safe and secure so the only argument is the document fees,I ask you again to let me know how much you can be able to assist from the total document fees than for us to go ahead and act as immature which may result in losing the funds.

I need your reply on the document fees on how best you can assist.
WE ARE BOTH GOING TO BENEFIT FROM IT BY USING THE FUNDS TO HELP THE POOR CHILDREN IN THE WORLD.
Regards,
SMITH

Still on May 19, Dr. Mashaal faxed the following letter to Nicholas, the employee at the Swiss bank who tended to his banking business. In it, he informed Nicholas of Linda Morgan's death and asked if it were possible to transfer the $10.5 million dollars to his bank. He inquired if the bank could hold the money until the documents were procured. You will see that he suggested that it would take about one week to obtain the documents before the money could be released for transfer to his Swiss account. He expressed his sorrow if he were to lose the money due to the Swiss

Dr. Agnes Chambers-Glenn

bank's lack of cooperation in assisting him. At the same time, he gave his appreciation in advance for help by the bank for assisting in solving this problem.

```
19.5.2007

Mr. (name omitted by author)
Assistant Director
USB AG.CHEMIN Louis Dunant 17
Box 2600 CH.11211 Geneve 2
Switzerland

Dear Mr. (name omitted by author)

Lady Linda Morgan already asked her bank to transfer the 10+
Million US Dollars to my account in your bank

You requested the lawyer Mr Smith to obtain:
        -MONEY LAUNDERING CERTIFICATE
        -ANTI-TERRORIST CERTIVATE
        -DRUG FREE CERTIFICATE
        -INSRURANCE BOND CERTIFICATE

The lawyer Mr Smith said these documents can be obtained but
at a cost of US$ 8400

Today the lady Linda Morgan died during a surgical operation
She died before authorize the bank to give Mr. Smith $8400
The lawyer informed me he has not that money.

Is it possible to ask the lawyer to transfer the 10+ million
dollar to your bank and kept suspended but to send from them
to the lawyer $ 8400 to get the above necessaey document
within a week time.Once you get the document ,then the money
can be deposited in my account.If not get the documents of
course can return back the money to its origin.But I am sure
you will get the douments in case $8400 are received by the
lawyer.

In case you cannot help and did this request I shall loose
the 10+Million dollars

I deeply appreciate to solve this problem

Yours sincerely
Dr.H.A.H.Mashaal
```

# CHAPTER 3

## ADAMS SMITH & DR MRS VIVIAN KAMARA

From the African side, there was often much confusion in date coordination of received e-mails and replies. Sometimes messages made one believe that perhaps there were a few people tending to the matter of extracting money from Dr. Mashaal as it appeared often that they were crossing up each other's messages. This appeared to be the problem on May 21 and May 22 with the exchanged e-mails and faxes. An e-mail sent to Vivian Kamara from Mashaal included the details of the European location where he wanted the money to be sent. On May 21, there was also a message—most probably a fax—sent from the Law Firm of Adams Smith and Associates.

**ADAMS SMITH AND ASSOCIATES LAW FIRM**
Barristers, Solicitors, Attorneys & Legal practitioners
C299/7 New Town Drive, New Town, Accra-Ghana.
Telefax: 00233-21-2382960     Mobile: 00233-243-243 493     Email: adam-smith@lawyer.com
: associate_lawfirm@yahoo.com

Our Ref: ASALM/COO-669/91     Your Ref...     Date: 21ˢᵗ May 2007

PROFILE:
Education:
LL.B., University of Ghana, Legon; Masters of Law degree from Temple School of Law, Philadelphia, PA.
Affiliations:
Member of the Ghana Bar Association.

...perience:
Mr. ADAM SMITH is a principal in the Proxy Chambers and Law Consultancy. He has conducted several financial seminars in collaboration with Databank Financial Services Limited, an investment brokerage firm on such topics as stock exchange listing, venture capital, finance leasing and portfolio management. Also served as co-legal counsel when the first Government of Ghana-owned bank, Social Security Bank, was privatized and its shares listed on the Ghana Stock Exchange. Recently appointed by UNIDO Ghana to advise on the implications of GATT for developing economies in the West Africa Sub-Region. Serves as a director on the Board of Social Security Bank Limited. A few of the firm's clients ...lude Societe Générale, Paris; Union Bank of Switzerland; United Nations Development Program, Ghana; UNIDO, Ghana; Ghana Australia Goldfields Limited; and Ghana National Petroleum Corporation. Areas of practice include corporate law, tax law, corporate finance and securities, conflict resolution, human resources and construction

In this message, Smith flaunted his curriculum vitae. Surely nothing could go wrong in this money transfer with a person of such sterling credentials handling the transaction! It does appear that a second page is missing as it appears incomplete with no closing.

This message was confusing because up to May 21, at 11 a.m. there had been no reference to a Vivian Kamara. However, there was an e-mail sent to her from Dr. Mashaal giving her his Swiss bank information and asking her for the necessary documents and the costs involved. He copied the same person with a different e-mail address likely to ensure delivery. There is no indication from where Mashaal got Vivian Kamara's name. Perhaps some e-mails had gone missing from time to time or this may have been dealt with in telephone contacts between Smith and Mashaal. With mixed up information and perhaps even missing information, one wonders why Dr. Mashaal did not catch on that this was a scam. If more than one African person was handling his case, there was likely to be a problem with mixing messages and possibly missing information.

In his message below, Mashaal addresses Vivian as *Mr.* He was determined to receive that money, so by this time he had contacted the bank directly and set aside his once trusted lawyer Smith and would now deal directly with Vivian at the bank.

```
Subj:  Late Linda Morgan
Date:  5/21/2007 11:01:09 A.M. Pacific Daylight Time
From:  Malara expert
To:    Vivian@ttbg.zzn.com
CC:    vkamara77@yahoo.com

Dear Mr Vivian Kamara

Late outstanding lady Linda Morgan selected me as United
Nation World Health Organization Expert to inherit her 10.5
million dollars to be utilizad to assist and help very poor
children in the World.She asked your bankto transfer the sum
to my account in Swiss Bank

    Account Dr. Hassan A.H.Mashaal
    Account No (deleted)
    Bank UBS AG
Address Bank Chemin Louis Dunant 17
         Box 2600
         CH-1211 Geneve 2
      Fax of Bank 0041 22 918 2660
Bank Ass Director who deals with my account
```

```
(name deleted)
There are some formalities required to transfer this sum Can
you please advise me Can the bank complete these formalities
and at what cost The cost may be taken from the deposited
money. Do you wish The Ass Director of the Swiss bank to
contact you ?

It is appreciated your early answer
Thank you for your assistance
Dr. Hassan A.H.Mashaal
International Malaria Consultant
Un-World Health Organization (Pen)
```

Dr. Mashaal on the following day received a fax—with an incorrect spelling of his name—from Dr. Ms Vivian Kamara, Management, the Foreign Remittance Department, The Trust Bank (ttb) in Accra, Ghana.

---

**TTB** *THE TRUST BANK*

Tema Business Centre
Hospital Road Com. 11 Junction
P.O. Box 1882, Accra

### FOREIGN REMITTANCE DEPARTMENT

22ND MAY 2007

Attn: Dr. Hassan AH Mashal

We acknowledge the receipt of your small message, However, we will like to you inform you that your late partner Mrs Linda Morgan has only authorized the management to wire her fund at Non Operation account No;0051 1699-23380-1187 to your nominated bank account at UBS (AG),Geneve 2 .Switzerland.

Hence, she was preparing on how to make change of ownership to your name before the death took her away, Therefore ,the funds is not on your name but since we have her authorization before death that the funds should be wire to you, this could easily be done but there is no way that will or any means be deducted from the said funds unless the late bearer has approved it. In which non of such has be applied in her file.

We are at your service to wire the funds to your nominated bank account as soon as you have all the legalization document covering the funds to avoid seizure or calling back of the funds.

We shall send copy of her deposit certificate for your perusal.

Thanks for your anticipated co-operation

Kindest Regards

Dr. Mrs Vivian Kamara
Manager

---

In the fax, she acknowledged having received an e-mail from him (a copy not given to me) and assured him that the $8,400 could not be withheld from the $10.5 million in order to release the funds to his bank in Switzerland. She insisted that her bank must have all the requested documents and she would procure them with the sum mentioned above. Page two of the fax was a copy of the proof of deposit of $10.5 million by Mrs. Linda Morgan of Freetown, Sierra Leone, deposited into The Trust Bank in Accra, Ghana. (*Mrs.* Linda who died as a result of cancer, an operation or in the auto accident that killed her parents and two sisters was a young single lady, not Mrs.)

The following fax from Kamara was to be proof of the deposit by Ms Linda Morgan.

Next day, Dr. Mashaal sent a message to Mr. Adams Smith with a cc to Smith's law firm. He sung praise for Smith's honesty and asked him to secure the necessary documents so the inheritance could be transferred to his (Mashaal's) Swiss bank account. This change in heart in reinstating Smith was only a few days after dismissing him as his trusted lawyer. Mashaal offered to send $5,000 and asked Smith to pay the balance which would be $3,400. He promised to return Smith's money *plus $10,000 as a reward for his honesty and efficiency* as soon as he received money from Ghana. See the following e-mail.

```
Subj:  ref your e-mail dated 22 May 2007
Date:  5/22/2007 &:58:32 A.M. Pacific Daylight Time
From:  Malaria expert
To:    adam-smith@lawyer.com
CC:    associate_lawfirm@yahoo.com

Dear Mr Adams Smith

I received your E mail and fax from the bank
I realized that you are honest lawyer and late honourable
Linda Morgan trusted you I completely trust you and request
you to obtain
        -MONEY LAUNDERING CERTIFICATE
        -ANTI-TERRORIST CERTIFICATE
        -DRUG FREE CERTIFICATE
        -INSRANCE BOND CERTIFICATE

I can transfer to you US$5000.Give me details for the
transfer The balance you manage to pay
As soon as the transfer took place to my account.I shall send
to the balance paid by you for the certifcates Plus $ 10000
as a reward for your honesty and efficiency

Kindly answer in detail. Thank you

Dr.Hassan A.H.Mashaal
UN-World Health Organization Specialist (Pen)
```

Also on May 22, Mashaal received a fax from Vivian at The Trust Bank acknowledging she was in receipt of his e-mail. However, there was a problem. Since Linda Morgan was dead, Vivian would be unable to authorize the transfer of the funds to the Swiss bank, so another complication had been placed on Mashaal receiving the inheritance that Linda intended for him. This was another time that one would have thought that Dr. Mashaal would have called a halt to this deceitful game. However, he did not. Perhaps, he believed that if he sent a little money, he would receive a lot!

Next day, Lawyer Smith sent a message to Mashaal and thanked him for his confidence in him and said he wished that the funds could be transferred by Western Union as a bank transfer takes from three to five days whereas the former method *is the easiest and the fastest*. He advised that the funds be sent that day and he included the names and addresses of two contacts. He said that these two persons were his *secretary*. He stressed the need for speed so he could get this process of transfer started as early as possible, and he solicited Dr. Mashaal's thoughts or ideas. The message follows. Why would Smith ask for the money to purchase the transfer documents be sent to people with addresses not that of his law office?

```
Subj:  Re: ref your e mail dated 22 May 2007
Date:  5/23/2007 6:35:47 A.M. Pacific Daylight Time
From:  associate_lawfirm@yahoo.com
To:    Malarexpert@aol.com

Dear Sir,
     Thanks for your confidence in me.However I whsh the
funds could be transfer via WESTERN UNION MONEY TRANSFER,it
is the easiest and fastest way of receiving low amount
of funds out side Africa. The funds can be send into 2
different names of my secretary,
1)NAME  ; FRED-ELABOR
ADDRESS; 12n NORTH RIDGE,ACCRA-GHANA

2)NAME ; MICHEAL-IKONO
ADDRESS. 20,SPINTEX ROAD,ACCRA-GHANA

IF YOU SEND TODAY,I WILL RECEIVE THIS SAME DAY BUT BANK WIRE
WILL TAKE ABOUT 3-6 DAYS BEFORE IT ENTER MY ACCOUNT AND I NED
TO START THE PROCESSING OF THE DOCUMENT AS EARLY AS POSSIBLE

LET ME KNOW YOUR TOUGHT OR IDEA
REGARDS,
SMITH
```

Dr. Mashaal was now showing signs of frustration as he was tired of waiting for Lawyer Smith to send what he believed to be the proper information for the money transfer. He did not want to send his money to either of the two names that Smith had supplied in his previous message because he had indicated earlier that his money must go to the bank, and he insisted on receiving bank details. We can learn from this message that phone calls had been occurring between these two men. Perhaps phone calls accounted for missing hard copy data in the past.

Now Mashaal really showed signs of frustration in the e-mail that follows. He insisted that Smith send a bank account number where he should send the funds to release the money. He was getting tough with his Ghanaian counterparts and appeared to mean business this time.

```
Dear Mr Smith
Sorry to say your administration very poor.Today Friday
Swiss bank is opened.On Saturday and Sunday bank is closed
If you send at once your account number ,Your name in the
account and bank address of your I an send the $ 5000 within
few hours
No more for nonsense information. I need only one line so
action is done

No more telephones Only answer this.

Dr Hassan H.A.Mashaal
```

Next day, the message that Dr. Mashaal was waiting for arrived from Lawyer Smith. First, Smith apologized for his delay in giving the bank coordinates and offered an explanation. He then gave the bank coordinates to which Mashaal was to send the money in order for Smith to procure the necessary clearance forms so Mashaal's inheritance of $10.5 million could be transferred to his Swiss bank. No longer were the names of Smith's two secretaries given as the persons to receive the money. The money was now to be deposited in an account in a bank in Ghana as requested by Mashaal. Smith said that this bank, Cal Bank Limited, was his bank, but the money was to be deposited to the account of *Good Rock Ventures*.

From the e-mail on May 25 until June 6 there appeared to have been no contact unless it was by telephone. At least, no copies of any paper communications were passed on to me in the two binders given to me by Dr. Mashaal in September.

```
Subj:  BANK DETAILS
Date:  5/25/2007 12:04:55 A.M. Pacific Daylight Time
From:  associate_lawfirm@yahoo.com
```

```
To:     Malaraexpert@aol.com
CC:     Malaraexpert@aol.com
```

DEAR SIR,
          AM SORRY FOR ALL THIS, I GUESS I DON'T KNOW MUCH ABOUT
BANKING PROTOCOL BECAUSE I BELIEVE IT TAKES 3-5 DAYS BEFORE
RECIEVING WIRE TRANSFER BY BANK THAT IS THE REASON WHY I
SUGGEST MONEY TRANSFER.
HOWEVER THIS IS MY BANK CO-ORDINATES AND AS YOU SAID THAT
SOONES YOUR BANK SEND IT ,HOPE CAN RECIEVE IT TODAY SO THAT
I CAN START THE DOCUMENTATION IMMEDIATELY
BANK NAME      - CAL BANK LIMITED
BANK ADDRESS  - 23 INDEPENCENCE AVENUE, P.O BOX14596,
ACCRA-GANA
SWIFT CODE:    - BK TRUS 33
ROUTING NO:    - 021001033
CAL SWIFT CODE - ACCCGHAC
CAL'S A/C NO: - 04089719
ACCOUNT NAME: - GOOD ROCK VENTURES
ACCOUNT NO: - 051020349216
WAITING FOR THE RECIEPT OF PAYMENT
REGARDS,
ADAM
```

For a lawyer who sent that very impressive curriculum vitae to now admitting that he knew little about banking seemed unrealistic. Notice that Adams Smith signed his message as Adam—without the *s*. Perhaps he had forgotten his own name. Several days later, on June 6, two forms arrived from Smith in a fax to Mashaal. During that week, Mashaal must have sent money from Europe, but at that time there seemed to be no bank papers or other indications that money had been transferred. He did mention to me later that the following two forms had appeared authentic to him, so he proceeded and arranged for the transfer of the requested money. I had believed that the Swiss bank had refused to take part in his transaction to move money to Ghana to pay for the documents required to legally move funds from that country and that he had turned to his German bank and was successful in having money transferred. This was revealed later not to be so. He told me that by putting pressure on the Swiss bank it did send some money as per his request. Later in a note to the Winnipeg Police he summarized all the moneys that he had sent to Ghana.
```

# CHAPTER 4

## ADAMS SMITH & SUSAN SMITH

As mentioned in the previous chapter, the two forms that arrived by fax are displayed below. Then after this flurry of e-mails and faxes, it appeared that life quieted down for Dr. Mashaal for a short time as there was no record of any contacts for about two weeks. This is unless they conversed by telephone which is a possibility.

Mashaal's money had procured a *Ghana Drug Enforcement Agency (G.D.E.A.)* form and a *State Insurance Corporation's Foreign Admittance Insurance Certificate* dated June 6, 2007.

Mashaal later told me that these forms appeared authentic to him, and he was excited at that time as he now believed that his inheritance would soon be flooding his German bank account. He gave Ghana a choice to send the money if they wished to his bank in Canada. He had told them that he would be leaving for Canada soon and staying there for up to six months.

*STATE INSURANCE CORPORATION (S.I.C.)*

Insurance House, F507/2 Nmetsobu Street, OSU, ACCRA-GHANA.

CONTRACTS (THIRD PARTY INSURANCE) ACT, 1948 (GAMBIA)
CONTRACTS (THIRD PARTY INSURANCE) ACT, 1958 (GHANA)
CONTRACTS (THIRD PARTY INSURANCE) ACT, 1949 (SIERRA LEONE)

*Foreign Remittance Insurance Certificate*

Managing Director
State Insurance Corporation (SIC)

On June 14 or 15, Mashaal sent an e-mail from Germany to Lawyer Smith in which he gave the details of his German bank to include his name, address, account number and the Swift Code as well as an International Account Number and Identification. Mashaal asked Smith for the fax number of his bank in Ghana so he could send the Swiss bank approval as at that point he anticipated that the Swiss bank would fulfil his request to send more money. In that message, he also included his good wishes to Smith for his help in executing this transaction. However, it was learned later that this transaction was never carried out as later Dr. Mashaal told me that the Swiss bank refused to be a party any longer to this money transfer and warned him that this was not bona fide. But Mashaal was still a believer and he turned to his bank in Germany and made the same request. To make the transfer from his German bank account was not as demanding as the Swiss bank had been. However, the German bank, too, cautioned him to be careful, but Mashaal told me that he was determined to continue as he believed his friends in Ghana, not the Swiss or German bank employees.

On June 15, Smith sent Mashaal a message stating that he had already paid for the two documents with Mashaal's money transfer and that he would give the account details to the bank in Ghana so necessary action could be taken. There was no indication in any documents given me of the amount of money he transferred through the German bank. That was confessed later as was the transfer made through his Swiss bank.

However, on June 18, he heard from Dr. Ms. Vivian Kamara, Vice President (Investment Services) on behalf of her bank management. She informed him that her bank now had the coordinates of his bank in Germany as well as those of his bank in Switzerland and now was able to supervise the transfer of the $10.5 million to his bank account. She then repeated all the information Mashaal had sent to her a few days earlier and informed him that the process had begun and that he could expect the bank transfer of the funds to be completed within three to five working days. She insisted that she must receive from him the cost of the transfer of funds and then her bank would immediately send a receipt for him to take to his bank. This message was sent via e-mail address Vivian@ icb.zzn.com and only one minute later, the same message but from

a different e-mail address and with a different format arrived from
vkamara77@yahoo.com. This was impossible! There had to be two
people working unknown to each other at different locations.

Perhaps the crime here is the fact that Vivian and others
continually convinced Mashaal that he would receive money. Dr.
Mashaal must have forgotten that Vivian had told him earlier that
the money could not be moved out of Ghana as Linda Morgan had
died approximately two months earlier and prior to changing the
ownership on the bank documents to Mashaal's name.

Next day, June 19, Mashaal sent the e-mail shown below. In
it Dr. Mashaal included the name, e-mail and fax number of the
employee assigned to deal with him in his German bank and asked
Vivian to contact this person.

```
Dear Dr Ms Vivian
Now I understood that the bank term to transfer the whole
funds and not possible to pay bit by bit particularly the
lady is not alive for any change
Also the term and conditions of your bank to receive 2.5%
($262,500.00) and this has to be 100% sure For this there is
a solution your bank can contact my German bank

E-mail; (name deleted)@sparkasse.osterode.de

Telefax : 0049 xxxx xxx xxx

And ask the German bank in case the 10.5 million $ are
transferred to the German bank. Will the German bank ensure
100% and confirm on receival to transfer at once $ 262,500.00
If this is confirmed by the German the problem is solved and
there is nothing against this solution in your bank
However once E.Mail the German Bank send to me a copy to
follow the case urgently

Thank you

Dr.Hassan Mashaal

Cc Mr Smith: Kindly send by e mail all documents obtained at
price $ 7000 except the two documents already sent
```

There had been a reference in a message from Mashaal to $7,000
that was to cover the cost of all documents, not just the two that he
had just received a few days earlier. He was also trying to negotiate a

deal, but Vivian's message the next day tried to set him straight. She said his bargaining was not at all favourable, and the only solution would be for him to pay 2.5% of $5 million for the first transfer then things could happen after she received that money. It appeared that messages from Vivian were inconsistent. As suggested earlier, there appeared perhaps to be two persons acting in the role of Vivian.

```
Subj:   Re: ref e mail 19 June 2007
Date:   6/20/2007 1:54:22 A.M. Pacific Daylight Time
From:   vkamara77@yahoo.com
To:     Malaraexpert@aol.com
```

Dear Sir,
      I just recieve a fax message on your proposal that yet
your german bank (GURANTEE) Hence,the bank here is finding
it difficult for you the reciever to come up with the
extension fees since you know the existence of the funds but
only trying to bargain which will not favour the bank in any
way.

We have alots of BANK GURANTEE/CD/LETTER OF CREDIT from
various offshore bank and our bank in encounter alots of
problems since the bank did not hour their gurantee letter,
many are god buyer after sending their bank letter of credit
or gurantee hoping for the seller bank that soonest they
deliver to the buyer the the bank will immediately in return
send the seller full payment till this moment we are facing
alots of court issue to recover seller funds back from buyer
bank as buyer fail to pay their bank for the bank to pay our
bank.

Therefore,your last solution was turn down except this which
was consider after an hours meeting that if you can pay
the charges of 2.5% of $5m for the first transfer then the
transfer can take effect immediately.

Am highly sorry for all this,
Regards,
Vivian

The next exchange of messages between Mashaal and Vivian started with insults about the useless banks in Ghana and the story told to him by his German bank employee of a similar story of a German lady and her pursuit of a grand inheritance offer from Africa. Still this bank employee was unable to extinguish Mashaal's enthusiasm and convince him to forget this entire *fantastic* offer of becoming the beneficiary of money from Linda Morgan. See message below from Mashaal to Vivian. Once more, it would appear that he was finished with this frustrating deal. But was he really?

```
Malaraexpert@aol.com wrote:

Dear Dr Mrs Vivian

I expected this answer as I was 100% sure Accra banks are
not only useless but hopeless in their administration
You said why the Swiss bank did not accept while the German
bank accepted.Actually at first the German Bank did not
accept and asked the same as the Swiss Bank but I requested
the director to mae exception.The director of the German
Bank said he will mae an exception in order to prove to me
that Accra banks are absolutely useless and will NEVER,NEVER
transfer money to me. The German Bank was correct
Also the similar cas as mine not by the Swiss Bank by by
the German bank who gave me a detail report about a similar
case of a German lady who was offered one million dollars
to be transferred from Accra Bank but whe she paid the fees
she never got the money. I shall print many copies of this
report to be circulated extensively

I am very happy I did not transfer money to your bank
otherwise I will be similar to that German lady who lost all
her transferred money. I am very happy not to dea with your
highly useless bank
Regards
Dr H.Mashaal

Thursday, June 21, 2007 America Online Malaria expert
```

In the message that followed, being dated the same day, Vivian voiced her rebuttals to his insults and a question for Mashaal to ponder.

```
Subj:  Re: ref your e mail dated 20 June 1007
Date:  6/21/2007 12"07:47 A.M. Pacific Daylight Time
From:  ykamara77@yahoo.com
To:    Malaraexpert@aol.com

Dear Sir,
     Thanks for the insult but we shall be very happy to have
copy of the report of the lady whom you claim that ghana
```

banks took her money and never transfer a penny to her,how
could this happen in a modern,you just turn everything down
only when the bank ask you for transfer charges ,this is
normal procedures the onwer of the fund is not alive then
how could you have authority to fell the bank to deduct
from the principal sum ,the funds is not on your name ,we
have arguer this so far previously before you understand
still yet the bank is not going to responsible for any loss
or damage ,the authorisation will recieve that we should
transfer $10.5 m in to the chosen beneficiary not to take
from the funds so if the beneficiary only want to recieve
the $10.5m into his account after the late decease and do
not want to spend a penny to recieve the funds them we count
it as you are only interested in the decease funds not what
her soul wishes.

Same day as the above messages, Dr. Mashaal received a
message from Lawyer Smith that opened with a prayer making it
appear that he believed Dr. Mashaal to be a wise person and had
great understanding. He apologized for Dr. Ms Vivian's attitude and
asked Mashaal to send the money to his account as he would ensure
that the transfer of the first $2 million took place. It is not certain
where the amount $2 million came from because the previous
compromise was to pay fees to receive the transfer of $5 million.
Smith gave his personal bank information as he had in an earlier
message dated May 25—nearly a month earlier—and indicated that
he was anticipating $50,000 being transferred to his personal Accra
account then he would pay the fees for Mashaal. He was hoping to
share the wealth—to be a part of the inheritance!

```
Subj:  BANK DETAILS FOR $50,000
Date:  6/21/2007 11:15:32 A.M. Pacific Daylight Time
From:  associate_lawfirm@yahoo.com
To:    Malaraexpert@aol.com
```

Dear Sir,
    Thanks for the wisdom and understanding that almighty
God has given to you though I understand the funds is meant
for the poor children and I will be glad if I can also be
part of the program when it start.

Am sorry for the Dr Ms Vivian attitude,she promises to
apologies if she has wrong you

Dr. Agnes Chambers-Glenn

```
Kindly send the money to my account just to ensure the
transfor of the first $2million take effect in my presence
and payment receipt is send to you or your bank,the bank
told me that it will take 3-4 days before the $2m will
arrive at your bank account in Germany

BANK NAME     - CAL BANK LIMITED
BANK ADDRESS - 23 INDEPENCENCE AVENUE,P.O BOX
14596,ACCRA-GHANA

SWIFT CODE:   - BKTRUS 33

ROUTING NO:   - 021001033

CAL SWIFT CODE: - ACCCGHAC
CAL'S A/C NO:- 04089719

ACCOUNT NAME  - GOOD ROCK VENTURES
ACCOUNT:      - 051020349216

WAITING TO READ FROM YOU.LET ME KNOW WHEN THE $50,000 IS
TRANSFER TO MY ACCOUNT SO THAT I CAN PICK IT UP AND PAY
IMMEDIATELY

REGARDS,
SMITH
```

June 21 was a busy day for message exchanges. Mashaal responded to Smith's earlier message and made a suggestion that they start with $1 million only, not $2 million as Smith had suggested. Mashaal appeared to believe that Smith could solve his problems, and he would no longer have to deal with the bank and Vivian as he found both very difficult to do business with. In the e-mail below, there was another change suggested: Mashaal proposed to get the transfer started with fees on only $50,000 as the 2.5% handling charges were more manageable until he received some of that $10.5 million to work with. He even suggested that perhaps he should not get himself involved any further in this project and thanked Smith and sent his best regards. It now appeared that he was bowing out like he made us believe two or three times earlier. See the message below.

Malaraexpert@aol.com wrote:

Dear Mr Smith
Many thanks of your e Mail
I wrote to you many times very gentle and polite becausr you
are practical person
Also I wrote many times to Dr Mrs Vivian very nice and
gentle but never she has a practical solution and always
insisted that I must pay 2.5% for 10.5 million dollars.When
I lost hope for any change I wrote strongly and criticised.
I wish to give example of the Swiss bank in case the bank
makes minor mistake example delayed an answer to any
request I criticize the bank bitterly for their delay. The
bank apologzes for the delay and took quick action. These
are banks who know their duties and great different from
Accra bank who cannot solve practically any simple problem
and do not accept criticsm. Criticism is well accepted in
highly developed countries but not in highly underdeveloped
countries.Iworked in more than 30 countries and I knew that
very well.
You suggested to pay for $2 million.I suggest as a start and
in order to respect the bank to pay advance 2.5% for 50,000
$ (namely 1250 $).In this case I must know detail Account to
transfer the money

You must realize this money will be used mainly to help
children and programs etc etc and will take a lot of time
from me.If it causes at the begging so many problems by the
Accara bank then it may be better not to involve myself

Thank you very much and best regards

Dr.Hassan A.H.Mashaal

Note: The word *begging* in the last paragraph above should have read beginning.
That correction was made in pen on the copy of the e-mail that was given to me.

More messages continued between the parties for the remaining
one and one-half weeks that Dr. Mashaal remained in German.
Vivian was not finished yet although she had not taken Mashaal's
insults very well. But as Smith had mentioned as being possible, she
sent a message on the same day as the above message apologizing
and blaming her actions on the bank rules. However, she said that
after meeting with Lawyer Smith and the bank management, the
sum of $2 million must remain as the amount for the first transfer

from her Ghana bank and that would require that Dr. Mashaal send $50,000 to Lawyer Smith's account at her bank.

Mashaal wrote Smith again the following day. It seemed that Mashaal had not yet put closure to this deal as he had indicated in the previous day's message. It appeared that he was hoping still for Smith to come to his rescue with some money to assist with the transfer charges. In addition, he repeated the German bank employee's story about the German lady who had been promised $1 million but had received absolutely nothing. Dr. Mashaal had been given a copy in German in an attempt to stress to him that he, too, was involved in a scam. But still he refused to give up and continued to pursue the $10.5 million inheritance that he was looking forward to receiving so he could *do good*. Mashaal's message of June 22 appears below. It appeared that he really believed Linda Morgan but it was Smith, Vivian and the Ghana banks that he was dealing with now that caused him all the problems by putting up barriers to receiving that inheritance. Once more, it appeared that Mashaal was finished with this exercise in futility as he again thanked Smith for his assistance and sent his best wishes. Just one more time!

Malaraexpert@aol.com wrote:

Dear Mr Smith

The honourable late lady Linda Morgan selected me to receive $10.5 million in order to utelize to help very poor children and people who are in great need of help.Also she asked me to contact you to assist in administration because she trusted you very much.

When I asked the Accara bank to deduct 2.5% (about US$ 262,500) and transfer the balance the unefficient bank indicated that this against the bank regulations.In case the administration of the bank is efficient ,the bank can have a special meeting and adjust the useless regulations to favour the clients but as it is well known the Accara banks are considered in administration the worst in the world.Their staff are not experience enough to adjust any stupid rules. Evidently the Accra banks are seriously deteriorated as this case proved it
Also I am pleased the German bank gave me a detail report of similar case concerning one million dollars.The concerned person after paid the fees never received any money which

100% confirmed the serious deterioration of Accara banks.I
shall translate this report from German to English and later
send to you a copy .Also it will be circulated extensively
in Germany and Switzerland.

Now I am very pleased not to deal with highly unefficient
Accara bank any more but it is regrettable that the money
if transferred to another person ,he or she Will use it
personally and never to help poor children as wished by late
Linda Morgan.I hope you follow the situation to see the
facts

Lastly I wish to thank you.You are very efficient and
reliable person but of course you cannot improve the
seriously deteriorated administration of Accara banks.

Best wishes

Dr.Hassan A.H.Mashaal

Friday, June 22, 2007 America Online: Malara expert

From the message above, take note that Mashaal appeared to
continue to believe that Linda's money really existed. However,
perhaps once more he was considering not pursuing it any further.
He did have some of his own money already invested to pay for
transfer forms and it appeared that he would like that money
returned. So, the *cat and mouse game* continued as Smith probably
was not about to let this source of income dry up. Read the message
below in which Smith indicated that he, too, was unwilling to go
along with the Ghana bank. He used the term *an internet scam* in his
attempt to have Mashaal see that there was a difference between his
case and that of the German woman. Also, Smith informed Mashaal
that he did not want him to copy any future messages to the bank.
They were to be sent only to him.

Subj:  Re: I am honoured not to deal with Accara bank
Date:  6/22/2007 3:47:00 A.M. Pacific Daylight Time
From:  associate_lawfirm@yahoo.com
To:    Malaraexpert@aol.com

Dear Sir,
    I do understand your predicament,if you have decide on
your mind that you will not fulfill the wishes of the late

lady ,I have nothing to say about this because she chose you
to do this project for her before his death.

My opinion is that I am here as a lawyer and I cant open my
eyes down for Accra bank not to transfer money after we pay
for the cost of transfer,this cannot happen.you know that
am a barrister and has since be practicing law for the past
18yrs, no bank here in Ghana can do a stupid thing,maybe
the case of the German women was a internet scam not a real
bank, you should understand this, it will never happen
either the bank will be close down or I sue the bank to pay
more for not complying to their word.

Pleas ,think about this and get back to me and if not I
will advise you to write a comprehensive email stating that
you are not interested in receiving the charity funds at
international commercial bank to the bank so that it will
enable me to look for another person to do the job.

I appreciate your concern and effort so far God be with you.
Regards,
SMITH

P.S.: NEXT TIME WHEN YOU ARE SENDING EMAIL TO ME,YOU SHOULD
ADDRESS IT TO ME NOT TO 'CC' WITH THE BANK EMAIL.

Messages continued and on the following day two messages were exchanged between Smith and Mashaal who were still hassling over how much of the inheritance money was to be sent at this time and how much money Mashaal must send in total to have the inheritance released. Would it be $10,000 or $100,000 after 2.5% was received at the Ghana bank? Smith insisted it should be enough money to release $1 million and asked Mashaal to trust in him. Sure, trust in a bandit!

It was on June 24 that I actually received that all important personal e-mail message from Dr. Mashaal who had not yet left Germany for Canada. Remember, it read: *An interesting story happened to me recently. No one will believe it. It is one of the extremely rare happening. I shall tell you details when I see you.* Perhaps this would indicate that he was still a believer two months after having received Linda Morgan's invitation to help her get the money out of Ghana. Although we can see from the exchanged e-mails that at times he was a doubter in believing that the money would ever be his.

The same day that I received that message, I later learned that contact continued between Mashaal and Smith. He told Smith that he was going to go to his bank in Germany and ask for a loan of $25,000, and if received, he would send that amount immediately to Ghana using the bank information that Smith had sent him a couple of days earlier. Mashaal then repeated the information that he had received in that message, and in addition he said,

*One more question Suppose after you receive the money and deposit it in the bank. Then the bank did not transfer $ 1 000,000 as the bank changes its mind. Then what action then I can do I hope the German bank accept to give me loan $25000.If the bank does not accept then I cannot transfer except after 3 months.*

There must have been phone calls concerning the sum of $25,000 needed for costs as I found no message prior to Mashaal's reply above where that amount was mentioned. The following day Smith's message below had the answers for Mashaal. Here is *The 100% Guarantee.* In addition to the guarantee, Smith advised his client to ask the German bank for a loan and not to mention the $1 million. It appeared that Smith's guarantee was that in the event that the transfer was not honoured, Lawyer Smith would send back the $25,000 and Smith would sue the Ghana bank.

```
Subj:  Re: Hallo
Date:  6/25/2007 12:45:26 A.M. Pacific Daylight Time
From:  ASSOCIATE_LAWFIRM@YAHOO.COM
To:    Malaraexpert@aol.com

Dear Sir,
    You need not to let the German bank knew that you are
sending the money purpose of transferring the $1m as they
already oppose you of sending money for the transfer so just
goahead and ask for a normal loan and they should send to
the bank details given to you same as follows;
Bank Name     CAL BANK LIMITED
Bank Address  23 Independence Avenue
              P.O. Box 14596 Accra ,Ghana
Swift Code    BK TRUS 33
```

Dr. Agnes Chambers-Glenn

```
Routing No      021001033
Cal Swift Code  ACCCGHAC
CAL'S A/C NO    04089719
Account Name    GOOD ROCK VENTURES
Account No      051020349216
```

Sir,I am given 100% guarantee and assurance that the bank
will Transfer the $1m moment I paid the cost of transfer.if
in case the transfer is not honor,I shall send you back the
25,000 usd and sue the bank to Ghana high court of justice .

Please.let the transfer be done today hopefully the bank
accept the loan.
Regards, SMITH

# CHAPTER 5

## GERMAN BANK INVOLVEMENT

Contacts continued. It appeared in the fax dated June 25 that Vivian was making contact with the bank person that Mashaal dealt with at his German bank. However, this could have been a trick. Vivian probably had faxed this to Mashaal only in Germany and simply noted that she was sending it to him in care of an employee at his German bank. This would have indicated to Mashaal that his banker had been notified by the Ghana bank about the money to be transferred. If his bank received this, Mashaal believed that this would help him get the required loan.

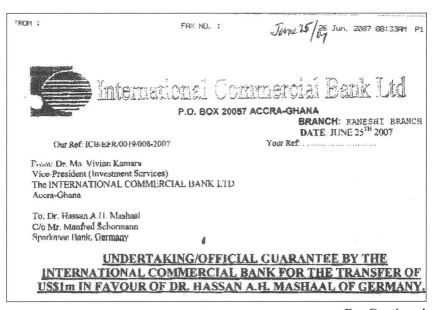

FROM :                          FAX NO. :          June 25/26 Jun. 2007 08:33AM  P1

**International Commercial Bank Ltd**

P.O. BOX 20057 ACCRA-GHANA

**BRANCH:** KANESHI BRANCH
**DATE:** JUNE 25TH 2007

Our Ref: ICB/EFR/0019/008-2007          Your Ref: ..................

From: Dr. Ms. Vivian Kamara
Vice-President (Investment Services)
The INTERNATIONAL COMMERCIAL BANK LTD
Accra-Ghana.

To: Dr. Hassan A.H. Mashaal
C/o Mr. Manfred Schormann
Sparkasse Bank, Germany

**UNDERTAKING/OFFICIAL GUARANTEE BY THE INTERNATIONAL COMMERCIAL BANK FOR THE TRANSFER OF US$1m IN FAVOUR OF DR. HASSAN A.H. MASHAAL OF GERMANY.**

**. . . Fax Continued**

THE INTERNATIONAL COMMERCIAL BANK LTD HEREBY MAKES THIS UNDERTAKING, THIS 25TH DAY OF JUNE 2007 IN REGARDS TO THE TRANSFER OF US$1m INTO THE NOMINATED BANK ACCOUNT OF DR. HASSAN A.H. MASHAAL AS STATED BELOW:

SPARKASSE BANK; Hauptstrasse 20/1, Im Bad-Lauerberg-Harz, Germany. ACCOUNT # / IBAN: DE25 2635 1015 0107 3304 58; BANK SWIFT CODE: NOLADE 21 HZB; BENEFICIARY ACCOUNT NAME: DR HASSAN A.H. MASHAAL

REMITTANCE PROCESS AND CREDITING OF THE ABOVE BANK ACCOUNT WILL COMMENCE AND TAKE EFFECT IMMEDIATELY UPON THE CONFIRMATION OF THE PAYMENT OF THE COST OF TRANSFER OF 2.5% OF THE AMOUNT TO BE REMITTED, WHICH HAS BEEN CALCULATED TO BE US$25000 ONLY.

THE INTERNATIONAL COMMERCIAL BANK LTD FURTHER RE-AFFIRM THAT THERE WILL BE NO OTHER REQUIREMENTS AND/OR MONEY REQUIRED FOR WHATSOEVER BANK PURPOSES AND THE FUNDS (US$1m) WILL BE TRANSFERRED TO THE ABOVE MENTIONED BENEFICIARY BANK ACCOUNT AS STATED ABOVE IMMEDIATELY THE COST OF TRANSFER CHARGES HAS BEEN PAID BY THE ABOVE MENTIONED BENEFICIARY IN THE PERSON OF DR. HASSAN A.H. MASHAAL.

DR. MS. VIVIAN KAMARA VICE-PRESIDENT (Investment Services) OF THE INTERNATIONAL COMMERCIAL BANK LTD UNDERTAKES TO SUPERVISE THE TRANSFER & REMITTANCE OF THE SAID US$1m FOR SUCCESSFUL CREDITING OF THE ABOVE BENEFICIARY BANK ACCOUNT WITHIN SEVENTY-TWO HOURS OF THE CONFIRMATION OF THE PAYMENT OF THE COST OF TRANSFER CHARGES.

MS. VIVIAN KAMARA
VICE-PRESIDENT (Investment Services)
INTERNATIONAL COMMERCIAL BANK LTD

BARRISTER ODBBO ROWLINGS
LEGAL DEPARTMENT, ICB

INTERNATIONAL COMMERCIAL BANK LTD    "YOUR SATISFACTION IS OUR CONCERN"    TELEFAX +233-21-7012205

However, in several previous messages, Smith had asked Mashaal not to mention the $1 million at his bank while attempting to get a loan. Why then would Vivian have sent this to Mashaal's bank? Perhaps this notation on the fax appeared solely to fool Mashaal and no copy had been sent to the Sparkasse in German, but only to him?

The following day, June 26, Dr. Mashaal sent a message to Lawyer Smith informing him that he had sent the $25,000 using the information that Smith had sent to him. In that message was the first indication that money had also been sent previously. There were no e-mails or forms from either bank among the material given to me by Dr. Mashaal, so there was no knowledge of any earlier transfer. Having sent $25,000 now, he was looking for the $1 million and demanded immediate action. Only later it was learned that he had sent from Germany to the Ghanaian bank a total of $32,000. We saw in earlier correspondence that he had sent $5,000 but there was no previous mention of the $2,000 that he showed in the message below.

```
Subj:  ref your e mail 26 June 2007
Date:  6/26/2007 11:22:48 P.M. Pacific Daylight Time
From:  Malara expert
To:    Associate_lawfirm@yahoo.com

Dear Mr Smith
I transfer the 25000 $ according to the data you gave to me
Previously when I transfer $5000 and $2000 you never asked
for receipt
Why now you make these complications..Your bank said in the
letter no more request once the money is transferred the
bank immediately will send the $ 1000,000
The bank in germany gave me a receipt.It has the following
Konto number (my account number)= (deleted)
Wahrung (Currency) USA
Betrag (sum) $25000
Name of my account:Hassan A.H.Mashaal
My Address: 37431 Bad Lauterberg
BIC(S.W.I.F.T) BKTR US 33
To:    C A L Bank limted
Street; 23 independence Avenue
       14596 Accra Ghana
No of account bank 051020349216
Name:  GOOD ROCK VENTURES

This was given by the bank to me as confirmation
Please take action .Enough too many letters. Take action to
transfer the $ 1000,000
Thank you

Dr Hassan A.H.Mashaal
```

Now it would appear that nothing would prevent Mashaal's receiving the first $1 million. Wait a minute! A message arrived from Vivian dated June 25, one day prior to the above message, in which she informed Mashaal that the funds had not arrived. Mashaal replied to Vivian asking her about the $9.5 million and how much money would be necessary to release that to his German bank account. Both persons seemed in much higher spirits now. For a change, they were very polite to each other.

Then on July 1—six days after the money had been sent—a message from Smith arrived informing Mashaal that the $25,000 still had not arrived at the bank in Ghana, but he was hopeful that it would soon. Smith also promised to take action to get $1 million transferred to Mashaal's German bank as soon as that money arrived in Ghana.

It appeared that Mashaal was too joyful too soon by the message he returned to Smith as the promised sum of one million dollars was not even on its way. See e-mail below.

```
Malaraexpert@aol.com wrote:

Dear Mr Smith
Now five days passed.I am sure the $ 25000 now in the bank.
Kindly take action so that the one million dollars is
transferred
When I receive the one million dollar I shall take the
following actions

1-Transfer to you 10,000 $
2-Inform your government about your name and honesty
3-Inform the Organization of lawyers in Ghana about your
efficiency
4-Circulate to all European Embassies or Consolates of your
country in Europe detal informations.Also to inform them
the informations received from Swiss Banks or Gereman banks
never to transfer to lawyers or banks in Ghana was wrong.

With kind regards

Dr.Hassan A.H.Mashaal
```

There was no date on the above e-mail. It had been trimmed off. I deduced that it had been sent between June 26 and July 1 according to the e-mail received just before and after it. Following is Smith's reply that was received by Mashaal on July 1 as he prepared to leave for Canada.

```
Subj:  Re: 25000$
Date:  7/1/2007 10:17:32 A.M. Pacific Daylight Time
From:  associate_lawfirm@yahoo.com
To:    Malaraexpert@aol.com

Dear Sir,
     Thanks for the confidence in me and I shall not
disappoint you, throughout Friday,the bank does not recieve
any funds in my bank account but I hope it will arrive this
week unfailingly, on Friday noon, I try several time to
reach MR MANFRED at your bank but I was told that he was not
```

```
on his desk but left a message because my bank could not see
the funds in my account but told me to wait till Monday.
Regards,
SMITH
```

Next day, Mashaal informed Smith that the German bank confirmed that the transfer of the $25,000 had been made. Once again, he quoted the information that his bank had given to him earlier and hoped that this information would satisfy Smith.

There were more messages from Smith concerning the non-arrival of the $25,000. It appeared that Mashaal's anxiety was getting the best of him as he sent another message to Smith confirming that the money had been sent and asked for the $1 million to be transferred immediately. Smith, too, appeared to be getting anxious and sent a message two and half hours later asking why the money had not yet arrived into his *Good Rock Ventures* account.

In a return reply, Mashaal told Smith that the money had been sent and that he had not forgotten his promise of giving him a reward of $10,000 as he had earlier promised for honesty in completing his legal duties. He inquired to where this reward should be sent as soon as he received his first $1 million. Smith informed Mashaal that the destination of the reward should be to the *Good Rock Ventures'* account—the same account that he had asked him to send the $25,000 that he was still waiting for.

The following day, Mashaal messaged Smith and revealed his annoyance of the long delay. He believed that the $25,000 should have arrived in Ghana and that the $1 million should have been on its way to his account in Germany. His frustration caused by *the waste of time* clearly showed, and he indicated that he should not have sent the money to Smith's account but that he should have had it transferred to the bank directly. You will recall that he had lost faith in Vivian on a few occasions so he had put his trust in Smith expecting him to make successful arrangements to have the money delivered.

However, Smith e-mailed back and rationalized that bank transfers do take up to three days while transfers by Western Union are received within hours. He did not say that transfers are more difficult to trace when sent through Western Union, nor that there is an extra relatively high charge for the transfer service. Smith explained that he wanted the funds to come directly into his account so as to ensure that the bank honor its promise to Dr. Mashaal. He repeated information that he had sent in a previous message; that is, he vowed to take the bank to court if it did not honor its commitment. You will probably recall that Dr. Mashaal was concerned earlier and told Vivian that her bank and all banks in Ghana were corrupt. Smith reminded him that the Swiss bank had sent $7,000 using the same system to wire it and after three days it had arrived at the Ghana bank. Smith was still hopeful to receive soon the latest transfer of $25,000. He would then pay the transfer costs so the $1 million could be released and transferred to Germany.

Now there was only one day remaining before Dr. Mashaal was to depart for Canada. Later in the day, Mashaal messaged Smith and thanked him for the earlier message and told him that he believed in his honesty as a lawyer and asked him to deposit the money as his money should arrive in Africa by July 2 for sure. Mashaal then left his home to take the train to Frankfurt to catch a flight to Canada for departure the following day. He had hoped to receive the $1 million before leaving for Canada but it was not to be. The following day, July 2, he arrived in Canada according to schedule. From his file it was learned that upon arriving in Canada, he immediately sent Smith a message to inform him that he was now in Canada. He also said that in checking further with his German bank, he learned new information; that is, he believed that the delay in the money arriving in Ghana was due to its routing through a Hanover bank.

As mentioned earlier, it was on July 4 at 10 a.m. that I learned about Dr. Mashaal's involvement in this money scam—*the unbelievable event that was occurring in his life*. The excuse for his visit to my home that day was the need for help to prepare a newly purchased cordless mouse for computer action. With the mouse problem solved, he excitedly told me about his good fortune and said that he was waiting for the $1 million to arrive any day now into his German bank account. I listened to his good fortune story, I shook my head, and then asked him, W*hy you?* I suggested to him that I believed it was a scam to obtain money from him. I could not believe that a person as intelligent as he could be so naïve. I suggested to him the old cliché: *If it sounds too good to be true, it probably is!* Those words did not appear to budge him in his belief. He insisted that he had been chosen because of his good works with the World Health Organization. I asked him how Linda Morgan knew about that. I did not know at that time that her first letter was not even addressed to him. He avoided giving me an answer. He said that she had asked him to distribute this money to poor children around the world. Next question: How was it that Linda had learned he was associated with World Health Organization? He did not disclose to me that he had told her about his association with the WHO when he replied to her invitation to assist her in moving her inheritance out of Ghana. To that point in time, I had not seen any of Mashaal's e-mails, but I would learn the answers from the approximately four hundred messages and forms after he gave them to me in September. Somewhat disappointed in my reaction that day, Mashaal left my home.

# C$\mathcal{HAPTER}$ 6

## ADAMS SMITH'S DEATH

The following day, while going to visit a friend in Dr. Mashaal's building, I met him in the hall and spoke with him for a few minutes. Nothing was mentioned of his good fortune as he was chatting with a Russian friend, the fellow who repairs his computer. After that, I e-mailed him from time to time and always asked if he had yet received the money. I never saw him in person again until July 14 when he came to my home to tell me that he was not well and had visited his doctor and was taking medication. It would appear that the stress and frustration of his involvement in this scam was taking its toll on his health. However, when he turned over to me his e-mails and forms in mid-September, I saw that messages had been exchanged continuously between him and the people in Ghana. I noticed that on July 6, Lawyer Smith wrote to him and indicated that the $25,000 that Mashaal had allegedly sent on June 27 had not yet arrived in his Ghana bank account, and he asked if Mashaal was *playing games*. Smith said that he was giving his Ghana bank pressure telling them that the money had been sent and asking for the reason why it had not yet arrived in his Ghana account. The bank had asked Smith to get proof that the German bank had actually sent the $25,000. Smith went on to say, *I am still wondering why the $25,000 transfer since 27 june still now never show up at my account,k don't know what you and your banker are up to. If real they transfer the money as they said in thier ;cc; email then let them send me copy of the TRANSFER SLIP/RECEIPT for my bank to trace it.*

Smith used the date June 27 but Mashaal's bank had sent the money on June 26 according to Mashaal's message that day. There was a message from Mashaal to Smith informing him that due to a mix up in routing, his bank told him that the money had been sent only yesterday, July 5. He blamed Smith for the delay as his instructions had been followed including Hanover as a clearance point. The money was now expected to arrive in Ghana on July 7.

```
Subj:  Re: ref your e mail
Date:  7/6/2007 8:22:12 A.M. Pacific Daylight Time
From:  associate_lawfirm@yahoo.com
To:    Malaraexpert@aol.com
```

```
Dear Sir/Ma,
    I have given my bank pressure that you actually transfer
the money but they are still insisting that there is no
money of such that arrives at my bank account, in other
word,they ask me to get PROOF OF TRANSFER PAPER which your
bank has use to issue the transfer.
In fact,I don't know who is playing game here ,if truly you
wire the funds since 27 June , the money should have be in
my account,I have never experience the kind of bank transfer
that takes more than 7 days ,PLEASE SEND PROOF OF TRSNSFER
SLIP.IF NOT I PUT IT ONTO YOU THAT YOU NEVER TRANSFER ANY
MONEY AND YOU SHOULD RETURN DR HASSAN MASHAAL MONEY BACK TO
HIM AS HE TOLD ME THAT YOUR BANK HAS ALREADY TAKE $25,000
FROM HIM.
HOPE THIS WILL LET YOU FIND THE SOLUTION TO THIS PROBLEM.
REGARDS,
SMITH Esq
```

On July 10, there was a very short message from Mashaal to Smith saying that he knew that the money had arrived and wanted to know what action Smith had taken. It was not clear how Mashaal learned that the money had arrived in Ghana unless he received the proof from his German bank sent to his home in Canada.

Two days later, Mashaal sent to Vivian at the bank a message informing her that Smith now had the $25,000 and would be making a deposit into her bank that day. With that information, Mashaal expected immediate action with the transfer of the $1 million. He mentioned that the 2.5% for the remaining $9.5 million would be transferred to her bank to save a long delay and asked for the necessary details for the transfer to be executed. He wanted these instructions to give to his German bank after the arrival of the one million. He thanked her for her cooperation and sent his best regards. See Mashaal's message below to Vivian.

```
Malaraexpert@aol.com wrote:

Dear Mrs Vivian

Mr Smith account has the $ 25000
I think he will deposit it in your bank today so that you
take immediate action to transfer the $ 1000,000 to my
German account

The 2.5% for the remaining 9.5 million US$ is better I
transfer directly to your bank in order to shorten the
period of transfer
Therefore please give me details of transfer direct to your
bank.The bank account to which the transfer will be made
and all necessary details to give to my German bank to take
action after I receive the $ 1000,000

Thank you for your cooperation

Best regards

Dr.HassanA.H.Mashaal
```

Before long, Vivian replied and gave Dr. Mashaal the shocking news that Smith had been involved in an automobile accident on his way to her bank with the money and was killed, so the money had not reached her bank. Notice here that she referred to Smith as Mashaal's client. Should it not be the other way?

```
Subj:  Re: $ 25000
Date:  7/12/2007 11:16:27 P.M. Pacific Daylight Time
From:  vkamara77@yahoo.com
To:    Malaraexpert@aol.com

Dear Sir,
   We are sorry for what has happened to your local client
the late barrister adam smith that has vital accident,we
just got the news from his chambers and his colleague ask
for us to give them your contact details.Should I give to
them? The money has not yet be paid to the bank.
Regards,
Vivian
```

On July 12, the day Mashaal received the shocking news of Smith's death, I answered a knock on my door and when I opened it there stood Dr. Mashaal. He had come to give me the news. I responded by asking him to date what was the total number of deaths of his African friends. It appeared that he had not given that idea a thought. I asked him if he did not think that six deaths in this saga were not somewhat unusual. I continued by saying, *Oh, come on! That is now six people related to your inheritance who have died from automobile accidents and all within only two and one-half months.* Again, I mentioned to him that this had to be a scam and it would be wise for him to drop it! At that time, I was not aware that he had sent $25,000 to clear the first $1 million of his $10.5 million inheritance. It is little wonder that he appeared so shocked. During that visit to my home, Dr. Mashaal told me that his health was not good and that he had been to the doctor again to learn that he had two major problems but had been given medication in an attempt to control these. It was obvious that this ordeal was taking a toll on his health. He was suffering from too much anxiety and frustration in his attempt to get the money transferred to his bank account or to recover his losses to date.

It was the following day that Mashaal replied to the news of his lawyer's death. First there were a few words of regret; then an inquiry of place and then on with the business of the money transfer. A few more questions were posed then a threat like what had often happened earlier.

```
Subj:  ref your e mail dated 12 July 2007
Date:  7/13/2007 7:08:50 P.M. Pacific Daylight Time
From:  Malara expert
To:    vkamara77@yahoo.com
```

Dear Dr Mrs Vivian

I am sorry for the news. Did Mr Adam died or in the hospital? Sometime ago you suggested to transfer the 2.5% for one million dollar (25000$) to Mr Adam Why you did not ask to transfer the sum to the account in your bank. This is I cannot understand. I hope you explain it.

Also is it possible that you request his bank to transfer the money to you Also who will inhert him ??? This one can

make this to be applied.Please give me the name who inherit
him and address and E mail etc

After I hear from you and no solution I shall contact Top
Embassodor of Ghana for intensive investigation

Thank you. Regards

Dr.Hassan A.H.Mashaal

Then the following day Mashaal sent another message asking
Vivian for the name, address and e-mail of Smith's next of kin.
Perhaps this was a mistake but he so badly wanted to locate the
$25,000 that was in Smith's possession when he was killed in that
automobile accident.

Let's return to the correspondence. With Smith's death, Vivian
appeared to be the major character again to deal with Mashaal and
his inheritance although earlier she had told him that she was no
longer in charge of his transaction. She had advised him that another
person had taken over his account at her bank. Vivian mentioned
that she could not disclose any personal information re Smith's
next-of-kin as requested by Dr. Mashaal in his previous message as
that would be against bank policy. She suggested that since she was
unable to contact the late lawyer's office, she believed they were out
for Smith's funeral ceremony. It would seem that Smith received
burial much sooner after death than Linda Morgan had. So we
cannot assume that burials are held a month after death in Ghana.

Subj:  Re: ref your e mail 14 July 2007
Date:  7/14/2007 9:20:03 A.M. Pacific Daylight Time
From:  vkamara77@yahoo.com
To:    Malaraexper@aol.com

Dear Sir,
     Thanks for the confidence in me but as soon as the bank
here confirm that they can transfer the funds to another
bank, then i shall give you our bank detail because there
is little that i can do this your transaction especially
when the person involve is dead, it will be difficult for
the bank to transfer the money in which we don't know if
the decease already cash the money from the bank before the
unfortunate death because I was inform that after he attend
court case he proceed to his bank after in which the vital

accident occur,I think the postal of the late adam smith is
out for funeral ceremony.
Sir,I advice you to be patience because you have lost a
dear person and his chambers are trying to find ou the
details of the funds in which they ask me about your contact
details,SHOULD I GIVE TO THEM OR NOT?
Regards,
Vivian

In a short message that I have not shown, Vivian asked
Mashaal to wire another $25,000 directly to her bank to the direct
account number that she had given him earlier. She would then
see that his first $1 million was transferred to his German bank.
She informed him that *it will take about two weeks before the final
burrier ceremony will take place*. It would appear that there had
been a delay and Smith had not been buried as Vivian presumed
previously.

Now with Smith gone—his sometimes trusted lawyer—Mashaal
was at a loss but knew that he must once more depend on Vivian to
move those funds, so perhaps he should be nice to her. He promised
compensation to her now that he owed no compensation to Smith.
Vivian should like $10,000 as a gift. He then offered his *best
solution*.

Malaraexpert@aol.com wrote:

Dear Dr Mrs Vivian

Many thanks for your great and honest efforts.It is deeply
appreciated the 25000 $ I sent to Late Mr Adam Smith was
borrowed from friends etc. Therefore any solution is
acceptable except to send more money as it is impossible for
me to obtain more money.

Therefore based on this fact ,Kindly find the best solution

I promise once I receive the money in my bank Sparkasse in
Germany ,I will send to you US$ 10000 personally for you as
reward
With kind regards and best wishes
Dr Hassan H.H.Mashaal

Vivian's reply that day gave no hope to Mashaal. He had suggested to her that she assist him in raising the second $25,000 and for that her reward would be $10,000. She replied as shown below that she did not have such an amount of money and that he was on his own to raise another $25,000. That was her sole solution to this problem. She showed no sympathy.

```
Subj:  Re: ref your e mail dated 15 July 2007
Date:  7/15/2007 10:01:58 A.M. Pacific Daylight Time
From:  vkamara77@yahoo.com
To:    Malaraexpert@aol.com

Dear Sir,
    Am sorry,i am ining solution but I dont have such money
with me if not i will love to assist even part of it so what
o you want to do now isince you don't have any more. If you
can find any moeans to get another $25000 ,then i can assure
you that we shall make a deal by trying to send all the
funds at once.
Very pity,i have no other solution.
Regards,
Vivian
```

Dr. Mashaal was not willing to give up that easily on the first $25,000 that he had transferred to Smith and told Vivian *I shall inform my German Bank to ask the bank who received the $25000 to transfer it to your bank,* and he asked her for the details of her bank so the money could be diverted from the Smith account. He closed with his best wishes and praises for her efficiency and help. Would Vivian accept these as sincere after having had many messages full of insults?

Several more e-mails passed this same day between Vivian and Mashaal. She responded to the above e-mail telling Mashaal that with the death of Smith, her bank could do very little. However only one hour later, Mashaal wrote to her and made a statement about trusting her honesty similar to a message he sent to her at the time of Linda's death. Now he asked her to find some person to put up another $25,000 to whom he would double the return to $50,000. Do you think that he really trusted her or was he trying to manipulate her? Read the following message from Dr Mashaal.

```
Subj:  ref e mail dated 15 July 2007
Date:  7/1/2007 2:44:03 P.M. Pacific Daylight Time
From:  Malara expert
To:    vkamara77@yahoo.com
```

Dear Dr. Mrs Vivian

Thank you for your letter
Already I had borrowed the $25000 I sent to Mr Adam Smith
based on your recommendation.I hope you manage to get them
it is not possible for me to borrow again
If one prepared to pay 25000$ ,after I receive the money I
can repay it double $ 50000
I hope you manage to get the $ 25000 $ I sent to Late Mr
Adam Smith

Or your bank can make a special meeting to approve to take
what is required from the available 10.5 millions Dollars on
exceptional basis

I appreciate you send me the name of the person who is in
charge of the finance of Late Adam Smith who received or
took the 25000$ his address and E mail

Thank you for your outstanding help
Best wishes

Dr.Hassan A.H.Mashaal

Following is Vivian's reponse.

```
Subj:  Re: ref e mail dated 18 July 2007
Date:  7/15/2007 11:22:19 P.M. Pacific Daylight Time
From:  vkamara77@yahoo.com
To:    Malaraexpert@aol.com
```

Dear Sir,
    Am sorry once again,i wish i could help but i am also
financially handicap,one of the second in command of late
smith chambers has your details he will contact you soonest
but i was inform that he went to the bank to withdraw the
$25000 and when he was on his way coming to pay in our
bank before he meet the sudden death,However those who are
the scene claim they o not see any money,definitely some
who among those who rush him to the clinic might have took
advantage of the money.

```
His chambers has nothing to contribute but only that the
$10.5 ,that is the reason why i am revealing all this to you
but i you insist that you don't have more money then there
is nothing i can do again.
Thanks an God bless
Regards,
Vivian
```

Unknown to me, e-mail and possibly phone contacts continued for nearly two weeks. We had lunch at least once a week, but Mashaal did not speak about his Ghanaian money business, and I never asked. I assumed that since I did not believe in his pending lottery, he was not sharing this matter but keeping it to himself as he had been asked on several occasion by his friends in Ghana. I just hoped that he would not send any more money.

Later I learned of more messages that arrived the same day as the above message. In one message, Vivian said, *I do not need any compensation from youbut the secret am reveal to you must be secrecy, the chambers of the late Adam smith want to get another representative to receive the funds of the late ms linda morgan in which you are the chosen by the late decease. However, i was inform that Mr. adam smith receive the funds from his account at CAL BANK before his unfortunate death.*

In that same e-mail, Vivian suggested that she would move the funds out of the escrow account in her bank and transfer at once the $10 million to Mashaal's bank in Germany as that bank had indicated that it was willing to accept all the inheritance at once. Vivian then asked for transfer fees of $50,000 for the full amount to be transferred. She said that she had turned over this matter to alhasan yakubu who is second in charge of the Adams Smith & Associate and says that yakubu will be contacting him, but he was not to tell yakubu what she had told him. It was not clear exactly to what she was referring. Perhaps she was referring to her intention of moving the funds out of the escrow account.

Mashaal was not about to finish this ordeal without trying again to get his money returned from Africa. In his message of July 16, he told Vivian that he had consulted his bank and they informed him that her bank could possibly make exceptions by changing some rules so it could take 2.5% from the available $10.5 million.

He suggested that if she tried this and was successful, he would compensate her as he had earlier told her with $10,000 once the money is received in Germany. Then he had a second idea. He asked Vivian, *Is it possible to put the $10.5 million in a cheque account on my name ? and to receive a check book from your bank on my name ?? I can send official letter signed and confirmed officially* and *Lastly I wish to thank you for your outstanding help* and signed *Best wishes*

Vivian replied shortly after receiving his message with a very curt one saying, *I don't want us to argue over this again as I already told you the situation of the funds, the only person who can authorize the bank to deduct a penny is the late Linda Morgan, it seens you do not inform the bank specialist the full story of the transfer.* Then Vivian admits that the bank could issue a cheque/ draft in Mashaal's favour but not until the money was paid *upfront* by him.

# CHAPTER 7

## BARRISTER MICHAEL MATHEW

Next day was a very busy day with messages flying back and forth between Dr. Mashaal in Canada and Vivian at the bank in Ghana. Four messages are shown starting below and on the following pages. First, Mashaal sent a message to Vivian, his once arch enemy, and offered what he believed to be a very practical solution to the money problem. No insults. Vivian likely made a reply either by e-mail or telephone as there was reference in the next message that Mashaal sent. I found no time printed on that message. Disclosed in this e-mail was the new representative of the law office with whom Mashaal was to deal. I could find no message in the files from Vivian concerning yesterday's mentioned message.

```
Subj:  Practical solution
Date:  7/17/2007 7:25:49 A.M. Pacific Daylight Time
From:  Malara expert
To:    vkamara77@yahoo.com

Dear Dr. Mrs Vivian
I realize that you wish to help me as much as you can
particularly after I sent to Accara 25000 US$ and were
stolen
You are honourable lady and I am sure you will do your best
to apply the present solution
Sometimes ago you requested full payment of 2.5% of 10.5
million US $ but repeatedly this was not possible for me
.Later you succeeded to modify this for the payment of $
25000 for one million dollar.but unfortunately the 25000
were sent but stolen in accra.Now also you suggested other
solutions to transfer all the 10.5 million $ but in a
practical way.
```

I hope you can help me if I send to your bank US$ 1000 which
is equivalent 2.5% of US$ 40,000. And as soon I receive $40
000 I can transfer to you 25,000 $ for further action
I do hope you can manage this and in this case send to my
the account number ,address bank etc to send the money
With high consideration to you

Best wishes
Dr Hassan A.H.Mashaal

And here is another message from the doctor to Vivian.

Dear Dr Mrs Vivian

Thank you for your E mail
You said the management gave the final consideration of
2.5% of $ 1m which is $25,000. The management can give
also consideration of 2.5% of 40,000 $ which is $ 1000
particularly if they realize I sent the 25000$ and was
stolen.

Mr Barrister Michael Mathew send an E mail in which he said
he sent yesterday e mail to me regarding the transaction
between Late Adam Smith and me. I send E mail to him that I
never received this mail and asked him to send it again as
may be he send it to wrong address.

Thank you

Dr Hassan A.H.Mashaal

Enough is enough! Vivian lost her patience with Mashaal and
became very angry with his attempting to manipulate her. Her reply
is shown below.

Subj:  Re: ref your e mail dated 17 July 2007
Date   7/17/2007 8:17:14 A.M. Pacific Daylight Time
From:  vkamara77@yahoo.com
To:    malaraexpert@aol.com

Dear Sir,
    I have only given you what the management can render, am
sorry if you cannot accept the final consideration as stated
previously 2.5% of $1m=$25,000.
Sir,i have devoted most of my time to ensure that the funds
enter your account safely but you are pushing me to the wall

```
in which i cannot do anything apart from the above decision
that was made by the management and i do not want anything
to jeopadize my sit because many question start arosing to
why am so much interested in your DEAL.
Sir,if you cannot do the above payment, pls,i will stop from
here.
Regards,
Vivian
```

If Vivian can blow off steam then what prevents Mashaal from venting his anger? He answered the question she had posed in her most recent e-mail about the reason for her great interest in his transaction. Once more he became angry and put the full blame on Vivian for his inability to receive those funds. (See the following message.)

```
Subj:  Re: ref your e mail 17 July 2007
Date:  17/7/2007 1:50:15 P.M. Pacific Daylight Time
From:  Malara expert
To:    vkamara77@yahoo.com

Dear Dr Mrs Vivian

You said many questions start arosing to why you are so much
interested in my DEAL.

The answer is simple because You are the one who 100%
responsible for the loss of 25000 US$. You suggested to send
the money to Mr Adam Smith and never gave the number to
which I was prepared to send the mone to your bank.WhY?????.

Evidently detail investigations will be soon done

I thought wrongly you can help but it is clear you are only
interested to cover your very serious mistake

Dr.Hassan H.H.Mashaal
```

A message arrived from micmathew_associates@lycos.com from Michael Mathew who claimed that yesterday he had sent a message and was waiting for a reply. In today's message, Mathew introduced himself and told Mashaal that he was contacting him on behalf of the late Adams Smith who died a few days ago. He said that he found the file on Adams' desk after his death, and he asked for Mashaal to contact him as soon as possible if he could be of any assistance to him. He included his telephone number in Accra and signed the message, *Best Wishes, Barrister Michael Mathew, LLB,HONS.*

Dr. Mashaal replied to Mathew's message (not shown) saying that he had not received any message from him yesterday and that was possibly due to an incorrect e-mail address being used. In his message, he briefed Michael on the payment he had sent recently and its loss and told him that he expected it was his office's responsibility to find that money. He said that his German bank warned him not to send money to Adams Smith as it would surely disappear. Mashaal proposed to Michael Mathew if that money could not be located then Mathew should get the equivalent from Smith's estate and deposit it into the bank so the African money transfer could take place.

Another message was sent to Mashaal by Vivian. In it she rambled on in poor English about trust, etc., and said she did not wish to work with him any more. She said that she was not afraid of losing her position if he launched an investigation as she had all the messages exchanged between them and knew she had done nothing wrong. She was not interested in the bonus of $10,000 but would accept it if Dr. Mashaal decided later that she deserved it for all the help she had given him. She closed her message as follows: *I guess i should be like a daughter to you ,am not afraid of any investigation because i do nothing wrong. Regards, Vivian*

In the message below, Mashaal suggested to Mathew to find someone to put up for a short time the second $25,000 and he would compensate that person. He said that he was unwilling to accept any alternative.

```
Subj:  ref e mail dated 18 July 2007
Date:  7/18/2007 6:00:23 A.M. Pacific Daylight Time
From:  Malara expert
To:    micmathew_associates@lycos.com

Dr Mr Barrister Mathew Mathew*

Thank you for your E mail

If you manage to find a person to deposit 25000 $ in the
bank so the bank can transfer one million dollar to my
account in Germany.If this is done I return to that person
```

```
instead of $25000 $ I return 40000 $ and in addition 10000 $
to you as a reward.

No other solution will be done.

Thank you and best wishes

Dr Hassan A.H.Mashaal
```

On a copy of the above message, I found a note showing the recipient's name should have been Michael Mathew, not Mathew Mathew.*

The following day correspondence was intense between Michael Mathew, Smith's replacement at the law firm, and Dr. Mashaal. In one message, Mashaal told Mathew that he believed that the money was stolen either at the scene of the accident or in the hospital where Adams Smith had been taken. In another, Mashaal asked Mathew to sell Smith's property to recover his $25,000.

Mathew responded that he had no authority to sell Smith's property to retrieve the money and return it to him. He asked Mashaal should he not look for another beneficiary who would complete the transaction. Mashaal then could be compensated after the transaction had been fully completed. Mathew closed indicating that he was awaiting Mashaal's soonest reply. Mathew offered Mashaal an out here but it seemed that Mashaal was not willing to take it as he still had hope of recovering some of his money.

Within two hours, Mathew returned a message to Mashaal saying that *it is not possible to transfer one million dollar into your account after I found another Beneficiary to complete the transactions.* He continued, *The Beneficiary will not give this amount out and I did not now how much is going to be compensated you after he/she completed the transaction.* Had Mathew really found another beneficiary? Are his firm and the bank finished with Dr. Mashaal?

Dr. Mashaal was waiting for Mathew's reply. Only a few minutes later there was an e-mail sent by Mashaal who said that there was no transaction as Michael would not accept the proposal he had sent him, and he threatened that this case would be dealt with *in future by International Court* as the solution he had given was the only one he would accept. It appeared at this point that Dr. Mashaal was unwilling to accept any further counter proposals that Mathew might make. He closed his message with *NO OTHER PLEASE* and *Thank you*. Have we not seen this same action several times already in previous messages from Dr. Mashaal?

Very early the next day, Lawyer Mathew responded with a message perhaps to show that he did not want to lose this source of money. He told Mashaal that it was possible to sell Adams Smith's property to replace the money owing him, and he believed that he could take legal action to uncover where the money was from and who is the rightful owner. This message was enough to get things moving again as Mashaal replied to Mathew's message same day, July 19. First Mashaal thanked Mathew for his *practical letter* and said that he was willing to postpone the court case he had threatened him with. This was to give Mathew time to work out a solution. He also repeated his reward of $40,000 for the person who put up the $25,000 on his behalf and, of course, an additional $10,000 to Mathew for his work. See e-mail below.

```
Subj:  ref e mail dated 19 July 2007
Date:  7/19/2007 11:13:14 A.M. Pacific Daylight Time
From:  Malara expert
To:    micmathew_associates@lycos.com

Dear Mr Barrister Michael Mathew

Many thanks for your practical letter
As you may know I am employee of Untited Nations World
Health Ogrganization Pen. Anything I promis must be done
100% to keep my status with United Nations I promise to
reward you heavily,.at least $ 10,000 or moe if you solve
my problems The problem to deposit 25000 $ in the bank
who promised to transfer One Million $ to my account in
Sparkasse bank in Germany

The 25000$ I sent to Mr Adam can be gained by sellin his
propery to replace the money I was the owner of the money
and was transferred from my bank in Germany You have the
details in the file Also if any agent interested to deposit
$ 25000 and I can receive the i million in Germany then I
shall pay the agent instead of $ 25000 I shall pay 40.000
$of course in addition to you 10,000 $ for your work
```

Dr. Agnes Chambers-Glenn

I hope you mange to solve the problem.I shall postpone the
court case for sometime to give you time to find any solution

Thank you and regards

Dr.Hassan A.H.Mashaal

In the following message, Mathew was changing his story
again as in an earlier message he had said that *it was possible to
sell Adams Smith's property to replace the money owing* him. Now,
Smith's property could not be sold to settle the debt of the missing
money that was presumed to have been stolen from Smith's dead
body. The rest of the message directed to *Dear Hon* seemed to be
just threats. It appeared that Mathew was informing Mashaal of a
court case his firm would undertake and would claim the $1 million
for themselves as costs or penalty, as Mathew described it. Was that
threat sufficient for Dr. Mashaal to drop this case?

Subj:   [Re]ref e mail dated 19 July 2007
Date:   7/19/2009 7:26:05 P.M. Pacific Daylight Time
From:   micmathew_associates@lycos.com
To:     Malaraexpert@aol.com

Dear Dr.Hassan A.H.Mashaal,

Many thanks for your respond!
Dear Hon. There is no law permits me to sell his property
or there is no power attorney allows to sell his property
to replace the Money because it was not griten that alter
his deat You,Dr.Hassan A.H.Mashaalshall sell his property to
replace the Money,if anything happen to it!

I strongly believe that you had my message as well and well
understood by you.

Dear Hon.This is only advise I can give and it will be
useful,if you comply with it can you be able to raise the
charges fee again,so that,it will be writeen that if Our
Chamber does not release the money to the Bank and we shall
make the penalty of $1,000,000 ($1m)dollar back to you as
the actual amount you were expected!

I shall be looking forward to read from you soonest.

Best Wishes,
Barrister Michael Mathew,LLB,HONS

64

Still Mashaal did not give up. He repeated his earlier response: He could not raise another $25,000 but would be able to find $1,000 and that should procure for him $40,000 of his inheritance. It appeared that he would be satisfied to receive just the return of at least his $25,000 payment. You will recall that he had sent two smaller amounts from his German bank in addition; but it appears that they are not as important to retrieve as the large payment. However, the $40,000 would also cover those amounts—US$5,000 and $2,000.

In his e-mail the following day, Mathew indicated that he was trying to get approval for Mashaal's latest request. He said that he had visited the bank on Mashaal's behalf. Then, offering no reason, he asked Mashaal for a copy of his International Passport. He had been asked for this early in his relationship with deceased Lawyer Adams Smith so the copy should have been in their office.

An immediate reply from Mashaal advised Mathew that he too had visited his bank moments earlier, and he assured Mathew that he would be able to send $1,000 from Canada which is 2.5% of $40,000. He said that if Mathew could convince the bank in Ghana to accept the $1,000 to release $40,000 the problem would be completely resolved.

The following day, July 21, I drove to Dr. Mashaal's home and drove him to his lawyer concerning another legal matter. He spoke very little of the scam to me during the trip, but he did say that Dr. Ms Vivian was planning a visit with him in Winnipeg as soon as he received his inheritance. Apparently she had spoken to him on the phone. I asked Dr. Mashaal if his wife was aware of his dealings with the people in Ghana and his bank. He replied that she did believe that he would receive this inheritance. I am not sure if this was entirely true as I never spoke with his wife about this matter thinking that perhaps she never knew anything about her husband's involvement in this money losing scheme.

Later that day, Mathew sent Mashaal the feedback from his bank from his previous day's visit. He said that the bank would not accept Mashaal's proposal to release $40,000 for the prepayment of $1,000. The bank insisted that the payment for transfer fees were $25,000 and that was it! There was no room for negotiations.

It appeared that Mashaal was persistent in that he would get things his way and again he messaged Mathew itemizing four demands. If not granted, he threatened to raise an international case against Vivian as he believed that she was the person responsible for the loss of his money. (Earlier when he spoke to me, he seemed excited that she planned to pay him a visit. However, according to the messages, he was angry with her as it was Vivian who asked him to transfer the $25,000 to Adams Smith and not to her bank.) The second point in his message was a repeat of asking Mathew to convince the bank to accept $1,000 from him to release $40,000 then he could pay a second $25,000 to the bank for the $1 million. He hoped that Mathew could convince the bank to carry out his wishes. He reminded Mathew that his German bank had insisted that he should not have sent the money to Adams Smith predicting that he would certainly lose it, and the bank had proven to be correct. However, with his insistence, the German bank had complied and sent the $25,000 to Ghana. His fourth point reiterated that it was impossible for him to send a second $25,000 as he could not borrow any more money, so there were only two possible solutions remaining to solve this problem. First, if Mathew could convince the bank in Ghana to accept $1,000 and transfer $40,000, the problem would be solved. He went on to say that *if the bank will not accept that solution then it is useless bank and rubbish.* Mashaal continued with a second possible solution. This was one that he had also put forward earlier; that is, Mathew was to *find a person prepared to pay $25,000 and as soon I get the one million dollar I pay him or her 40,00 instead of $25,00 beside for you for your reward*

There appeared to be no correspondence after the above message until four days later when Lawyer Mathew sent a very short message asking if he, Mashaal, were *the one who send another Lawyer to investigate about the fund with the bank?* He demanded an urgent reply. With no reply, Mathew sent a second message to Mashaal the following day. In that message, he gave the results of his very recent visits to the bank and showed a concern that the person that visited the bank and inquired about the funds in Mashaal's name was possibly sent by him, and he wanted to know if this were so. He also wanted Mashaal to tell him what proportion of another $25,000 as requested by the bank that he would be able to provide.

On July 28, two days later, Mathew had become very impatient and sent another message to Mashaal who had not made contact with him for several days. Mathew asked again how much money he could send as the bank had asked him to find out. He advised Mashaal that he wanted this issue to be a secret between only the two of them. See the repeated request for secrecy in the following e-mail.

```
Subj:  Dear Dr.Hassan A.H.Mashaal
Date:  7/28/2007 10:40:00 A.M. Pacific Daylight Time
From:  micmathew_associates@lycos.com
To:    Malaraexpert@aol.com

Dear Dr.Dr.Hassan A.H.Mashaal,

As I informed you already that the Bank refused to accept
$1,000 dollar and I would like you to tell me what amount
which is more than half of the demanded amount,so that,I can
try as much as possible to inform them that this is what you
can be able to raise at this moment!

Let this issue between you and I.Let me know how much you
can be able to provide to solve this matter amicably and the
said fund will be transferred into your designated account
successfully.

I shall be looking forward to read from you soonest.

Best Wishes,

Barrister Michael Mathew,LLBHONS.
```

Finally, Mashaal replied that with the greatest effort he would be able to transfer $2,500 which would be 2.5% of $100,000 to be transferred to his bank in Germany. This was nearly a month after I insisted to Dr. Mashaal that he was mixed up in a money scam and should drop it. However, for his own personal reasons, he refused to bow out. From his actions, I observed that it appeared he now realized that he was involved in a transaction that was less than honest.

The following day Mathew's message arrived informing Mashaal that $2,500 was too small an amount, but he would do his best *to confuse* the bank and would get back to him with its reply the following day.

As promised, Mathew sent his reply concerning his visit to the bank. He said that he tried to convince the bank to accept Mashaal's offer of $2,500, but the bank held firm in its refusal. The following three paragraphs are copied from Mathew's message.

*Now, I would like to contribute to this transaction because I have seen that it is genuine and I am also giving 100% assurance that it will be done as soon as the said amount of $25,000 dollar is provided.*

*Let me know how much you will be able now to raise from your end as at now I can provide $5,000 dollar*

*Please what is my compensation after the fund is transferred into your said account.*

Mathew had said repeatedly that the bank would only accept $25,000, and Dr. Mashaal had been just as firm in saying that he could afford at the most $2,500. So why did Mathew ask him again how much he *will be able now to raise* when the bank insisted that Mashaal must provide $25,000?

Mashaal replied to the above-mentioned message within two hours telling Mathew that the compensation for his assistance in raising the necessary money would be 100% or more than the amount that he paid into the deal. Mashaal insisted that he could never raise more than $5,000. From $1,000 to $2,500 and now to $5,000, Mashaal had raised his possible financial contribution in partnership with Mathew. Now what do you think Mathew's reply was? Read the message below that must have raised anew Mashaal's hopes.

```
Subj:   [Re]ref e mail 30 July 2007
Date:   7/30/2007 10:20:23 P.M. Pacific Daylight Time
From:   micmathew_associates@lycos.com
To:     Malaraexpert@aol.com

Dear Dr.

Good Morning,I believed that you have done your best so
far!When the said amount will reach me,so that,I will
```

```
give it to the bank and they should transfer the fund of
$1m dollar in your account and after the $1m dollar is
transferred you shall make the remaining payment.

I shall be looking forward to read from you soonest.

Best Wishes,
Barrister Michael Mathew,LLB,HONS.
```

Mashaal's message the following day simply repeated Mathew's message of the previous day. It appeared that Mashaal thought that the offer was *too good to be true*. For proof, Mashaal asked Mathew to e-mail him a letter from the Ghana bank to confirm this. He wanted this letter before he transferred the $5,000. Mathew replied asking Mashaal to brief him on how he wanted the bank to write the letter that he had requested a day earlier. Then Mathew made a promise to get the letter for Mashaal from the Ghana bank by the following day. He summed up the state of the funds: $5,000 from himself and $5,000 from Mashaal to make a total of $10,000. Will Mathew deliver his promise? So often we have seen that the party in Ghana reneged.

Within two hours, Mashaal outlined the letter for the bank as requested by Mathew, and he sent it in the e-mail that follows.

```
Subj:  [Re]ref e mail 31 July 2007
Date:  7/31/2007 5:38:45 P.M. Pacific Daylight Time
From:  Malaraexpert
To:    micmathew_associates@lycos.com

Dear Mr Barrister Michael

The bank can send E mail to me as follow

Title full name of bank
Address Bank
E.Mail bank & Phone Number & Fax No
Account Number of Bank
_____

Then the letter include

The bank fully agreed on receival of 10,000 US$: $ 5000 From
Mr Barrister Michael which will be later returned by Dr
Mashaal with 100% compensation and transfer of $ 5000 from
Dr H.Mashaal
```

Dr. Agnes Chambers-Glenn

On reeceival of US$ 10000 the bank will transfer One Million
US Dollars to the account of Dr. Mashaal in Germany .On
receival of the one million Dollar by Dr Mashaal he will
send the remaining balance of 25000 that is 15000 $ to the
bank and as well another 10,000 US$ for Barrister Michael.
which includes compensation
The bank is fully responsiple for the action.
Also the bank confirm receival of $5000 from Mr. Barrister
Michael and waiting for receival of $ 5000 can be
transferred from Dr H.Mashaal.The bank should give the
account number of the bank to which the $ 5000 can be
transferred from Dr H.Mashaal

As soon as I receive this from the bank I shall send the $
5000

Thank you.Best wishes

Dr.Hassan A.H.Mashaal

# C#APTER 8

## Michael Mathew, PATRICK ANSAH ET AL

The following day, there was a flurry of messages exchanged between the two men. Mathew's first message informed Mashaal that the late Linda Morgan's bank refused to release the money with a payment of only $10,000. The bank wanted $25,000 as earlier requested. However, Mathew said he would discuss with his bank if it would be willing to loan him more money, but he asked Mashaal to look for more money also until they have a combined total of $25,000 to satisfy the bank. You will recall that Dr. Mashaal was to send the money to an account at the bank where Mathew did his banking. Mathew was to take Mashaal's transferred funds from his bank to Vivian's bank where Mashaal's inheritance is being held. This was the same procedure that had been used when the late Adams Smith received the first $25,000 payment from Dr. Mashaal. That did not work but Mashaal still seemed willing to repeat the procedure as directed by Vivian and Mathew.

Mashaal replied immediately that he would attempt to borrow $6,000 and send it as soon as he received word that Mathew had borrowed $19,000 from his bank. Then as soon as the $1 million appeared in his German account, Mashaal would return to Mathew $38,000, doubling the amount he had put up for the release of that first $1 million. This money would be sent to the same bank, Vivian's, but in Michael Mathew's name.

71

Mathew replied after a short time stating that he had never mentioned that he could raise $19,000. He said that he could raise another $5,000 from a Mr. Patrick Ansah. That would bring his contribution to $10,000. So, it is now up to Mashaal to raise the balance of $15,000. He tried to convince Mashaal that by pooling their money, they would achieve their goal, the release of the $1 million to Mashaal's German bank account. Of course, Michael expected his compensation for helping raise that money.

Then Mashaal wrote to Vivian's bank and told them that he was willing to send $5,000 and that Mathew would also put up $5,000, so the two deposits would be sufficient to release the $1 million and have it transferred to his German bank account. He then promised that immediately upon receipt of the money from Ghana he would transfer the balance of $15,000 to the bank so the total sum of $25,000 as requested would be paid. However, he wanted a guarantee from the bank that Mathew had deposited his share before sending his. He asked that the bank also send him the account number where his payment would be deposited. Had the bank not advised Mashaal through Mathew that nothing less than $25,000 would be sufficient to procure the $1 million? Most probably to Mathew a little money was far superior to none.

Mathew learned of Mashaal's message to the bank and in his e-mail he appeared to be at his *wits end* with this transaction and told Mashaal, *it seems that you don't want me to involve anymore.* And signs off *Best Wishes,*

An hour and half later, Mashaal replied with the subject line: *3rd letter on 1 aug 2007.* In the message he said, *i WANT YOU TO BE INVOLVED but I cannot pay more than $6,000 Any one assist he will get double what he pays in few days*

Now according to the e-mails given to me, it appeared that the intensity of communications had subsided as the two men took two days off before any more messages were exchanged.

Early on August 3, Mathew sent a short message to Mashaal in which he said, *Good day!Since I have not heard from you please can I return the money I borrowed back? Ho*wever, Mashaal made another desperate appeal to Mathew to put up $19,000 that would be repaid double after the $1 million arrived in his German bank.

```
Subj:  ref e mail 3 August 2007
Date:  8/3/2007 6:28:52 A.M. Pacific Daylight Time
From:  Malaraexpert
To:    micmathew_associates@lycos.com
```

Dear Mr.Barrister Michael Mathew

I told you the maximum I can pay now is $ 6000
Already I paid Mr Smith 25000$ + 5000 +2000 Total $ 32000
$.All were lost in vain
In case you can manage 19000$ so that with my 6000$ the
total 25000 to the Bank
Of course the 19000 $ will be repayed as $ 38000
I repeat I cannot pay maximum 6000$
If you have no other solution then the situation ends

Thnnk you
Dr.Hassan A.H.Mashaal

Only 30 minutes after receiving the above message, Mathew e-mailed Mashaal and begged him to try harder to find more money—$10,000 from his end. He said that he had discussed the matter further with Mr. Patrick Ansah. Perhaps he is indicating that Ansah would be willing to lend him more money. He asked Mashaal to tell him by what method he would be sending the money, a money gram or by Western Union. He closed by saying, *Lest I forget, Do not forget your promises! Please, response soonest. Best Wishes,.*

Within two hours, Mashaal returned a message to Mathew reminding him that the total he would be able to raise was $6,000 as he had already paid Mr Smith $32,000. And, all had been lost. He said if Mathew could raise $19,000 then he would send the $6,000. He reminded Mathew that he would be repaying him double; that is $38,000. He closed thanking Mathew and saying, *if you have no other solution then the situation ends.* Here are these words repeated again!

However, the drama continued. It appeared that there was a message missing among those given to me as the next one on file was from Mashaal to Mathew telling him that the bank must send a message informing him that Mathew had deposited $15,000. Only then he would send his $10,000 (not $6,000) to make up $25,000 that the bank insisted upon. This would be the replacement of the previous $25,000 payment lost during Adams Smith's accident. When the $1 million was safely in his German account, Mashaal would transfer to Mathew a 100% profit, $30,000.

Little time was lost as just two hours later Mashaal received Mathew's reply shown below.

```
Subj:  [Re]ref e mail 3 August 2007
Date:  8/3/2007 10:59:47 P.M. Pacific Daylight Time
To:    micmathew_associates@lycos.com
From:  Malaraexpert@aol.com

Dear Dr Hassan,

I did receive your email content and well noted by me.I will
deposit the money with the Bank tomorrow morning by 8.00 to
8.00am,so that,the email will be sent to you that the sume
of $15,000 dollars is received by me.
Please,Iwould like you to draft a letter that the sum of
$15,000 dollar has been given by Barrister Michael Mathew
and after the the sum of $1m dollar is transferred into you
said account I will be paid back by #$30,000 dollar.

I shall be looking forward to read from youn back.

Best Wishes
BarristerMichael Mathew,LLB,HONS.
```

Mashaal's reply that follows confirmed his receiving Mathew's previous message.

```
Subj:  ref e mail of 3 August 2007
Date:  8/3/2007 12:46:21 P.M. Pacific Daylight Time
From:  Malaraexpert
To:    micmathew_associates@lycos.com

Dear Mr Barrister Michael Mathew

Many thanks for your letter
You mentioned tomorrow that you will deposit in the bank
15000.The bank should inform me that the bank received 15000
$ and ask for additional 10000 $ to have 25000 $ so that the
bank transfer one Million Dollars to my account in Germany.
The bank should give reference account number for transfer.
I confirm the 15000 $ in case are received by the bank to
be utelized as above,This money will be returned back as
$ 30000 (15000$ paid +15000$ rewards) on the name of Mr
```

Barrister Michael Mathew. This action will be taken once I
receive the One million Dollar in my German account.

Best Wishes
Dr. Hassan A.H.Mashaal

Next day, a fax arrived at Mashaal's Winnipeg home—a deposit slip. The form shown here below has no date, no bank name, etc. It appears that the right side has been cut away. That was the condition I found it among all those messages that were given to me in September. I suppose the purpose of this form was to indicate to Mashaal that the $15,000 promised by Mathew and borrowed from Patrick Ansah was on deposit now. In the message, Mathew did identify the bank as Zenith Bank Ghana Limited. This was proof to Mashaal that Mathew had kept his promise and it was his turn to keep his and send his $10,000. In his message, Mathew asked if he should give his bank account number in which the additional $10,000 could be placed. He reminded Mashaal that he agreed with his earlier promise of a reward equal to twice his contribution, so would be looking for $30,000 in return for his part in putting up the $15,000.

For some time, there were no messages exchanged between Vivian and Mashaal, but after receiving the deposit slip, it seemed that Mashaal's excitement was rejuvenated and he wrote Vivian with a copy to Mathew. (You may recall that this is one thing that Mathew earlier had requested Mashaal not to do. He did not want copies of Mashaal's e-mails going to the bank, and he asked Mashaal not to send any to Vivian.) In today's message Mashaal disclosed that Michael Mathew was taking part in raising the replacement $25,000 as demanded by Vivian's bank before releasing $1 million and transferring it to Germany.

He asked Vivian to confirm that Mathew had indeed deposited his share in the amount of $15,000 as agreed. Then Mashaal asked Vivian to give him the answers to two concerns he had. Did her bank receive the money from Mathew to be loaned to him? If so, give him the following details so he could send the balance of $10,000 to her bank:

- Name and number of bank account where money to be sent
- Name of the bank and detailed address
- Fax, telephones, e-mail, etc., of the bank.

Vivian's reply came the following day informing Mashaal that Mathew had made the deposit of $15,000 and that the bank was now waiting for his transfer of $10,000. She sent him a long list of bank details where the money was to be wired. As we can see on the bank deposit slip, the bank account's name where the money was to be deposited was Patrick Ansah. She said as the guarantee stated earlier that as soon as the full amount of $25,000 was in her bank, the $1 million would be transferred to his German bank. She suggested that he ask Michael Mathew to send him a copy of the deposit receipt of $15,000 that he paid to her bank's affiliate. This receipt was shown on the previous page.

Still on August 5, Mashaal messaged Vivian thanking her for the letter in which she acknowledged receipt of the $15,000 from Michael Mathew. He informed her that he was now in Canada and the first Monday of that month was a civic holiday, thus it was a long weekend, so the bank would not be open until Tuesday morning. At that time he would be able to send his $10,000 from his Canadian bank. He asked confirmation that the account name that was to receive his transfer was that of Patrick Ansah. Mashaal promised Vivian that he would not give his Canadian bank the Citibank New York's Swift Code as she had earlier asked him not to disclose this information. However, immediately, Vivian returned a message to correct the details. Mashaal was to give the details of the Citibank New York, and she repeated all the details.

Within a very short period of time, Mathew returned a message to Mashaal confirming he had received word that the bank had sent him proof of his money being deposited and was only waiting for Mashaal's money to arrive in Ghana. Mathew requested that Mashaal advise him when the $10,000 had been transferred from his Canadian bank.

The following day, at least seven e-mails were exchanged between Ghana and Canada. The first one of the day was from Mashaal to Vivian with a copy to Mathew's law firm. In this message, Dr. Mashaal had serious questions to which he needed answers before sending his $10,000. From this message, it appeared that Mashaal by that time suspected that his windfall may *not be for real*. It may be *too good to be true*! Perhaps my insistence that he withdraw from the scam before losing any more money was sinking in. Read the following message. Again Mashaal makes reference to his lawyer. I had introduced him a few years earlier to my lawyer and friend. This was likely one of his tricks since at that time, the lawyer knew nothing of the scam that Dr. Mashaal had gotten himself mixed up in. It was two weeks later that I asked my lawyer friend if he knew about the scam that Dr. Mashaal was involved in, and he said that he had no knowledge of it. It was obvious that both sides were playing games.

```
Subj:  transfer of 10000 US$
Date:  8/6/2007 7:02:47 A.M. Pacific Daylight Time
From:  Malaraexpert
To:    vkamara77@yahoo.com
       micmathew_associates@lycos.com

Dear Dr Mrs Vivian

My lawyer asked me why the US4 10000 is not transferred
directly to your bank or Zenithe Bank Ghana Limited.Why it
will be transferred to PATRIC ANSAH account no. 6020203409
Who is Patrick Ansah and why he is involved in this transfer
I deeply appreciate detail elaborated answer In case it is
transferred to your bank or Zenith Bank Ghana Ltd I need the
account number of any of these banks.

Also I asked you in the transfer should I omit the following
            CORESPONDENCE BANK :Citibank New York
                          Swift Code Citius 33
                          IBAN/FEDWIRE :FW021000089
This you did not answer
Sorry to bather you but I appreciate your answer before I
send the $ 10000
Dr Hassan A.H.Mashaal
```

Dr. Agnes Chambers-Glenn

Within a few hours, Mashaal sent a message directly to Mathew repeating his earlier inquiry about transaction matters that were of concern to him. Mashaal must have forgotten the name Patrick Ansah as it had been mentioned a few days earlier that he was the person who was putting up the money for Mathew. It appeared that perhaps Mashaal's bank in Canada had asked this question as they had not seen any e-mails, nor had he disclosed to his bank the money losing web that he was entangled in. Mashaal's reference to legal advice in the above e-mail was part of the game.

```
Subj:  hallo
Date:  8/6/2007 10:26:06 A.M. Pacific Daylight Time
From:  Malaraexpert
To:    micmathew_associates@lycos.com

Dear Mr. Barrister Michael Mathew
The bank asked me to transfer the $ 10000to the mane of
PATRICK ANSAH
Why not on the account of the bank. Who is PATRICK? And why
transfer on his name ? it seems to me there is a trick in
this subject

Please explain to me in detail why this wrong action
Incase the transfer to the account of the bank I will do it
at once
If I transfer to PATRICK ,he will die or sick or money
stolen etc etc etc

Please explain in detail

Thank you

Dr Hassan A.H.Mashaal
```

Vivian replied addressing Mashaal's concerns. She repeated earlier information and informed him that *the family of the late adam smith has file a petition to our management that we are trying to divert her late husband funds to one Dr. hassan of Canada which her petition was turn down because the letter of authorization receive from the late ms liinda morgan that we should transfer her fortune to your nominated bank account in germany before her sudden death, etc.*

She continued by saying that the $15,000 had been received from Mathew and now it was up to Dr. Mashaal to make his payment of $10,000 as instructed in a previous message. This message was certainly convincing as usual with the promise of transferring $1 million as soon as Mashaal's funds were received at the Ghana bank.

Less than 30 minutes later, there was a message from Michael assuring Mashaal that everything was okay and that he, too, had wondered why he had been asked to deposit the money with the Zenith Bank of Ghana instead of in the bank where Vivian worked. He explained that since deceased Smith's family was after the total transaction of $10.5 million claiming it as their own, that was the reason for the funds to be deposited into the other bank. (Does this really make much sense?) Mathew continued by trying to ensure Mashaal that everything was being done correctly. In the middle of the message he said, *Dear Dr. Hassan, I am Ghanian and no one can use any trick as far as I am Lawyer here and I know everything details regarding this Transfer now. I also paid the payment to Zenith Bank of Ghana after I asked a lot of questions regarding the money I deposited at Zenith Bank of Ghana Ltd.* He asked Mashaal to take the e-mail with the bank details to his bank and *make the transfer of $10,000 as I have given you 100% assurance that there would be no problem at all.* Is Mathew to be believed?

The next message was from Mashaal to Mathew with a copy to Vivian. Mashaal was still wondering who Patrick Ansah was, and why had his bank account number been given as the destination for the money transfer rather than a number of a bank escrow account. He feared if he sent the money to Ansah that *he will have an accident and the money will be stolen or disappear.* And Mashaal told Mathew that he had asked this question earlier both to him and to Vivian, but neither had answered his question concerning that matter. He said that he still hoped *to get a clear answer.*

Michael replied at once telling Mashaal that he had been informed that *Mr. Patrick Ansah is a presentative to Zenith Bank Gh.Ltd. We were informed to transfer the money to the name given by them.* Michael insisted that Mashaal just go ahead and send the money, and the $1 million would be credited to his German account without delay.

Do you recall that some days ago, Mathew said that a Mr. Patrick Ansah would loan him the money that he proposed to put up as his share at that time? It seems that Mashaal and Mathew as well had forgotten about the e-mail in which Mathew first mentioned Ansah's name. But worse still, it seems that Mathew had also forgotten from whom he had borrowed the money!

The final e-mail of August 6 was from Mashaal to Mathew with a copy to Dr. Mrs Vivian. In it, Mashaal showed that he was very hesitant to send money to Ansah's account. He reminded Vivian and Mathew that when he sent money earlier to the private account of Adams Smith, he lost it. His bank in Canada had warned him—like the European banks—that this would most probably happen if he sent money to the private account of Patrick Ansah. So Mashaal had a new proposal for Vivian and Mathew. He asked Mathew to raise another $10,000 for a few hours only and as soon as the million dollars was released to his Canadian bank he would then authorize Dr. Mrs Vivian of the Ghana bank to deduct $50,000 and give it to Mathew before the transfer of the balance of $995,000 was made. He said that would mean the repayment to Mathew of $25,000 with a $25,000 reward.

There appeared to be a miscalculation in mathematics on Mashaal's part as $995,000 plus $50,000 totals $1,045,000. Of course, most probably Mashaal intended this to have read $950,000.

The following day, August 7, was another day of busy business communications. The reply to Mashaal's latest proposal came early from Vivian. There was no mention of the wrong figure in Mashaal's calculations and offer. She said that *the late Adam Smith insist of you sending the funds to his account to be sure that the bank will honor its promise.* Smith was dead now nearly a month and Vivian says *he insists.* She continued that it was necessary for Mashaal to send the money to her bank to the account she gave him earlier as Michael Mathew paid his money into it. She said that any loss would be taken by her bank. And she insisted that he go ahead and send the money quoting the correspondence number that she had given him in earlier e-mails and asked him not to waste any more time.

Just fourteen seconds later, the same message quoted above arrived supposedly from Vivian but with a different type face and in italics and bold. She meant business as she said, *Don't waste time.*

Today saw the entry of another character's involvement into this confusing episode of who owns this money and who will get it. Susan Smith, the wife of the late lawyer Adams Smith, wrote to Dr. Mashaal saying that the bank would not answer her questions about the funds they were holding that really belonged to her husband and thus to her and to her children. She asked Mashaal to reply and to clear up matters.

Same day, within a few hours, Mashaal replied to Mrs. Susan Smith and sent a copy to Vivian at the bank. In this short message, Mashaal issued a threat to Susan. The message appears below.

```
Subj:  ref e mail 7 August 2007
Date:  8/7/2007 8:55:17 A.M. Pacific Daylight Time
From:  Malaraexpert
To:    susansmith233@yahoo.com
       vkamara77@yahoo.com

Mrs Susan

Your husband received from me $ 25000

This has to be repaid back to me.in case not,a case in the
international court will be raised
Your husband planned to take the money illegally.Many things
we know now.The accident happened to him was well planned to
steal the $ 25000. Government will be informed in details.

Dr.Hassan A.H.Mashaal
```

Soon after responding to Susan Smith's message, Mashaal wrote to Mathew sending a copy to Vivian Kamara. Did Mashaal at last see that he was involved in a scam? Was he now a doubter like he indicated on a few earlier occasions? Still it appeared that he was not willing to give up as he believed that he could recover at least the amount of money he had sent to date. (It was by this time in excess of a month that I first tried to convince him that his good fortune was not for real; that it was simply a fantasy.) There was an indication here that there may have been another message or more that were not given to me by Dr. Mashaal. He shared very

Dr. Agnes Chambers-Glenn

little of his money game with me as it was unfolding. There were phone calls at this time also as he spoke about some. Once very excitedly he told me that Vivian would be visiting him by the end of the month. Another time later in August he asked me if I thought he should send more money. He should have known my answer without asking. I do believe his involvement was somewhat embarrassing and frustrating for him as he could not make much headway in getting his hands on that money.

```
Subj:  ref e mail of August 2007
Date:  8/7/2007 9:14:35 A.M. Pacific Daylight Time
From:  Malaraexpert
To:    micmathew_associates@lycos.com
CC:    vkamara77@yahoo.com

Dear Mr Barrister Michael Mathew

I promised to deposit $ 10000 in the Bank once the bank give
me the account number of the Bank but Dr Mrs Vivian claimed
that was not possible because Mrs Smith requested the money
etc etc.This does not prevent I deposit my 10,000 $ in the
bank but Dr Mrs Vivian gave another Bank even in the other
bankI was asked to deposit the money to MR PATRICK ANSAH
which was very wrong procedure
Because of these wrong procedures I was advised that these
wrong procdures to take my 10000 $ illegally as Did Mr Smith
who took illegally 25000$.I knew many things now in detail
which will very useful to take legal actions.

I said in case there is 10.5 Millions on my name (which
I have prove not correct),However in case it is correct
I suggest to deposit the 10,000$ only for few hours to
receive 50,000 $ in few hours when the one million dollar is
released. This is very practical as deposit of 10000 only
few hours. But as you know that all this case to receive
money and never give money that is why you do not like to
apply this to get $ 500000 in hours. You know very well all
these case is not real but to steal money from clients.

D r Hassan A.H.Mashaal
```

From the above message, one would believe that Mashaal had finally *seen the light*, but had he? A message from Mathew to Mashaal told him that he could not put up the additional $10,000 even for a few hours as he had already borrowed the $15,000 *from*

82

*somebody* and if Mashaal did not reply really soon, he was going to *withdraw from the transaction*. He reminded Mashaal of his promise to supply the $10,000 if he (Mathew) borrowed $15,000. Now Mashaal had reneged. Mathew signed off, *I do hereby thank you so much and May God bless you abundantly(Amen)*. Finally, it appeared that Mathew had withdrawn his involvement. However, Mashaal always intending to have the last word, sent a message to Mathew with a copy to Vivian. (Refer to message below with subject line *Group pf theives*.) Notice the very strong rebuttal included in that message, a threat to Mathew and Vivian that they must return his money or else!

```
Subj:  Group pf theives
Date:  8/7/2007 1:59:56 P.M. Pacific Daylight Time
From:  Malaraexpert
To:    micmathew_associates@lycos.com
CC:    vkamara77@yahoo.com
```

M.Barrister Michael Mathew

Linda Morgon supposed to be died but after the date of her death a letter by her name was sent to a person in middle East country.The letter was the same which was sent to me.Also she stated to that person to contact her lawyer Mr Adam Smith.I am glad to receive this informations which is clearly and 100% proved that you are group of organized theives to rob many persons
Please inform Mr Adam Smith in case he return US$ 25000 I will close my mouth and the story ends but in case not I have now many evidence to proove you and Mr Adam Smith and some in Banks are cooperated together to be highly organized theives. Certainly I shall manage to proove that and certailly this group wil be put in prison for many years because they ruin the reputation of Ghana.Your Government and many Embassadors will help me to get rid of this corruption. As I said I shall stop in case Mr Adam smith return the $25000 but if not you will get all of you severe punishments.

Dr.Hassan A.H.Mashaal

Vivian's blistering message below was sent to Mashaal in response to his previous message. Mashaal had told Mathew and Vivian that Lawyer Smith was not dead and that their entire scheme was a trick for robbing him. Vivian, referring to the Smith family,

Dr. Agnes Chambers-Glenn

also said that *the family now given the bank pressure that you are
only after their late father money*. She was making reference to what
she had mentioned earlier. She had told Mashaal that Smith's widow
was a nuisance at the bank trying to claim the money that Mashaal
believed to be his and not that of the late Adams Smith's family.

```
Subj:  Group pf theives
Date:  8/7/2007 4:00:29 P.M. Pacific Daylight Time
From:  vkamara77@yahoo.com
To:    Malaraexpert@aol.com
```

Dear Sir,
    I will advise you to take action immediately because we
all know that adam smith is dead even the death certificate
should be out soonest because they will burry him soonest.
Also, lawyer micheal has vow to come and take back his money
which he deposited with zenith bank because you accuse
him of what he doesn't know anything but we are ready and
prepare for your international court action because you
create the problem by asking lawyer micheal to contact the
late adam smith next of kin to go to the bank and get money
so this create suspicious to the family that the funds
belongs to them,never the less,if lawyer micheal come for
his money we shall return to him since he paid the money to
the account that we advise him so you can continue to look
for adam smith in the grave or anywhere you claim he is.

The question is how many do you know that the same letter
send to you goes to someone far away in the middle east, the
family now given the bank pressure that you are only after
their late father money,am sorry we shall stop communicating
with you as soon the lawyer micheal withdraw his money as
find a way to send the late linda morgan funds to states
treasury vault or give to late adam sith family

BYE FOR NOW
VIVIAN

---

FOOTNOTE: I first learned of this message of August 7 along with all the others after Dr. Mashaal gave me the materials in September. This was sent about three weeks before he finally went to the police on August 30 to report the loss of his money. After reading this message, I was surprised that Dr. Mashaal had kept his doubts to himself all the while speaking positively to me about the deal. It was early October that I went on line and read about the corruption in Ghana. According to the articles, corruption is as prevalent within the government itself as it is in the population in general. It is considered a way of life in Ghana to outwit your neighbour with a *better* way of making a living through such money scams. (Google *Corruption in Ghana* on the Internet.)

84

# C H A P T E R 9

Messages continued. Mashaal returned a message to Vivian telling her that the $10.5 million was in his name and for that reason the bank could not transfer it to anyone else. He closed repeating one more time his threat that *the subject will be studied by international organization.* That day, August 7, was another very busy day with messages concerning Mashaal's inheritance and the problems that it had created.

The following day was just as active with at least seven messages exchanged starting very early in the morning. Vivian from the bank was back in action again. She reminded Mashaal that he was wasting his time by making excuses about Lawyer Smith's death. She assured Mashaal that there was 100% security in sending the money to the account given as the bank had given him that number. What a guarantee!

```
Subj:  Re: 10.5 Millions $
Date:  8/8/2007 12:12:02 A.M. Pacific Daylight Time
From:  vkamara77@yahoo.com
To:    Malaraexpert@aol.com

DEAR SIR
    I DON'T WHY YOU ARE WASTING YOUR TIME IN FAULTERING
FACTS, THE MAN DIED AND DEFINITELY THE FAMILY MUST RAISE AN
EYESBROWS TO KNOW WHERE ALL HIS FORTUNE CAN BE LOCATED.

OUR BANK ALREADY PROVIDE YOU AN ACCOUNT AT ZENITH BUT IF
YOU ARE INSISTING ON GETTING ANOTHER BANK ACCOUNT,THEN AM
SORRY WE CANNOT PROVIDE IT,THERE IS 100% SECURITY ON THE
```

Dr. Agnes Chambers-Glenn

```
ACCOUNT NAME GIVEN TO YOU BECAUSE WE ASK YOU TO SEND THE
MONEY INTO IT.

YOUR CHOICE
REGARDS
VIVIAN
```

Then Mashaal sent Susan Smith the message that appears below. He insisted that the money he had sent to her husband must be repaid to him, or he would raise a case in the international court.

```
Mrs Susan

Your husband received from me $ 25000

This has to be repaid back to me.in case not a case in the
international court will be raised Your husband planned to
take the mony illegally.Many things we know now.The accident
happened to him was well planned to steal the $ 25000.
Government will be informed in details.

Dr.Hassan A.H.Mashaal
```

Susan replied immediately. This was another feisty lady, Vivian being the other. Perhaps this was an indication that both messages were written by the same person as their anger and diction appeared very similar. Also, it appeared to me that it is really a male doing the writing but pretending to be a female. Certainly they do not appear to be very culturally groomed. Notice that Susan mentioned that she would bury her husband tomorrow. What is tomorrow's date? What day was lawyer Smith killed in the accident?

```
Subj:  WE SHALL SEE
Date:  8/8/2007 2:12:26 A.M. Pacific Daylight Time
From:  susansmith233@yahoo.com
To:    Malaraexpert@aol.com

HELLO,
    I AM ALSO WORKING VERY HARD WITH MY LAWYERS TO ENSURE
THAT YOU DID NOT TAKE MY LATE HUSBAND MONEY BUT THE ONLY
PROBLEM IS THE BANK IS NOT PROVIDING ME ENOUGH DETAISL OF
THE FUNDS BUT I KNOW THAT WITH TIME I SHALL GET TO THE
BOTTOM OF THIS.
```

WHATEVER YOU CLAIM ABOUT MY LATE HUSBAND THAT HE STEAL YOUR
MONEY AND INTENTIONALLY GET ACCIDENT AND DIED IS A PURE
LIE,WE SHALL BURY HIM TOMORROW.

LISTEN,WE GOT ALL THE INFORMATION THAT SINCE WHEN THEY
ANNOUNCE THE DEAD TO YOU,YOU ASK ONE HIS LAWYER TO CONVINCE
THE NEXT OF KIN TO COLLECT ALL THE DOCUEMENTS, I BET YOU
THAT YOU WILL NEVER SUCCEED, I AM READY T GO INTO WAR WITH
YOU AND FIGHT IN ANY INTERNATIONAL HIGH COURT BECAUSE NOW I
KNOW THAT MY LATE HUSBAND HAS $10.5M WHICH YOU WANT TO USE
YOUR OPPORTUNITY OF HIS ABSENCE TO RETRIEVE.

I WILL GET THE WHOLE FACT VERY SOON, LEAVE MY HUSBAND
PROPERTY ALONE.
SUSAN

A few hours later, Susan fired off another message demanding that Mashaal denounce his claim to the $10.5 million inheritance from Linda Morgan by writing a letter to Vivian at the bank. After he did that, she would return the $25,000 that Mashaal claimed he paid to her husband. Susan insisted that this money belonged to her and her children.

Subj:  Re: your husband received 25000$ from me
Date:  8/8/2007 5:58:32 A.M. Pacific Daylight Time
From:  susansmith233@yahoo.com
To:    Malaraexpert@aol.com

HELLO SIR
   HANKS FOR YOUR EMAIL, I HAVE NO PROOF BECAUSE HE IS
DEAD,HOWEVER I AM READY TO PAY BACK YOU $25,000 AS YOU CLAIM
THAT MY HUSBAND RECEIVED FROM YOU ONLY IF YOU WILL INFORM
THE BANK IN THE PERSON OF DR MS VIVIAN KAMARA THAT THEY
SHOULD RELEASE THE $10.5m OF MY HUSBAND FUNDS TO ME.

OR YOU BETTER STAY AWAY FROM THAT FUNDS BECAUSE IT BELONGS
TO MY LATE HUSBAND AND OUR FAMILY.
JUST A LETTER FROM YOU TO THE BANK THAT YOU ARE NOT
INTERSTED ON THE $10.5M THAT THE SHOULD RELEASE ME AND I
PROMISE THAT I WILL PAY YOUR $25,000 BUT IF NOT AM SORRY I
AM READY TO CHALLENGE YOU IN ANY INTERNAIONAL COURT OF LAW

AND ALSO PREPARE AND TO LET YOU KNOW THAT THE FUNDS BELONGS
TO OUR FAMILY

REGARDS,
SUSAN

The messages continued to flow that day. Lawyer Mathew sent a reply to an earlier message from Mashaal saying *I did receive your email with an insultive words and I did not learn to insult in my profession.I do hereby to inform you that I have withdrawn the sum of $ 15,000 dollar back today. I wish you the best of luck. Bye.* There was no signature.

Same day, Mashaal messaged Susan Smith explaining to her that her late husband, Adams, was simply working for him to help the administration of transferring the $10.5 million to his German bank account and that Smith had cashed the $25,000 to release the first $1 million to be transferred to Germany, but with his death, the money had been stolen. So he concluded that 100% of the inheritance was his but he was prepared to ask the bank to give her a half a million dollars as a donation in the memory of the late Adams Smith. In return, she must be prepared to give him that $25,000 that he had sent to her husband to clear the funds. It was obvious that Mashaal assumed that Susan had stolen the money from her deceased husband's body.

Susan Smith responded saying that she was *still investigating the truth of the fund which the person incharge of the transfer Dr Ms Vivian is not given me enough details, I assume that the late lady authorize you as the receiever which i assume that the late lady authorize you as the reciever which i don't have any proof but as far as i am concern,i still stand on my words that the funds belongs to my late husband.*

Susan continued, *in other words,we are capable of handling the burrier ceremony which will take place tomorrow and friday night for final ceremony therefore i am only prepare to send you $25,000 even though i have no proof that my late husband receive the said money which you claim only if you can write to the bank that they should release the funds to late adam smith family because my great concern if that i got information they you have contact our his associate that they should contact my son who is the next of kin to assist you in securing the funds.*

Susan had more to say. *Sir,am sorry ,youcannot go free with this money as i am still saying despite i am a woman but ready to battle with you in any length of any higher international court of law to retrieve back what belongs to my late husband,OUR FAMILY.*

*If you want any compensatiom,we are ready to render it to you as you claim,my late husband has your $25,000 so i advise you to kinly write a short letter to the bank indicating that you are no longer interested in the transfer that they should release the funds to smith family ,i promise you with the name of ALLAH,GOD that i and the entire family will reward abundantly for your great effort and honesty. Regards, susan*

By now, I am sure that from reading all the messages, you have noticed that all persons involved are lacking good business and English writing skills. It seems that banker, lawyer, doctor, as well as the others typed their own work. There appeared to be no secretaries involved in any correspondence as there would normally be in situations involving professionals in Canada and most other countries.

The following day, Mathew replied to a message from Mashaal in which he had called him and others *a group of thieves.* It appeared that Mathew was finished and perhaps had withdrawn his $15,000 deposit. Now if Mashaal wanted that inheritance, he would have to put up another $25,000 of his own money to ensure the transfer of his inheritance to his German bank. See below.

```
Subj:  [RE] ref yiour e mail of 8 August 2007
Date:  8/9/2007 4:30:16 P.M. Pacific Daylight Time
From:  micmathew_associates@lycos.com
To:    Malaraexpert@aol.com

Dear Dr.Hassan A.H.Mashaal,

I thought I have done the best I can do at this point and I
also guarantee you 100% assurance that I am Lawyer who tells
you the truth that I was instructed to deposit the sum of
$15,000 dollar with the Zenith Bank of Ghana with the Name
of Mr.Patrick Ansah and when you called me Group of Thieves
and I suggested the best thing to be done,I must call back
of the money i deposited with them which is $15,000 dollar.

If you are interested to receive the sum of $1m dollar just
go ahead and transfer the money to the Name and Account
information provided by Bank to you.

I wish you best of Luck!

Bye,
Barrister Michael Mathew,LLB,HONS.
```

In Susan Smith's message of August 10 shown below, she said that her late husband was buried that day. Her message two days earlier had informed Mashaal that her husband would be buried the next day, August 9. Perhaps it was the difference in time zones that caused this discrepancy. You will recall that he was killed on July 12. It appears that his body has been kept for over a month. Probably in this scam Susan and the others involved had not realized the time passing so quickly, or they may have gotten details mixed with other victims from whom they were extracting money. An entire month before burial seems like a long time to keep a corpse in any country but especially in the equatorial Africa region.

```
Subj:  Re: ref e mail dated 10 August 2007
Date:  8/10/2007 9:52:49 A.M. Pacific Daylight Time
From:  susansmith233@yahoo.com
To:    Malaraexpert@aol.com
```

Dear Sir,
    I know that you are only pretending about my husband stole your money,we finally burry him today ,therefore I do not know anything about the funds and cannot pay any money which I do know the truth of it ,what am after now is the $10.5m,my lawyers are keeping their eyes on account officer in charge of the funds, as i have told you earlier,youstay away from my children funds, my husband told me something about the funds but you think because he is dead and you want to take advantage of it,am sorry this will not work out, if you know the money is on your name why do you ask the $25,000 only and why dont you go for it if it belongs to you truly,there are alots of holes in your story,i bet you,it will not work out
Regards
Susan

These messages were followed by one from Mashaal to Vivian. In it he asked her if it were possible for her to open a *cheque* account, either in her bank or another bank, in his name and transfer $10.5 million into it.

In a forceful message replying to his above request, Vivian answered as follows: *Sorry ,we cannot open a cheque account on your name because we have authorization from late ms morgan that the funds should be transfer to your account ,therefore the family of late adam smith also saying that the funds belongs to their father because you have ask of his barrister to contact his next of kin on this transaction so they are thinking the funds belongs to their father.*

Vivian continued, *As I said we provide you an account to send the money as lawyer micheal has call that he will come for his $15,000 deposit previously and the bank will have no alternative to send the whole money to the STATES TRESURY VAULT ,am sure by then you will be able to come down and explain yourself to BANK OF GHANA as it seems you dont want to understand and listen to instructions.* She signed off with *Thanks Vivian*

It was not clear if what Vivian meant here was that her Ghana bank would be sending Mashaal's inheritance from Ms Linda Morgan to the Ghana State Treasury Vault, or did she mean to a United States of America Treasury Vault in New York City? It appeared that she no longer planned on having any further dealings with Mashaal and indicated that he might have to fly to Ghana to straighten up this financial mess.

Mashaal replied to Vivian and repeated what he had told her earlier; that is, she could not transfer the $10.5 million to anybody else as it was in his name, and if she should attempt to, *the subject will be studied by international organization.*

The following day, there was less activity but still business continued. Mashaal wrote to Mathew explaining why he had not sent the $10,000 as he had earlier agreed to. He told Mathew that his banks in Switzerland, Germany and Canada had all insisted repeatedly that he not transfer any money direct to any individual in Ghana, but rather to a bank. He mentioned that earlier the European banks did not want him to transfer money directly to lawyer Smith but due to his insistence, the banks complied. His insistence had been based on the recommendation of Dr Mrs Vivian whom he had faith in at that time. All that money was lost as all three of his banks had predicted. Vivian had told him that she had not given him a bank account in which to deposit the $10,000 as she believed that Mrs. Susan Smith might create a problem. Vivian insisted that he should send the second payment of $25,000 to a Mr. Patrick Ansah's account. Mashaal told Mathew that the reason he did not transfer $10,000 was Vivian's insistence again on the money going to an individual's account in place of into a bank's account. He said he was prepared to send $10,000 but that he required a bank account number. Mashaal believed that having a bank account number would solve the chance of loss. He repeated an earlier offer saying that if Mathew would give the bank the total required, $25,000, just for a few hours to ensure the release of the $1 million, he would reward him with a return of $50,000 on the same day. Mashaal directed Mathew to claim his $50,000 as soon as Vivian at the bank made arrangements to make the transfer and send the balance to Germany.

Mashaal then sent a message to Susan Smith and told her that he had the letter from the late Linda Morgan that stated that her inheritance of $10.5 million was to become his inheritance. He said that Linda asked him to *use the money to help children and poor people in different countries.* Mashaal was referring to that first e-mail that Linda had sent him dated April 24.

He then proceeded to suggest to Susan Smith *a very practical suggestion.* He later offered to take only $1 million and to give her the balance of $9.5 million. Was this not extremely generous of Dr. Mashaal? He told me later that he only needed $1 million to carry out a malaria eradication program in Yemen. He felt that he might not have enough energy at his age to attempt the same for other malaria infested countries. However, his offer was not without his placing conditions on Susan Smith receiving it. He asked her to deposit the $25,000 that he earlier sent to her husband as he really believed she had that money. That would have covered the cost of transferring $1 million to his German bank. Good planning? Then Susan was to inform Dr. Mrs Vivian that she was making this deposit so the bank would transfer the $1 million to his account in Germany. If Susan reached an agreement with Vivian, then Mashaal would be willing to correspond with the bank and make the request to Vivian to transfer the funds, then he would send a copy of this correspondence to Susan. He also insisted that she must use some of *her $9.5 million to help poor children and poor people as late Linda Morgan wished.*

The following day, Susan Smith replied to the message from Mashaal in which he said he would give her $9.5 million of the inheritance and he would be satisfied with only $1 million. Susan did not appear happy even with that offer and told him again that she had no proof that her late husband owed him $25,000 and that she had shown his e-mail to some of her family on the way to the funeral. They advised her *not to allow him to take advantage of $25,000 that belongs to our family.* She went on to say that she knew how to use the funds for poor children as her entire family belong to a NGO (non-government organization) orphanage program. She said that since he insisted that her husband took the $25,000 that she would refund it *if* he wrote to the bank and advised it to release the $10.5 million to the family of Adams Smith. When the bank released the funds to her family, then she was ready to send him the $25,000.

Then Vivian messaged Mashaal and told him that the account number that the bank gave him in which to deposit the $10,000 was for his security as the Smith family and associates were now giving the bank plenty of pressure to be the recipient of the $10.5 million. She said that from his message she now knew that lawyer Mathew had withdrawn his $15,000 so Mashaal would either have to reconcile with Mathew, or send the entire $25,000 that was needed to release the $1 million. She continued that if he listened to his bank in Canada that most probably he would lose the $10.5 million. Vivian said that she would not tell the late Adam Smith's family any information and then said that if she did not receive a positive reply that day, the transaction was finished. Do you suppose this was Vivian's final threat?

Mashaal wrote Susan again saying that he could give her the account number into which he transferred the $25,000 and from which her late husband withdrew the funds. But he said that the most important thing to him was that she made a deposit of $25,000 and agreed that he receive the $1 million. He continued by saying that if she refused his suggestion, she would receive nothing instead of $9.5 million as *officially* the total money was in his name and the bank could not change this without his permission. As soon as he received the $1 million, he would write the bank and give it authority to give the balance to Mrs. Susan Smith. Mashaal signed off, *In case you do not agree on the above sorry I shall not write again.I am very bussy and I have no time to waiste.*

Vivian sent a message to warn Mashaal if he did not raise the $25,000 transfer charges within a week that the money would be sent to the *United States Tresury Vault.* She continued to say that the Smith family were sending insults in e-mails and in phone calls saying that their late friend's funds (deceased Smith) were deposited with her bank and his family wanted the money now. She continued by telling Mashaal that she had given him his instructions but it seemed that he refused to follow them so her bank had no choice but to send this large amount of money to the *States Tresury Vault.*

The same day, about six hours later, Mashaal wrote Vivian and told her that she could take the transfer charges from the $10.5 million if the bank would call a special meeting and adjust the regulations to help a client. He said that this was done in advanced banks in Switzerland and Germany and many other countries. He suggested that Ghana should not be so backward that adjustments cannot be made. And he offered if her bank would make a special rule for him that he would give the bank $1 million and the balance of $9.5 million less the charges of 2.5% can be transferred to Germany to his account.

It would appear now that Mrs Susan Smith's receiving Mashaal's inheritance was no longer on his mind. He felt that she had no legal right to the money so why should he worry. Again he offered a threat to Vivian saying *In case you swift the funds to the STATES TRESURY VAULT, This will be very serious and you will responsible for the great errors done.*

For the reader, the meanings of statements in a message may not always be clear, but the gang of thieves and Dr. Mashaal had been corresponding since April 24, about four months, and they seemed to assume things and know what to write next to play out their drama. Many of the messages used very poor English language; however, the individuals seemed to know how to respond and keep this deceitful game continuing.

Again, Mashaal reminded Vivian that her bank made a very serious mistake by insisting that he transfer the $25,000 to Adams Smith and not to the bank. This money was lost following the bank's instructions, so he believed that the bank should be able to make an exception to the rule in this case. He reminded Vivian that the bank stood to receive $1 million as he promised.

Within hours, Vivian replied to Mashaal's message and declined his offer of compensation if her bank changed the rules for his transaction. She bluntly informed him that *accepting such compensation from a client is against the rules and regulations of Ghana banks and is called bribery and corruption in sectin a4, article 1 and 6 in the bank of ghana form A2.* She insisted that her bank could not transfer any money to his bank account until the 2.5% charges had been paid for the first $1 million, and she gave him seven working days to make the transfer, or the money would be sent to the States. She signed off with *Your Choice, pay the money due or fly to the United States for the release of the funds.*

The drama continued. Mashaal replied to Vivian's message thanking her for her reply and told her that he chose to fly to the USA for the release of the funds since he had worked for the United Nations and is now a pensioner of UN.

Later the same day, Vivian had a new twist in information for Mashaal. She told him that she was sorry to inform him that the funds were not yet in his name and that was the reason the bank requested the transfer charges in the first place having assumed that Linda Morgan would be alive and could authorize the deduction of the transfer charges from the principal sum. However, since she was dead, the receiver must pay the charges in advance. She went on to tell him that the funds would be sent to the States in Linda's name and it may be difficult for him to have access to them because there is no legal document showing that he is the beneficiary of the funds, only a receiver according to the documents left with her bank. Vivian said that she did not understand why Mashaal was wasting his time. She explained that Lawyer Mathew was trying to be of help to him, but Mathew was angry now and had withdrawn his deposit of $15,000. She expressed her sorrow for Mashaal's position and gave him another week to get the money, another $25,000, to her bank.

Mashaal replied immediately reminding Vivian that she had officially written a letter to employees in his German bank and had sent him a copy of the letter in which she had told them that the $10.5 million was in his name. *This is confirmed,* he said. He is referring to the letter of some days earlier that Vivian had sent to the German bank employee in care of Dr. Mashaal—not directly to the employee. Thus, Dr. Mashaal believed that the bank had received a copy of the letter and was informed of the ownership of that $10.5 million. Vivian tried everything to trick and confuse Mashaal.

Next day, Vivian replied and told Mashaal that the funds were in his name in Ghana only, *but as soon as they leave the shores of Africa for the States Tresury Vault, they will no longer be in your name.* Vivian repeated that he had only one week to get the money to her bank. She related how she was under pressure from the Smith family who had even visited her home earlier that day. She finally had called the police to make them leave. She insisted that there was no other method now for the release of the $1 million except for him to abide by the bank's instructions and get the second $25,000 to the Zenith Bank.

Mashaal's e-mail reply shown below was written two hours after receiving Vivian's above information.

```
Subj:  ref e mail 12 August 2007
Date:  8/12/2007 7:56:38 A.M. Pacific Daylight Time
From:  Malara expert
To:    vkamara77@yahoo.com

Dear Dr Mrs Vivian

In case the funds are on my name and therefore by law in
case the funds are transferred to STATES TRESURY VAULT
should be also on my name.I was informed by specialists that
these funds must be always on my name.I hope your bank is
honest to apply this similar to banks in Switzerland and
Germany Or you would like to say your bank cannot follow
Swiss or Germany banks for their honesty and the bank prefer
to be dishonest so that not follow foreign banks.

Thank you & best wishes

Dr.Hassan A.H.Mashaal
```

Next morning I received a message from Dr. Mashaal in which he told me that he was ill and had to go to the doctor at the oncology department and would update me on his health when next he talked with me.

Finally on August 13, Susan Smith replied to Mashaal's generous message dated August 9. This lady replied as usual, the greatest bully. See message below.

```
Subj:  Re: ref e mail dated 9 August 2007
Date:  8/13/2007 12:15:01 A.M. Pacific Daylight Time
From:  susansmith233@yahoo.com
To:    Malaraexpert@aol.com
```

HELLO SIR,
    HERE YOU GO,YOU THINK YOU CAN ASK THE BANK TO SEND THE
FUNDS TO UNITED STATES,WE ARE WATCHING EVERY STEPS YOU TAKE.
MY INFORMANT REVEAL THAT THE FUNDS WILL NOT BE ON YOUR NAME
WHEN IT LEAVE AFRICA,I WILL BE IN THE STATES NEXT WEEK ,SO
IF YOU CAN MEET ME FACE TO FACE THEN YOU SHOW ME DOCUMENT
PROOFING THE FUNDS BELONGS TO YOU.

REGARDS,
SUSAN

How safe do you believe Dr. Mashaal would have been meeting
some people from the Nigerian mafia in New York City? In her
message to him on the same day, Vivian appeared to have had
enough. She seemed really fed up, but she replied to his argument
that his name of ownership would not be on the funds the minute
they left Africa as she had informed him in her previous message.

```
Subj:  Re: ref e mail dated 12 August 2007
Date:  8/13/2007 12:14:57 A.M. Pacific Daylight Time
From:  vkamara77@yahoo.com
To:    Malaraexpert@aol.com
```

Dear Sir,
    I will not exchange anymore words with you as i have
inform you that you have only this week to comply with the
bank terms,either you send the $25,000 to bank account that
we provided to you ,this is not late smith account,the bank
purposely provide this account for you and gurantee leter
can still be issue in your favor that soonest we receive the
payment control number of $25,000 ,the bank shall remit $1m
immeidiately to your bank in german or swiss bank but if you
are still comparing german or swiss bank with Africa bank,am
sorry you are going no where.
The funds rest on your name here in Ghana but soonestit left
the shore of africa,it will comes back to the owner name
because document the authorisation that was send to us by
the late linda was only a mere email letter that was not
sign but yet we recongnise so you can inform your specialist
about this that we only receive an email from the late linda
that we should transfer the said funds to your account which

Dr. Agnes Chambers-Glenn

```
the UNDITED STATES AUTHORITY will not depend or accpet an
email letter not sign or seal by COURT OF LAW.
You are wasting your time ,i will not from today reveal
anything to you because smith wife has got the information
that the funds will be send out of the country and i dont
want because of your case to lose my sit.
Bye for now,contact me only when you are ready to pay the
2.5% of $1m and we shall give you bank irrevocable gurantee
sign and seal.
Vivian
```

It appeared from most of the e-mails being exchanged now that tempers were elevating for everybody. All the African players were angry with Mashaal's delay in putting up the second $25,000 that was necessary to clear the $1 million for transfer to his bank. He continued to insist that the $10.5 million was in his name and that could not be changed. Now the bombshell! Vivian informed Mashaal that Linda Morgan's letter of April 24 had not been signed. This would mean that it was not legal.

Mashaal was not about to give up yet. He continued to have hopes that the money, at least $1 million, was within his grasp. He wrote to Vivian saying, *In case the money is on my name in Ghana. It is not possible to change that if transferred to another country unless there is serious corruption in administration. Also in case I pay 25000 $ your bank will say the money to go to Germany will not be on my name as it is not in Ghana. This is a serious corruption in administration hopefully can be corrected.* Mashaal showed signs of serious frustration as he was not in control as he was accustomed to being most of his working life.

Later in the day, Vivian replied although earlier she had indicated that she had had enough of Mashaal's nonsense. She emphasized that if he had sent the money to the bank as outlined some time ago, there would be no delay in transferring the money to his German account within 72 hours. She repeated that there was no corruption in her bank system and went on about things that Mashaal and she had discussed earlier about procedures in the European banks versus Ghanaian banks, etc.

Mashaal always wanting *to get another word in*, replied to Vivian with reference to her e-mail of August 11 and quoted her as saying that it would be easier and better to fly to the United States for the release of the funds since he had worked for the United Nations office, and he had indicated that he agreed with her and was willing to fly to the USA and solve the problem, but he asked her if the Ghana bank would act upon what it had promised like Swiss and German banks would do.

Now just when we thought this was over, next day Vivian replied and stalled on her suggestion for Mashaal going to the States to claim the money because of what she had told him earlier; that is, the funds would be sent in the name of Linda Morgan, not his. She said that she would no longer be corresponding with him as she was leaving her bank position as Account Officer to the funds. In addition, she reminded him that he had only until Friday to send the $25,000. (The request had been sent on Tuesday.) Vivian said that Susan, the late Smith's wife, was waiting for the funds to be transferred to the USA and her lawyer was visiting her bank (Vivian's) from time to time. However, Vivian said that since Mashaal was *like a father* to her, she would not give Susan's lawyer any information. She assured Mashaal that she needed his reward as promised earlier and at the same time she wanted to assist him. She added that she was looking forward to visiting him either in Canada or in his home in Germany.

So that set Mashaal off again with a reply to Vivian. He again described to her the hopeless situation of the Ghanaian banking system. He asked her how could the bank put money in the name of a deceased person and then transfer it to the United States. He told her again that her bank was not to be trusted and gave his examples as he had earlier. He told her that she was not assisting him by asking the bank to put the funds in the name of a dead person. Then he said, *By the way, I have very high pension from United Nations. The Money of Linda Morgan will never used for my benefit only to help others as she wrote..Now the money will help no body because of the useless administration of Ghana bank.* And he sent best wishes.

A day passed and Vivian replied with a short, curt message in which she wrote, *THANKS FOR THE INSULT. I HAVE TOLD YOU THAT THE BANK WILL BE RESPONSIBLE FOR ANY LOST THAT MAY OCCUR BY GIVEN YOU A BANK GURANTEE LETTER BUT SINCE YOU REFUSE TO DO THIS. I WISH YOU GOOD LUCK BY*

(Notice the usual errors in spelling and in sentence structure. As I informed the reader in the Introduction, I always quoted material exactly as it was written, repeated words, misspellings, incorrect punctuation, missing punctuation and capitals, incorrect spacing, etc.)

Always to get the last word in, Mashaal replied with his short insulting message as follows:

*Dear Dr Mrs Vivian*
*I cannot trust a bank who transfer money on name of DEAD PEOPLE. No doubt must be the worst bank in the world with the worst staff*

*Thank you*
*Dr.Hassan A.H.Mashaal*

Not waiting for a reply, the next day Mashaal sent off another message—using very large red print—and informed Vivian, *This is not an insult but FACTS.* In her reply, Vivian again told Mashaal that she was being removed from managing his account transactions. She wished him good luck and suggested that he *write a comprehensive e-mail to the new manager advising him to the location in Canada to divert the funds.* However, Vivian did not inform him of the name of her replacement nor give an e-mail address for the new manager.

# CHAPTER 10

Vivian's announcement that she would no longer be in charge of the inheritance transfer had caused Dr. Mashaal some anger. Not even waiting for the name of the new person he was to work with, Dr. Mashaal sent an e-mail to Vivian's e-mail address but directed it to the Director of the Bank telling him that Vivian had advised him to write a comprehensive e-mail to the bank so that the bank would freight the funds as consignment to his address in Canada. He included his Canadian address, gave his post office box, and closed with *thanks*.

The following day, August 19, Mashaal received a reply from the bank from a Kofi Banson who appeared to be the new bank director who had taken over from Vivian the managing of Dr. Mashaal's account. The Subject of this message was *NON INSPECTION CERTIFICATE NEEDED*. In this message, Kofi told Mashaal that the funds were now scheduled to leave for the USA since Mashaal's application letter indicating that he wanted the money to be freighted to his destination had been received. Kofi repeated the Canadian address that Mashaal had given in the previous message to the former bank director. He rambled on about the funds being claimed also by the family of the late Adams Smith; however, earlier Vivian had made it clear to him that he was the first beneficiary as Linda Morgan had sent an e-mail to him to be the beneficiary. It would appear that Kofi believed the route to ship funds from Ghana to Canada was through the USA then take them over the border into Canada.

So now Mashaal must obtain the required certificate, the A2, from the office of the president (He did not say whose president.) to allow his *special diplomatic carrier to enter Canada without any hindrance due to the 9/11 incident it patriotic act as be send to Africa not to freight any huge mount of money outside the west Africa nation without proper documentation covering, attach is the form a2 of Non Inspection Certificate,which you will fill and send back with the required fees to for the funds to be freighted unfailing next week. Please fill the form and return with the required fees to obtain the document.* " And Kofi signed this *FOR ICB (hisnk).*

We had not heard the last of feisty Susan Smith yet. Next day, August 18, she sent an e-mail as she had heard that Mashaal was trying to have the money sent to Canada.

```
Subj:  HELLO
Date:  8/18/2007 8:39::14 A.M. Pacific Daylight Time
From:  susansmith233@yahoo.com
To:    Malaraexpert@aol.com

DEAR SIR,
    WHERE DO YOU WANT TO DIVERT THE MONEY THAT BELONGS T
MY LATE HUSBAND TO, GERMANY OR CANADA, THE FUNDS DOES NOT
BELONG TO YOU SO LEAVE OUR INHERITANCE ALONE.

SUSAN
```

First thing next day, Mashaal messaged Susan thanking her for the message above and telling her that the bank was sending the money to the United States *Tresury* Vault and if she sent her USA address, he might be able to meet her in the USA.

Within six minutes, Mashaal messaged the Bank Director in Ghana to whom he had just been introduced. He asked him to give him the detailed address of that location of the United States *Tresury* Vault since he understood that the $10.5 million had been sent there.

Vivian, after having been relieved from her position of tending to Mashaal's inheritance, sent Mashaal a message in which deciphering the meaning of the content was difficult. She may have been trying to tell Mashaal when replying to the Director, not to use her e-mail but she had not yet given him an e-mail where the

Director could be reached. An attachment was mentioned but I was unable to find it. Probably Dr. Mashaal did not print it. At that time he was not forwarding messages.

High praise went to Kofi from Mashaal who had just very recently met him through an e-mail. Mashaal wanted to proceed with business and get his hands on the money that he believed was rightfully his. He mentioned the amount of $3,750. (I presume that there was a missing message or two, or a phone call, asking for that amount to pay for another form that would be necessary to move that money.) An early message from Mashaal to Kofi follows:

```
Subj:  Ref your E mail
Date:  8/19/2007 8:06:58 P.M. Pacific Daylight Time
From:  Malara expert
To:    kofi@icbb.zzn.com

Dear Kofi
I wish to thank you very much for your letter.Yor efficiency
is very high
I have few questions to help me
1-What address to send the form
2-The staturory official mandatory fee of US $3750 to what
address to be send,Account number etc
3-From where i get letter from the Presidency
4-From where i get Diplomatic non -inspection certificate

Regarding the 10.5Million Dollars it was on my name.Never on
the name of Mr. Smith.Mr Smith was only the lawyer to help
administration BUT NOTHIN ON HIS NAME.His wife claimin this
wrongly

Many thanks and best wishes

Dr.Hassan A.H.Mashaal
```

Perhaps Dr. Mashaal believed that *a little bit of sugar could go a long way* when establishing his new relationship with Kofi. The message that arrived the following day from Bank Director Kofi spelled out the instructions for Mashaal after telling him that he was *not to reveal any of this to a third party*. This transaction must be kept secret as per the instruction from the previous Ghanaian bank employees and the two barristers that had worked on the case. See the following e-mail that contained the answers to Mashaal's

Dr. Agnes Chambers-Glenn

questions posed in his earlier message. Kofi closed by asking him *to act as soon as possible*.

Notice in the message below the introduction of the two new names, Micheal-Ikono and Annor-Kumi Richard. Mashaal had a choice to which one of the two persons he could send the money. However, that would be determined by whether he sent the money via Western Union or chose to transfer it directly to an account at the Ghana bank. To ensure delivery, Kofi sent the message and a copy to the same recipient, Dr. Mashaal.

```
Subj:  NOTE
Date:  8/20/2007 2:09:05 A.M. Pacific Daylight Time
From:  kofi@icbb.zzn.com
To:    Malaraexpert@aol.com
CC:    Malaraexpert@aol.com

Dear Sir,
This need to be handle diplomatic manner so i decline you
for revealing to third party because it will be difficult
for our bank to move the funds by wire transfer for now
unless you pay the 2.5.% for the $1m that is why the moving
by freight is easy and fasted way.

I WILL ANSWER YOUR QUESTION AS FOLLOWS BRIEFLY.
!-What address to send the form:-P.O BOX AT 542
ACHIMOTA,ACCRA-GHANA
2-The statutory official mandatory fee of US 3750 to what
address to be send,Account Number etc :YOU EITHER SEND BY
WESTERN UNION MONEY TRANSFER SINCE IT'S A LOWER AMOUNT AND
CAN BE RECEIVE WITHIN AN HUR TO THIS NAME :MICHEAL-IKONO,
ADDRESS;12N INDUSTRIAL AREA,ACCRA-GHANA OR

YOU SEND TO ISSUING ACCOUNT OFFICER ACCOUNT:
BANK NAME;STANDARD CHARTERED BANK,GHANA LTD
BANK ADDRESS:P.O BOX 20 TEMA-GHANA
ACCOUNT NAME: ANNOR - KUMI RICHARD
ACCOUNT NUMBER:870152136-54300
SWUFT CODE:SCBLGHAC

3-From where i got letter from the Presidency : Letter will
be issue at office of the presidency that the funds could be
allow to freighted to your destination
4-From where I get Diplomatic non-inspection
certificate:Same from office of the presidency soonest the
mandatory fees is paid
```

```
Also,i want to alert your fear that we have strongly warn
the late smith wife that i did not in any form see her late
husband name on the document presented to my desk so she
should stop accusing our bank wrongly or she will face the
law court.

Please you need to act as soon as possible.
Regards,
Kofi
```

Mashaal received another message from Vivian the following day although she was to have been relieved of her duties related to him. She wrote, *Congratulations the management finally sue the late smith wife and associate to court that the funds is no on thier name and they should stop communicating with you.* It appeared that the court case was settled in a big hurry. It would appear that Vivian sent this information as an excuse to keep the funds in Ghana and not to freight them to the United States Treasury Vault as had been threatened on at least two occasions.

Of course, early that same day, Mashaal replied to Vivian's message. In his message, besides tending to business, he suggested that he would send an invitation to her to come and visit him in Canada or in Germany. So perhaps Vivian was no longer the dishonest person that he had been accusing her of being. Read Mashaal's message below that he wrote to her.

```
Subj:  ref e mail 21 August 2007
Date:  8/21/20077:19:31 A.M. Pacific Daylight Time
From:  Malaraexpert@aol.com
To:    vkamara77@yahoo.com

Dear Dr Mrs Vivian
Many thanks for your letter indicating that the funds is not
on the name of late Smith and associate I realized you are
very fine and reliable person.Please I am sorry for some
letters I wrote wrongly before.

Now I am asked to fill the form titled THE PRESIDENCY
REPUBLIC OF GHANA
NON-INSPECTION CERTIFICATE APPLICATION FORM "A"

And pay US$3750 to Standard Chartered Bank Ghana Its Account
8701521354300 etc
```

```
What I wish to ask you,in case I send the $ 3750 will the
10.5 Million $ or one million dollar will be transferred to
my account in Germany or Canada without paying 2.5% Iwish
very much to know that

Many thanks.I wish one day to invite you to stay with us in
Germany or Canada

Best wishes

Dr.Hassan A.H.Mashaal
```

Vivian replied to the idea of the invitation that Mashaal offered in his message and said that she would be taking vacation by the end of next month, and by then she expected he would have received the money. She asked if he could send her the invitation that he mentioned so she could apply for a visa. Vivian also asked Mashaal to fill out the forms she sent and return them to her. Again, she insisted that he stop communicating with Susan Smith and family. She told Mashaal that he still had the option of paying the 2.5% ($25,000) and receiving the $1 million instead of paying this latest charge of $3,750 that would have the funds sent to his Canadian address as a consignment. (Whatever she meant by a consignment was not clear. Probably this was another idea to further confuse Dr. Mashaal.)

That evening, I had a call and a visit from Dr. Mashaal wanting to discuss the sending of more money to Ghana. He suggested he might send $10,000 to the bank. He did not give the reason, but perhaps I did not give him time to as I simply said, *No! No! No!* Later I did learn at the police station on August 31 that he did send money the morning following that visit. He sent $3,750 from the Bank of Montreal in Winnipeg. The receipt was dated August 24. It would seem that he could not stop himself from attempting to recover at least the lost $25,000 by paying more.

According to e-mails I was given in September, I learned that on August 21, Mashaal also wrote to Kofi who was suppose to be tending to his money affairs and now had his own e-mail address, so it was not necessary any longer to use Vivian's to reach Kofi. In this message he told Kofi that the Canadian post office told him that it would take two weeks for the completed form to reach

Ghana. For the sake of time, he thought it would be best to send the original by post and at the same time a copy by fax, but he required a fax number. He also asked if he were to send the $3,750 would he, Kofi, and his bank send the $10.5 million without asking for anymore money from him, and would the money inheritance reach his Canadian residence in cash or would it be deposited into his Winnipeg bank account. He also inquired about those two forms that were costing him the $3,750 to obtain: a *Letter of Mandate from the Presidency* and a *Diplomatic Non-Inspection Certificate*. Mashaal was not satisfied with the information in Vivian's earlier reply.

The message the next day from Mashaal to Kofi informed him that his Canadian bank was delaying the sending of the $3,750 until they, the Bank of Montreal, received from Dr. Mashaal the answers he had requested in the previous day's message to Kofi. In other words, Mashaal was telling Kofi to hurry with his reply so he could send the money and have his inheritance on its way from Ghana to Winnipeg.

After early September when I was given the nearly 400 e-mails and forms by Dr. Mashaal, I started to collect information relating to scams. I e-mailed alerts to many family members and friends suggesting they be aware and not get trapped like Dr. Mashaal had and requested them to send me any they received as scams have not gotten through my filter system into my e-mail.

Dated August 22, was an e-mail from me to Dr. Mashaal. This was among the stack of messages and forms he gave to me in September. In that message, I had warned him that I believed he was involved in a scam and it would be best for him to discontinue his involvement and not to send any more money. A day earlier while visiting my home, he had again told me that he had developed a health problem and his heart specialist had diagnosed it and given him the results. I suggested that he take his stack of information and pay the police a visit because it was obvious that his involvement in this scam was destroying his usual good health. Perhaps the police would be able to track these Ghanaian thieves. Then I told him about my losing many thousands of dollars to a friend who had borrowed nearly $100,000 from other friends and me, and my friend had lost all of it to some clever Middle East tricksters in Australia. Actually, thirty thousand dollars was what I had invested in *the get rich scheme.* I had received absolutely no compensation from this one-time friend. This fellow even lost his car to another person that he had borrowed from for that *high paying business deal* he had been promised. With Dr. Mashaal, I was having a very difficult time getting through to him. However, he appeared to have heard my warning and indicated he would comply. But had he really? I found out later, he had not.

Messages continued from Kofi. The message of August 22 arrived with a cc as well. Kofi included a fax number as Mashaal had requested and assured him that once the $3,750 was received the consignment would be forwarded in the form of cash to his Winnipeg address by a diplomatic carrier who would assist him to deposit it into his chosen bank. Would a recipient not wonder what this deal was all about when given this information? A million dollars cash delivered to his home? Can you imagine a legal shipment of $1 million cash from Ghana to Winnipeg? I am sure that Dr. Mashaal knows the law about importing money in access of $10,000 requiring a declaration completed at Customs upon arrival. I wonder what his thoughts were of receiving $1 million. But, then he had checked this with his bank and seemed to believe this was possible. Perhaps it is with proper documentation. Kofi said that this method of a consignment had been chosen by Mashaal by paying only $3,750 instead of paying the second $25,000 as the bank had requested from him for so long. Kofi also said that *the two forms will accompany the consignment/funds to your end but we need to apply for this as soon as possible that is the reason i suggest that you use western union money transfer since it's the fastest way to receive low amount of money as it take only an hour to receive if you send it but bank to bank takes about 72 hours, you are free to send through any of your choice.* Then Kofi asked for Mashaal's direct phone and fax number.

Messages continue to be exchanged. Mashaal contacted Kofi and told him that his bank in Canada informed him that the addresses given to him earlier from Africa were not sufficient to send the funds requested. So Mashaal asked for a more specific address—a street address, not a post office box. The Canadian bank also wanted the telephone, fax and e-mail of the Ghana bank. They also asked for the private address of Annor, his telephone and e-mail. You will recall that Annor-Kumi Richard was one of the persons that Kofi named to receive the funds into an account at the bank. Mashaal said that his bank needed these items for *security reasons*. He suggested a very quick reply from Kofi because he would like to get the money on its way the following day, Friday. Most probably the bank was being extra cautious and as well as were stalling Mashaal on sending that money. Later you will learn the reason that Dr. Mashaal gave to the bank for needing that money to be sent. His reason was certainly far from the truth.

Kofi replied only one hour later, but he did not give any additional information that Mashaal's Canadian bank had requested as necessary before sending the $3,750. See the message below.

```
Subj:   Re: ref e mail 23 August 2007
Date:   8/23/2007 2:08:52 P.M. Pacific Daylight Time
From:   kofi@icbb.zzn.com
To:     Malaraexpert@aol.com

Dear Sir,

The bank gave us the follwoing :Standard Chartered
Bank,Ghana Ltd.
Address: P.O box 20 Tema-Ghana
Tel/Fax: +233 21 7012205
Telex: 2671
E-mail: Not Known
Account Name: ANNOR-KUMI RICHARD
Acc.No: 870 152 135 4300
Swift Code: SCBLGHAC
Account Address:P.O box nt 12 community 20,tema-ghana
Account Holder phone number:002332977878
E-mail:sakimatti@yahoo.com

Sir,I send your request to the bank and this is all they
could offer that Canada bank should check their telex,they
will realize that Ghana use only p.o box as contact address,
am sorry this is all i can do for now, i await your positive
reply.

I have requested that you should send your phone number and
fax but till now no reply ,please send this in your return
email.

Regards,
Kofi
```

In Mashaal's file of e-mails exchanged I found the following two forms. No date appeared on either of these so-called important business documents that were required to move the money out of Ghana to a country of Dr. Mashaal's choice. *The United Nations Non-Inspection Certificate* and *The Presidency Republic of Ghana Non-Inspection Certificate Application Form "A"* are shown below and on the following page. Dr. Mashaal remarked that these forms were very realistic so he thought they must be official documents. They were stamped *Certified* and *Approved*. Certainly they looked authentic to him he remarked to me much later. Since one was suppose to come from the United Nations, he asked later, how could they have possibly obtained those forms falsely?

The form below required some enhancing as original, a fax, did not scan well. No words were altered.

# THE PRESIDENCY

## REPUBLIC OF GHANA
### NON-INSPECTION CERTIFICATE APPLICATION FORM "A"

NAME OF BENEFICIARY: Dr. HASSAN. A. H. MASHAAL

NATIONALITY: CANADIAN

PASSPORT NO.: BD 118282

ADDRESS OF BENEFICIARY: Apt. 1502 SUSSEX HOUSE.
230 ROSLYN ROAD. WINNIPEG. MB. CANADA. R3L-0H1

TEL: (1-204). 284-2448      FAX:

EMAIL ADDRESS: malara expert @. aol. com.

ITEM(S) TO BE FREIGHTED: 10½ Million US DOLLARS

REQUIRED DESTINATION & DELIVERY POINT (COUNTRY/ADDRESS): Apt. 1502.
SUSSEX HOUSE- 230 ROSLYN Road WINNIPEG - Manitoba - Canada R3L-0H1
Bank Accnt. D. H. A. H. Mashad. Bank. af. Montrnl. Acct. Nr. = 0573 4507 785
330 Portage Avenue Winnipeg - Manitobr Canada R3C DC4
BENEFICIARY SIGNATURE & DATE: ..... H. Mashaal

THIS FORM MUST BE ACCOMPANIED BY THE FOLLOWING, IF THE FREIGHTED ITEM
SHOULD BE CASH:

1. LETTER OF MANDATE FROM THE PRESIDENCY.
2. DIPLOMATIC NON-INSPECTION CERTIFICATE.

### For Official Use Only

Name, Signature & Date of Official To Freight Items:

......

Sign of Approving Officer                    Sign of Operations Director

This form is to be submitted with a statutory official mandatory fee of US$350 only.

---

Mashaal replied an hour and a half later to Kofi and sent him all the information that he thought Kofi had asked for. This included his phone and fax number in Winnipeg, his residence address, his Winnipeg bank account number and address. Then he promised to post the Presidency form the following day as the fax number, 0047-005-981-869, that Kofi had sent did not go through. If Dr. Mashaal was really in doubt, one would wonder at his sending this very personal information. It appeared since the beginning of this business whatever he was asked for, he complied. This seemed to be proof that the Nigerian scam group and others are able to convince people that they are honest people and are to be trusted.

The Letter of Request made the following day by him to the Bank of Montreal is shown below. In addition to his letter, he also completed the Canadian bank's form asking that the money be transferred. With these, the bank complied and sent the money probably because of his insistence. However, he told me later that the bank, like both European banks, advised him that there was little doubt but that this was lost money but he refused to listen to them. All this took place only two days after my conversation with him in which I had advised him to send *NO* more money! The action from this day would later haunt him as he acknowledged at the police station that he had sent more money, the latest from Canada, $3,750 and he opened his binder to the bank form. When I checked the date of the form, I saw that it was sent the day after I had tried to convince him that he was involved in a scam and had tried very hard to suggest to him that he should not send any more money to that gang of thieves. Perhaps involved in a money scam such as this may be synonymous with compulsive gambling. One just cannot stop and denial is part of it also. You will notice that the bank address and the account number have been omitted on the letter below. I learned later that all account numbers, etc., had been changed and that deleting them was not really necessary. Noted is the fact that the Ghana bank shows a Telex number after saying it had none.

```
24 August 2007

Bank of Montreal
xxxx Xxxx Street
Winnipeg-Manitoba
Canada RxX xXx

Dear Sir,
Kindly transfer today from my US% Account #...... a total of
3750.00 US$
Three thousands, seven hundreds and fifty US Dollars. The
transfer is urgent & today

To:    Standard Chartered Bank,Ghana Ltd
       P.O.Box 20 Tema-Ghana
       Tel / Fax +233 21 7012205
       Telex 2571
       Account Name: ANNOR-KUMI RICHARD
       Account Number: 870 152 135 4300
```

```
Swift Code SCBLGHAC
Address:P.O.Box nt 12 community 20,tema-ghana
Phone No: 00233242977878
e-Mail: sakimatti@yahoo.com

Appreciate confirmation. Thamk you

Dr.Hassan A.H.Mashaal
P.O.Box Winnipeg
Manitoba.CANADA RxX xXx
```

I found the customer receipt concerning the mailing of the above originals to Ghana. It was a REGISTERED Canada Post form to P.O. Box AT 542, Achimotz Accra, Ghana with a Declared Value of *zero*. A handwritten note on the form was the date, *24/8/2007 and Letter to Ghana*. You will recall that Mashaal faxed both forms after receiving a valid fax number but for safety sent the originals by registered mail *to ensure valid documents were placed on file*.

Shown on the following page is the form prepared by the Bank of Montreal requisitioning the wire transfer to Ghana as Dr. Mashaal requested. Notice the reason given on that Canadian bank form was *to pay for estate and medical expenses*. Did Mashaal tell an untruth in order to get the money on its way to Africa? He was from Egypt, so his reason given here most probably would have been acceptable to the bank employee.

| BMO ☻ Bank of Montreal | Requisition for Wire Transfer | | 24/AUG/2007 |
|---|---|---|---|

| Serial Number 057366992 | Value Date 24/AUG/2007 | Amount USD | 3,750.00 |
|---|---|---|---|

**ORDERING CUSTOMER**
Name     DR HASSAN AH MASHAAL                    *Note: 4017# — whited out.*

Source of Funds   ACCOUNT
QUOTED RATE & EXCHANGE
N/A

**BENEFICIARY**
Name     ANNOR-KUMI RICHARD

Address   P.O. BOX NT 12
City      TEMA
Region    COMMUNITY 20                           Postal Code
Country   GHANA

**BENEFICIARY BANK**
Bank Name STANDARD CHARTERED BANK GHANA LTD

Address   P.O. BOX 20
City      TEMA
Region                                           Postal Code
Country   GHANA                                  Bank ID      SWIFT SCBLGHAC

**CORRESPONDENT BANK**
Bank Name WACHOVIA BANK NA                        Code 1000106

**DETAILS OF PAYMENT**
Notify by Phone  NO                   Regular  Number
Credit Account   YES  Account   )1F   54:        Pay on Application & Identification   NO
Remittance Information TO PAY FOR ESTATE AND MEDICAL EXPENSES -
- PH NO. 00233242977878

**WIRE TRANSFER AGREEMENT**

In consideration of the Bank of Montreal (the "Bank") processing and receiving wire transfers ("Transfers") from time to time for our account, we agree as follows:

We acknowledge that the Bank is not responsible for and we agree to indemnify and save the Bank harmless from and against any and all charges, expenses, losses, errors, damages, penalties, costs or inconvenience resulting to us or any other person arising from any delay or failure ofperformance due to causes beyond the control of the Bank, including, without limitation, the acts or omissions of or the insolvency or bankruptcy of other financial institutions or systems failures respecting the processing and receipt of Transfers. The Bank is not liable to us or any other person for incorrect or improper payment to or from us or any person arising out of the processing of any Transfer, unless caused solely by the negligence or willful misconduct of the Bank.

We acknowledge that the Bank may delay the sending of a Transfer in the event that any restrictions applicable to the Bank in any clearing system used to effect the Transfer, including, without limitation, insufficient credit or other limits delay the Bank from sending the Transfer. We acknowledge that the Bank and other financial institutions involved in processing Transfers may rely solely on any account or identification number (s) provided and will not seek to confirm whether the number (s) specified correspond with the name of the payee or the payee's financial institution provided in the payment order and are not obliged in any other way to verify the information contained in the payment order. The payee may be required to provide identification to the satisfaction of the paying financial institution.

Transfers executed by the Bank are irrevocable. While the Bank shall use its best efforts to request a return of funds upon our instructions, the Bank cannot guarantee a return of funds or a return of funds without charge or fee to us. If the Bank is able to obtain a return of funds, the Bank will credit our account less any applicable charges or fees, at the bank's quoted rate of exchange (where foreign currency exchange is requested by us) on the date such credit is made. The funding account number information may be provided to the beneficiary's financial institution as part of processing this Transfer.

We agree to pay any Bank charges or fees and to reimburse the Bank for any fees or deductions charged by other financial institutions, withholding or other taxes, interest and penalties that may be paid by the Bank, in connection with any Transfers. We acknowledge that other financial institutions may charge or deduct a fee for processing Transfers (including fees for refund requests and corrections).

Transfers are subject to cut-off times, time zone differences and local laws and regulations of the destination country, including Canada.

| _____ | D. GROSS | _____ |
|---|---|---|
| Customer Signature | Completed by | Authorized by |

Form 90135                                                    Customer Copy

No messages between August 24 and August 28 were found in the material that Dr. Mashaal turned over to me. It appeared that it was August 24 that Kofi contacted Mashaal and told him that he had been away from his desk and Mashaal was to try that fax number again. Then he said that the *Letter of Mandate* would be ready tomorrow noon and he would send Mashaal his diplomatic flight itinerary as that would inform him when they (whoever Kofi means by *they*) will be arriving in Canada to deliver the money to his home. Kofi thanked Mashaal for his patience and understanding. (Perhaps the business terminology confused Dr. Mashaal as he seemed to accept whatever Kofi said and continued with *business as usual*!)

I had to drive Dr. Mashaal's to his lawyer's office as he was involved in a property sale with him managing the legal work. I also had to take him to his tax accountant about a tax settlement. Due to Dr. Mashaal's aging, when staying in Canada he depends on my help driving him to his appointments and assisting him with his business matters. I was considered a trusted friend by both him and his wife who usually remains in Germany but visits Winnipeg occasionally. This contact with his lawyer was my opportunity to tell him (a personal friend of mine you will recall I mentioned earlier) about the web that Dr. Mashaal was entangled in. His advice to me was to get him to the police and fast. He suggested I take him to the neighbourhood police office immediately.

I knew from experience that I had to make a plan that he would accept as I had been suggesting to him for almost two months that I believed he should go to the police but with no success. First thing I did was inform Dr. Mashaal that I had told his story to his lawyer, but I had not used his name. I simply said it was a friend of mine. Mashaal told me that he found no problem with my telling his lawyer that he was the person involved in this story. I believed at this time that he wanted help to get out of the tangled mess. However, he likely continued to hope he would be able to recover his money or at least the biggest portion of it. This conversation between Dr. Mashaal and me took place that Tuesday over a cup of coffee in a restaurant after he had completed his legal business. It appeared that he was now warming to the idea of going to the police but no date had yet been set. Nor was he sharing any copies of e-mails or forms with me at that time. I knew very little of what was occurring.

From the e-mails that he passed on to me a couple of weeks later, I learned that on that same day Kofi had sent a message advising him to try another fax number that he supplied in a message. So, at 2:16 in the morning, Mashaal had sent Kofi a reply telling him that *it was a very good fax number* and listed the two items that he had just faxed to him. Those were the *Presidency Form* (reminding Kofi that the original had been sent by registered airmail a few days earlier) and the confirmation from the Bank of Montreal that $3,750 had been sent as requested. Mashaal closed his e-mail: *From my side I completed all your requests. I do hope to receive the money soon. Many thanks and appreciation. Best wishes. Mashaal.*

# $\mathcal{CHAPTER}$ 11

## KOFI, JAMES MARTINS & MASHAAL
## ARRANGING TO MEET IN WINNIPEG

On August 30, I made the following entry into my diary; *I am really worried about Dr. Mashaal.* A day or two earlier he had briefed me on the latest plan that he was making with Kofi via e-mail and phone calls between Canada and Ghana. Kofi wanted him to fly to Toronto to meet with a James Martins and pay him a payment of $7,800 US, in order for him to take possession of the money that was on its way from Ghana to Toronto. It seemed that this payment was required for Kofi's representative, Martins, to clear *the consignment* from Customs at the Toronto Airport. Can one imagine Dr. Mashaal clearing $1 million at the Toronto Airport? Earlier plans were for the money to be delivered to Dr. Mashaal's home in Winnipeg with no extra charges after he had sent the $3,750 by the Bank of Montreal. Now Kofi had made a change in plans for delivery with another person added to the delivery process, a Mr. James Martins.

Kofi continued to play a major role in the arrangements to move that money from Ghana to Canada but James Martins who resided in Toronto would be Kofi's representative in Canada. Kofi's plan for Mashaal to meet Martins in Toronto came early the next morning, August 31. Dr. Mashaal phoned me and told me that he had just received an e-mail from Kofi saying that Martins would now be flying into Winnipeg from Toronto the following day to pick up US$7,800 to be used for the clearance costs at the Toronto Airport. Another $1,000 Canadian to cover the cost of his Winnipeg/Toronto return air ticket would also be necessary. He asked me during the phone call if he could come to my home and discuss this new development. This I took as an indication that he was becoming frightened. He arrived at my door within minutes and I invited him in. He lost no time in announcing *Let's go to the police, NOW!* I agreed and drove him to the Tuxedo neighbourhood police office where we were met by a constable to whom I introduced Dr. Mashaal and myself. Dr. Mashaal briefly told the constable the reason for his visit. He said that somebody was coming the following day to collect more money from him and he was concerned for his safety and wanted the police to protect him.

At first the constable did not appear interested and told us that he could do nothing about this problem because as far as he understood all the money had been sent from Switzerland and Germany. It would be a matter for the police in those countries, he said. From what I had been told by Dr. Mashaal up to that time, all money sent had gone through his German bank. I learned later this was not so. It was at the moment that we were being dismissed by the constable that Dr. Mashaal spoke up sheepishly and told me that he had sent money last week from his bank in Winnipeg to an account in a bank in Ghana. That was shocking as that was after continually advising him not to send any more money. That happened only a day or two after he had come to my home that evening to discuss sending more money, and I had advised him against doing so.

He leafed through his binder and found the bank form. This binder contained a selection of about 50 e-mails chosen from the approximate 350 or so that had been accumulated to that date. He opened his binder at the Bank of Montreal form shown on page 114 and displayed it to the constable. The original had accompanied the money transfer from the Winnipeg bank to the Ghana bank on August 22. The constable said, *Oh that makes a difference!* He excused himself and we waited for about ten minutes while he spoke on the phone.

When he returned to the counter, he said, *I have made arrangements with the main police station downtown for you to meet with a detective.* Although it was noon, we were to go immediately and ask at Information for a specific detective as he would be expecting us. We would be invited into a secured area where Dr. Mashaal would give his report. We were told that we should not be surprised if the detective met us in shorts or other casual attire as it was not necessary for him to dress in uniform.

We drove immediately to the main police station and at Information we identified ourselves and requested to see the detective. Soon he appeared and invited us into an interrogation room where Dr. Mashaal gave his report. This room was void of furniture except for a small wooden table and three chairs. It was obvious it was used to take statements from people. We were not offenders, but we were hopeful that an arrest would be made soon and the fellow arrested would be sitting in the chair that Dr. Mashaal now occupied. Mashaal dictated to the detective his statement that filled three pages. He then asked Mashaal to read it carefully before signing it to ensure the written statement was accurate. By this time, it was after one o'clock, so after reading and signing the report, we hurried to Mashaal's home where I dropped him off as he wanted to tidy up his apartment before the detective arrived at 2:30—the agreed time to visit and take information from his computer. As the detective had asked for me to be there also, I hurried to my home and returned to Dr. Mashaal's before the appointed time for the computer search.

The detective arrived at Dr. Mashaal's residence accompanied by a colleague. The officer stood beside the detective seated at the computer while he selected and printed out a stack of messages—at least fifty. After they discussed the printouts, he said that he believed the messages had originated in Toronto but upon further examination, he said that he now believed that they had originated in Africa. The detective dismissed the idea that anybody would be arriving the following day and would not agree to Mashaal's request that police be at his home to protect him and possibly arrest the fellow that was to come for more money. With that statement, Dr. Mashaal appeared very disappointed and frightened. He had been convinced from the correspondence and phone calls that somebody would visit his home the following day. Unknown to me, he later asked a neighbour to help him develop a protection plan. The following day, they shared their plan with me. I was not happy about it and told them so. I shall not reveal the full details as I felt it could get us into great trouble if executed. I told them that I would have no part in their plan as it existed. They could count me out!

That Friday afternoon, Mashaal was waiting for further word from Kofi in Ghana and James Martins in Toronto as to when Martins would be arriving. Mashaal had been informed by Kofi that a parcel of 32 kg would be delivered to Winnipeg. In another phone conversation from Kofi around 4 p.m., Mashaal was told that he must pay US$7,800 shipping costs plus the cost of a return air ticket Toronto/Winnipeg for Martins. In that same conversation, Mashaal was told that people would be arriving in Toronto from Ghana the following day, Saturday, with the $1 million but Martins would not be flying to Winnipeg as there were no flights out of Toronto to Winnipeg on Saturdays. Of course, that was not correct. There are several flights by airlines flying this route every day. Kofi told Mashaal to wait for a phone call the following day at noon as he would deliver further instructions. This information had given Mashaal cause for concern.

Part of the plan hatched by Dr. Mashaal and his neighbour George included all three of us in Mashaal's apartment on Saturday, so he would not be alone. Immediately, I was to check the Internet for all incoming flights from Toronto and record the arrival times, so we might have an indication of a possible time for Martins' arrival into Winnipeg. We would then allow Martins up to one-half hour to arrive at Dr. Mashaal's residence from the airport as we believed that there would be no checked baggage to wait for and the taxi ride would take about twenty minutes. Mashaal had been told by Kofi that the money was now at the Toronto Airport as a consignment. He said that Martins would visit him in Winnipeg only to pick up the cash and return to Toronto to pay for the release of $1 million. It was not mentioned at this time when Martins would return with the consignment and help Mashaal take it to his bank as was earlier promised. Of course, the likelihood of $1 million was only a phantom, so Martins would have collected the American cash to clear the consignment plus the Canadian cash for a return Winnipeg/Toronto air flight and probably would never have been seen again. For Martins, it would have amounted to a free return flight and a gift of US$7,800.

The detective had not entirely abandoned Mashaal as late on Friday afternoon he phoned and said that he was on his way home for the weekend. He advised us if there were any new developments occurring over the weekend, Mashaal or I should call 911 and give the Police Report Number that he had given us. Then we were to call his cell phone number if needed.

Still fearing that Martins might arrive unannounced on Saturday to pick up the cash, the three of us were ready to put into action Mashaal and George's revised plan. My part was to go to the guest parking area outside the building and sit in my car facing the front entrance. I would have a camera, a cellular phone, the detective's cell number, and the Police Report Number for 911. While seated in my car, I received a call from George requesting that I come to the apartment and contact the detective for them. While in Mashaal's home, several e-mails and several phone calls came in with George sometimes answering the phone and pretending to be Mashaal because of Mashaal's hearing problem. In one phone call, Martins insisted on $7,800 being sent to Toronto that day and he gave two ladies' names that were to receive $4,000 each. Mashaal said he needed an e-mail with the names. He also corrected Martins on the amount. Each lady should receive US$3,900.

In my conversation with the detective, he asked me to convince Mashaal that he must not send any money to Toronto that afternoon. He also said that Mashaal must insist that the *Nigerian thieves* keep their promise to deliver the money to him in Winnipeg. In conversation between Mashaal and Martins, the latter said that he would be unable to deliver the money parcel to Winnipeg if he received no money to clear it from Customs at the Toronto Airport. By refusing to send the money, Mashaal was told that he would have to travel to Toronto.

Finally a call from Martins at 5 p.m. said that he had missed his plane so would be coming early the following week. In an earlier conversation, Kofi had informed Mashaal that there were no flights between Toronto and Winnipeg on Saturdays. Now he was told that Martins had missed his flight. At any rate, Dr. Mashaal must wait for another time for the arrival of that parcel of 32 kg to be delivered in exchange for US$7,800 plus the cost of the Toronto return flight. The waiting game being over for that day, George and I left Dr. Mashaal alone and returned to our homes but not without stressing that he must not allow *anybody* unknown to him to enter his home. If somebody that he did not recognize arrived, he was to phone immediately for George as he lived in the same building and could arrive at once. This was an extremely exciting but very nerve-wracking day! Dr. Mashaal's face revealed his anxiety.

As I exited the building, I saw a large crowd of people outside the building attending an occupants' yard sale. Was Martins in the city but deterred by the crowd? Might he still arrive later in the evening? However, as predicted by the detective, there was no visit from James Martins that day.

Over the next few days, there were many phone conversations but few e-mails between Mashaal and Kofi or Mashaal and Martins except Kofi's messages shown below. Two of these messages, according to the time shown on them, had been sent only 34 seconds apart. What a swift typist! Or was there more than one person tending to this matter in Ghana? It was actually in one of these messages that Mashaal first learned of the new and additional amount of US$7,800 required for handling charges. Earlier Mashaal had been told that all costs had been paid. Are there signs now that Mashaal might be willing to forgo his large inheritance?

From Kofi's two messages that follow, one can notice that his patience was wearing thin. It seemed that he just wanted to get this money moved. He had no time for any of Mashaal's stupid questions. His diplomatic crew had a limited time to spend in Canada and this money must be claimed by Mashaal within that limited time or it would necessitate Mashaal's travel to Ghana to claim the money if it were returned there.

```
Date: Sunday, September 2, 2007
Subject: Fwd: ref e mail of 1st Sept 2007

Dear Sir,
I have try my best possible as i said in my previous email
that things need to be done in a diplomatic manner,we have
try to move the funds/consignment out of Ghana west Africa
to your destination,at least the bank will have rest of mind
with the pressure that Susan smith and smith associate at
law firm are given to us so you don't need to bother about
airline or craft that move the consignment to Canada as at
now but you should be only rather interested to receive the
parcel,sir,if the funds/consignment comes back to Ghana it
will be a long process to get it our or you will be require
```

to come to Ghana to make claim on it .Tey have only from now
till next Tuesday,the choice is your's

Thanks,
Kofi

No time was shown on the above message nor on the one that
follows:

Date: Sunday, September 2, 2007
Subject: Fwd: ref e mail of 2 Sept 2007

Dear Sir,
What i know about the flight details has be given you
previously because there was no flight direct to Winnipeg
from Ghana, i will have to check this tomorrow morning at
their office because I was in the bank working that time
before they signal that they have leave to Canada.

My understanding is that you should suppose to be
communicating with the carrier that arrive at Toronto since
you have their phone number with you for full details,i am
here and i do not know the next connecting flight which they
took,all i know is that they arrive at Toronto safely ,if
you are not satisfy for their arrival,i will advice them to
phone on Monday that they should prepare their self and come
back to Ghana,maybe you will have to come down by yourself
and make the shipment by yourself since you have documents
covering the consignment with you then you will know the
charges that flight takes on this type of consignment.

I thought is that you should be finding ways to receive the
consignment than wasting time for questions that is not
necessary the most important is that the consignment has
arrive then go for it,i guess you are not ready to receive
it,call them and find out yourself.

I have done my best here,i am not in Canada they are their
with you,you are free to call them and ask them any question
you wish.

Thanks
Kofi

Still another message from Kofi is shown below. Kofi wanted to
have Mashaal believe that he had done his best and now it was up

Dr. Agnes Chambers-Glenn

to Mashaal to pay up and take possession of that large shipment of money that was in Toronto waiting for him: 32 kilograms!

```
Date: Sunday, September 2, 2007 12:34:12 PM
Subject: Fwd: No answeer

Dear Sir,
Your question has be answer if you want to take action,you
have the time to do it now because they have only now
till next week Tuesday to stay in Canada,they are there
to deliver and come back,all what i am doing is on your
favour because the funds/consignment is no more with our
bank,therefore i am only to ensure safe-delivery is take
effect because the bank will not be responsible for any loss
or damage that may occur.

Regards to the flight,my understanding is that they left
with Delta air lines FLIGHT NO DL167 but i do not know the
next connecting flight to Toronto because there was no
direct flight to Winnipeg but the most important issue which
i thought you need to sort out is the release delivery of
the consignment than rather wasting much as they come to
Accra-Ghana by then you will take the consignment out by
yourself because i explain to me that you will need to pay
handling clearing charges of $7,800 when they arrive so i
don't know why you said you are not aware of it
MY NUMBER IS HERE IF YOU WANT TO REACH ME 00233207713756
Thanks
Kofi
```

Same day, September 2, Mashaal sent an e-mail message to me saying that *they continue to contact me by phone. I inform them to contact me by e-mail as my hearing not good. They did and that is better in order to have records. Since yesterday and today I had many records. Mainly it is concentrated on payment but other informations. I do not know wether to fax all these to the police or not. Best regards. Mashaal*

Many phone calls were also exchanged that day between Mashaal and Martins in Toronto. I was in Mashaal's home when several of those calls arrived. Martins repeated the names of two ladies in Toronto to whom Mashaal was to split the $7,800. The address he gave was 1400 Dixie Road, Toronto. From experience, we knew that the address was nearby the airport and was most probably in an industrial area rather than it being a private residence.

So Mashaal asked Martins for the specific suite numbers for the two ladies in that building, but Martins refused to give these to him and instructed Mashaal to send the money and somebody would be waiting at the entrance to receive it. Again he told him to simply split the $8,000 between the two ladies and send as soon as possible today. As per the detective's insistence, no money was sent.

The following day, I received another message from Dr. Mashaal in which he informed me that he had asked Kofi again not to contact him any more by phone as his hearing was not good. As well as being a reason, it was also an excuse as Dr. Mashaal was attempting to ensure that he had written proof of what was happening so he could present this to the detective. Every incoming message that day was forwarded to him at the police station and also a copy forwarded to me. The message that follows was from Mashaal to Kofi that same day. The names given by James of the two ladies in Toronto to receive the $7,800 split were Mrs. Diana James (perhaps James Martins' wife) and Mrs. Margaret Wood.

```
Date: Sunday, September 3, 2007 7:20:30 PM
Subject: Fwd: To send $ 7800 to Toronto

Dear Mr Kofi

1-When When the 10.5 million $ was in the bank in Accra
Ghana, I asked Mrs Dr Vivian to take 2.5% from the 10.5
Million $,the charges of the bank to transfer the money to
my account in Germany or Canada.Mrs Dr Vivian state that
this was not possible accourding to the rules & regulations
of the Bank

2-When you released the 10.5 million $ from bank,packed them
(32 Kgm) and went to airline to send them to Canada.On the
way why you did not take from these cash money the necessary
handling charges. By that time the bank in Accra has no
control of the money

3-Also at Toronto Air Port,the airline will accept (based
on my communication),. The air-line will accept that Mr
James Martins can open one of the packages and take $ 7800
required for Handing Charges. Still this can be done today.
The Canadian Airlines has no objection to this action if it
is requested by Mr James Martins
```

```
4-Mr James Martins in Toronto on the telephone,he asked
me to transfer $ 3500 to Mrs. Diana James (perhaps James
Martins' wife) and $ 4500 to Mrs. Margaret Wood in Toronto
address: 1400 DIXIE ROAD TORONTO
The total is $8,000 and not $ 7800. I do not understand why
I transfer the money of handling charges to these families.
What is the role of these families in my case

5-Still today I am prepared to transfer $ 7800 Handling
Charges direct to the air-line at Toronto to release the
consignment and send it to Winnipeg. This is of course
can be done only if I receive details of the flight
number,arrival date and hours etc.

Your comments are highly appreciated as Mr James Martins
informed me in the Telephone you are very good person and
reliable.Many thanks for your efforts to help me

Best Wishes

Dr.Hassan A.H.Mashaal.
```

At first, Kofi tried to convince Mashaal to go to Toronto to claim the shipment of money. After some thought Mashaal agreed he would go as by now the detective believed he would be able to accompany Mashaal. Nobody wanted Dr. Mashaal to go alone.

To stall for time, Mashaal told Kofi and Martins that he was ill and must stay close to his bed other than visiting his physician, so there would be no meeting in Toronto soon. Unfortunately, at this time, Mashaal was truly becoming ill. From the stress, he had developed a racing heat beat and had visited his heart specialist who had sent him to the hospital to have a 24-hour monitor placed on his chest. The following day, the hospital employee reported to him that his heart was racing at over two times its normal rate. A few days later, he reported to his heart specialist with whom he discussed his condition. He was advised to take life easier. Actually the physician was unaware of Dr. Mashaal's involvement in the money scam as Mashaal had not revealed anything about it to his doctor.

# C*H*A*P*T*E*R 12

## KOFI, MARTINS & MASHAAL
## MEETING CHANGED TO TORONTO


On September 4, the detective contacted Dr. Mashaal and told him that he had been informed by his office that there was no money available for flights to Toronto. That same evening, Mashaal sent a message to him saying that *you are working very hard on my case.* He believed the Winnipeg police would be responsible for catching the criminals, so he said that he would be happy to pay for two return tickets to Toronto for the detective and himself and even for a second police officer if necessary. He suggested he could pay either by Visa or cash, whichever would be more suitable, and he suggested that they *travel tomorrow or after tomorrow.* He closed with *I hope you accept my suggestion.*

Then an e-mail with the subject *Go to Toronto* arrived for Mashaal from Kofi. In it he told Mashaal that he was very busy but would check his e-mail twice daily until Mashaal received the packages. By *packages*, it was presumed Kofi meant the money shipment. He also asked Mashaal to send copies of his flight details for his trip to Toronto and to cooperate with the diplomats from Ghana so the delivery and release of *the packages* would be smooth. And he asked Mashaal to *compensate them for the great effort after delivery* to his address in Winnipeg. He said that he had given Mashaal's e-mail to Martins and had asked him to keep him *informed of every single conversation so I can give directive from here.* Then he said, *God is great? everything is finally concluded no any charges acumulated or whatever,you need to go there with the cash amounting to $7,800 usd not $8,000. I wait for your comment*

*Regards, Kofi* This message is a rather confusing one. The package was to be delivered to Mashaal's home in Winnipeg, but Kofi spoke of Mashaal's flight plans to Toronto. Also, it is difficult to believe that Ghanaian diplomats had brought this personal shipment to Toronto as Kofi had mentioned. What would be the relationship between Ghanaian diplomats who were delivering this money to Canada and Linda Morgan who died in Ghana but was a citizen from Sierra Leone?

No decision had yet been made about going to Toronto. However, another message arrived from Kofi assuming Mashaal was making the trip as ordered by him. In that message Kofi asked Mashaal to send his air flight details and he would forward that information to Martins in Toronto. He assured Mashaal that Martins would definitely contact him that day.

The detective responded to Mashaal's offer to pay for the Toronto flights saying he would discuss, in the morning, this offer with his sergeant. He cautioned Mashaal that perhaps the suspects may not even come to the Toronto Airport and continued by saying that *these people are experts at manipulating people to get the money they want.* He also said that if Mashaal was still willing to try to meet Martins in Toronto that he was certainly willing to go with him. He closed by saying that he would speak with Mashaal the following day about this matter after discussing it again with his superior.

Still that evening, Mashaal sent a message to Kofi. He informed Kofi that he could get a flight to Toronto either the evening of the fifth or the morning of the sixth, but he had not booked as he needed more details from him. He needed to know where he should go to meet Martins and suggested that the Toronto Airport was a very big place in which to try to meet someone. He said he knew because he often got lost in it. He then asked Kofi to give him Martins' e-mail so he could communicate directly with him and determine where they could meet. He said that after he heard from Martins, he could send Kofi his flight number and time of arrival at Toronto. And he told Kofi if he did not give him Martins' e-mail then he would not go to Toronto, nor would he send the $7,800 to Mrs Dianna James at 1400 Dixie Road, Toronto. He informed Kofi that at any rate, his bank could not send money to an apartment building without a suite number. He said that perhaps Martins had given him the suite number over the phone, but due to bad hearing, he had not gotten it.

Then early the next morning, the detective contacted Mashaal and told him to change his story and inform Kofi that he was ill and would not be able to go to Toronto for a day or two. However, he would be able to make the Toronto trip shortly after that and would then inform Kofi of his flight plans.

Then many e-mails arrived from James Martins in Toronto. After Mashaal sent the following message to Kofi in Ghana, a string of messages arrived from Kofi also. From the following message, it seems that Mashaal had advised Kofi of a flight but had cancelled it. Of course, he really had not booked. He was only playing a game. Mashaal had suggested a new meeting place. The message that follows was sent to the detective to keep him informed of the communications he was having with Kofi in Ghana. Dr. Mashaal was determined that with the help of the detective Martins would be arrested. (For protection, the detective's name has been omitted in all e-mails.)

```
From: Malaraexpert@aol.com (Malaraexpert@aol.com)
To: (the detective) @winnipeg.ca
Date: Wednesday, September 5, 2007 9:01:52 AM

Subject: Fwd: My E Mail sent yesterday

5 September 2007

Dear Mr Kofi

You did not answer my E Mail sent yesterday .Iasked you:
        1-E.Mail of Mr James to communicate with him about
where we can meet in Toronto
        2-Detail Address Mrs Dianna James (the suite number)
so that if I did not come to Toronto I can send $ 7800 to
her

Also I add a third idea
        3-In case the above two suggestions are not
applied.Mr James can fly to Winnipeg and visit me in my
residence To receive $ 7800 and in addition the cost from
Toronto-Winnipeg & return
```

Dr. Agnes Chambers-Glenn

```
My flight today afternoon is cancelled but still I can fly
tomorrow 6 Sept 2007 in case I get detail answer today.
In case I do not receive any answer and none of the above
three suggestions are applied. In this case you are
responsible

Thank you. Best wishes
Dr.Hassan A.H.Mashaal
```

As promised, a reply arrived that morning from the detective to Mashaal. He said that if Mashaal *can get them committed to meeting at the Winnipeg Airport that would be wonderful.* He asked Mashaal to keep him updated and said, *Perhaps we can get those guys.*

A message from Mashaal to Kofi that day informed Kofi that Mr. James Martins had just a few minutes earlier phoned him from Toronto saying he had sent an e-mail yesterday but Mashaal insisted he had not received it. He promised to send it again but still it had not arrived. Although communication was good between Kofi and Mashaal, he wanted to hear from Martins, and he again asked Kofi to send Martins' e-mail address to him so they could communicate by the Internet rather than the telephone. Mashaal closed his message saying, *Urgent action is required to arrange meeting Mr. James to deliver $7800 Thank you*

Shortly after that, Mashaal did receive Martins' e-mail address from Kofi with advice for Mashaal to send Martins an e-mail using keriost@yahoo.com. Kofi continued saying that Martins would answer the remaining questions that Mashaal had posed in a previous message and that he, Kofi, would give Mashaal and Martins directives from his bank office in Accra, Ghana.

Using the e-mail address that Kofi had just given him, Mashaal sent a message to Martins telling him that he had received his address from Kofi but that he had never received any messages from Martins himself. He informed Martins that he would be able to go to Toronto the following day but he was afraid of losing his way in the Toronto Airport as he had in the past since it is a very big airport. He also told Martins that now he thought that meeting in the Toronto Airport seemed too difficult for him and suggested that instead of him meeting Martins there, it would be better if Martins flew to Winnipeg the following day where he could meet him in the Winnipeg Airport. There would be very little difficulty there as that airport is small and it is easy to find people on arrival. He would have with him the US$7,800 in cash plus the price of his return ticket. Then he offered an alternative plan saying that if Martins preferred to meet him in his home that would be okay. Mashaal gave his street and apartment number along with the name of his condominium building. He informed Martins that the cost of a taxi would be about $15 and the time needed to reach his home would be about 15 minutes. The message closed with *Appreciate urgent answer to take necessary action Best wishes and regards and thanks to highly efficient Mr Kofi* Of course, this was all a game in an attempt to deceive Martins and have him arrested in Winnipeg.

Mashaal then sent another message to Martins repeating his e-mail address and drawing to Martins' attention that probably he had misspelled his e-mail address and that was the reason that Martins' e-mails were not reaching him. Later the same day, Mashaal finally received the long awaited message from Martins in which his only words were: *am still waiting for you sir, James*. Then another message arrived within one minute as most probably Martins had pushed a wrong key and the first message was on its way before it was finished. In the second message Martins wrote, *am here still waiting for you, for your air line schedule for tomorrow. James*

Meanwhile, Mashaal had sent a message to the detective telling him that within the period of one hour he had received four e-mail messages from Martins from Toronto. Mashaal had forwarded these to the detective for him to study and asked to be advise of what to do next as he was hoping that through the police and his guidance the criminals would be caught.

A very short time later, Mashaal sent the following message to Martins with a copy to Kofi. Mashaal then forwarded a copy to the detective so he would advise him of the next move he should take.

```
Malaraexpert@aol.com wrote:
Cc: Mr Kofi

Dear Mr James Martins

Can you come tomorrow to Airport Winnipeg to receive $ 7800
+ price of ticket Toronto Winnipeg & return
```

Dr. Agnes Chambers-Glenn

I must have an official receipt of $ 7800 when you receive
the money

Or if you prefer to come to my Apartment,it is OK. I will
try not to leave my home till you come Apt # (Details were
omitted.)

To come to Toronto Airport not easy as very difficult to
meet you in Toronto Airport.it is very big and complicated
place.I usually loose my way in Toronto Air-Port

Appreciate urgent answer.Best wishes
Dr.Hassan Mashaal

Note to Mr Kofi all your mail I received but not single time
I received any mail from Mr James Although by phone Mr James
said he sent to me E mail.I do not understand why I never
receive E.Mail from Mr James

Finally communication was established between Martins and
Mashaal and a copy of each message was forwarded by Mashaal to
the detective. From the message below, it appears that the problem of
not receiving e-mail messages from Martins was probably that Martins
was not very literate in English writing and the use of e-mailing.

To:    Malaraexpert@aol.com (Malaraexpert@aol.com)
Date:  Wednesday, September 5, 2007 4:32:24 PM

Subject:Fwd: no mail received from you

i dint have money for the ticket,
if you can send me a ticket fees but I what you to come you
can open your article com firm if it is complete,,and will
come with the next available flight with you or by myself .
to Winnipeg,
James

Two hours later Kofi sent the following message to Mashaal
who forwarded a copy to the detective. (The reason for the headings
of most recent messages having missing parts is the fact that Dr.
Mashaal forwarded all messages now to the detective. I have also
deleted some personal information where necessary.) Notice that
Kofi once more asked Mashaal to handle this *confidential matter* in
a mature way.

```
Date: Wednesday,September 5, 2007 6:15:16 PM

Subject: Fwd: no mail received from you

Dear Sir,
I am sure that you finally got james online,however i
will prefer you to travel downthere to meet them ,this is
confidential issue that need to be handle in a mature way.

You either decide what to do either you go to toronto or you
snd flight ticket for james to come and collect the money
for him to bring the package to you.

I wait for your reply
Regards,
Kofi
```

It appeared that an agreement had been reached for Mashaal to travel to Toronto as shown by the following message. He said, *at the Air-port Toronto there are many ways out In order to find you,is it possible to send to me by e –mail any of your photos However in case I did not find you,Ithink I will take a taxi to your home Can you give detail of your home so that I can give it to the Taxi Driver in case I could not find you in the very busy Toronto air-port Appreciate urgent answer Thank you and best wishes*

It was early the next morning that I received a phone call from Dr. Mashaal asking me to please come to his home as he needed help in contacting the detective. This was due to his lack of effective hearing. So I went. Details still had not been established but it was learned from Mashaal's message to Martins very early that morning that Mashaal had told Martins although he had booked his flight to Toronto for that day, September 6, it was necessary for him to cancel as he developed a throat infection with a very high fever and he had gone to his medical specialist for treatment. He said that his doctor had advised him to stay in his home until his throat condition improved and the fever had disappeared. This was simply an alibi so he could convince Martins to fly to Winnipeg as an arrest could be made much easier there. According to the detective, the Winnipeg Police had already contacted the Toronto Metro Police and asked for assistance if they and Dr. Mashaal decided to travel to Toronto and set the trap there.

Dr. Agnes Chambers-Glenn

Following is a forwarded copy of the e-mail that Mashaal sent to Martins concerning his flight to Toronto. He pretended he had booked for that day, September 6. From the message it appears that Dr. Mashaal even at his age was really no fool.

```
From:    Malaraexpert@aol.com (Malaraexpert@aol.com)
To:      (the detective)@winnipeg.ca
Date:    Thursday, September 6, 2007 6:45:46 AM
CC:      (e-mail address deleted)
Subject: Fwd: Forced to cancel my flight
```

Dear Mr .James Martins

I booked my flight to Toronto today 6 Sept 2007 but very unfortunately I was obliged to cancel it because I got throat infection and high fever.The Medical Doctor Specialist gave me treatment and asked me to stay at home till my condition improves and no fever.

However if you wish,you can come to Winnipeg.I cannot meet you at the Air-Port Winnipeg.You can visit me at home.May be I can send a Taxi to the Air port if you wish.Or you can take yourself any Taxi (about 15 $) to come to my home. Apt # (etc., details omitted). I have the cash with me $ 7800. You can buy a plane ticket one way Toronto Winnipeg about $ 300. I shall give you in addition to 7800$ the 300$ and ticket back from Winnipeg to Toronto

I hope you can manage to pay 300 $ for the ticket,even if you borrow them.I wish to settle this situation as early as possible .I hope my medical situation will not oblige me to be hospitalized.

Sorry for these unexpected events. Wish you good health Dr.Hassan A.H.Mashaal.

# CHAPTER 13

## KOFI, MARTINS & MASHAAL
## MEETING REVERTED TO WINNIPEG

Mashaal had planned his excuse of illness on the direction of the detective who decided he should not go to Toronto but should play along with Kofi and Martins and entice Martins to visit Winnipeg. For most of that day, both his neighbour George and I were in Dr. Mashaal's home and heard the telephone conversations with Dr. Mashaal acting out his inability to speak over the phone as he wanted communications by e-mail. He was trying his utmost to convince Martins to fly to Winnipeg and come to his home to pick up the money that he had withdrawn from the bank to have ready for a visit by Martins.

Mid-morning, Mashaal received a message from the detective who asked him to book a flight for Martins to Winnipeg. He still insisted that he did not believe that Martins would actually come but gave Mashaal instructions on how to purchase the ticket so it could not be cancelled for cash by Martins. The detective's message appears below. After receiving the detective's message, Mashaal immediately notified Martins that he would book a return flight for him since Martins had said that he had no money to buy a ticket. However, Martins replied without delay saying that he did not want Mashaal to book a flight but would borrow money for a one-way ticket and Mashaal could reimburse him in Winnipeg for the return flight.

Dr. Agnes Chambers-Glenn

```
From:    (the detective) @winnipeg.ca
To:      malaraexpert@aol.com
Date:    Thursday, September 6, 200710:26:32 AM
CC:      (e-mail address deleted)
Subject: Flight to Winnipeg
```

Dr. Mashaal,

Please book flight #WS475 - West Jet flight departs Toronto
at 12:15 pm on Sept. 7, 2007 and arrives in Winnipeg at 1:47
pm. After you have booked this flight you will get what is
called a PNR number. I need that number and I will then put
the proper securities in place so that this ticket cannot be
changed or the suspect cannot convert it to his own use in any
way. If the suspect does not get on the flight you will not
be out any money as you could change the name on the ticket
and use it for yourself. Given the circumstances I would also
contact West Jet for you and attempt to get you a refund.

After you have booked the flight please advise me. DO NOT
ADVISE Mr.MARTIN of the flight details until you have
contacted me.

Thank you,

(name omitted)
Commercial Crime Unit
Winnipeg Police Service

Following is the message in which Mashaal responded to
Martins after Martins had informed him that he wanted to book his
own flight. Martins would borrow money for a one-way ticket that
Mashaal could reimburse as well as pay the cost of his flight back
to Toronto. The reason most probably that Martins did not want
Mashaal to book his flight was that the name James Martins was, of
course, the name by which he conducted his Nigerian business and
it would not match his photo ID.

```
From:    Malaraexpert@aol.com (Malaraexpert@aol.com)
To:      (the detective)@winnipeg.ca
Date:    Thursday, September 6, 2007 1:25:52 PM
Cc:      (e-mail name deleted)
Subject: Fwd: ref your e mail 6 Sept 2007
```

Dear Mr James Martins

Many thanks for your e mail.I am pleased you will come to
Winnipeg tomorrow 7 Sept.As I promised all costs of travel

from Toronto to Winnipeg to Toronto will be paid cash to
you. The $ 7800 as I told you are available in cash.

I am glad to tell you,under intensive treatment , now I have
no fever but still cough and has pain in my throat

Please give detail of your flight which will arrive Winnipeg
Tomorrow and hours of arrival.
In case my health is progressing better I shall come to the
air port But if still the health is not good I will stay in
my apt# (etc., deleted) and you take a Taxi (about 15$)

I appreciate to have an official receipt of $ 7800

Thank you.Also I wish to thank Mr Kofi for his efficient
communication. (There was no signature on this message.)

Accepting the detective's advice, Mashaal sent a message
to Martins in which he told him that he would be unable to meet
him in the Winnipeg Airport, but could send a taxi to the airport
to pick him up and drive him to his home, if he so wished. He
repeated to Martins that he would reimburse him for the cost of
the taxi and gave his residence address again and as well he tried
to assure Martins that he had in his home the US$7,800 cash and
the Canadian dollars to cover the cost of his airline tickets. He
told Martins that a one-way ticket generally costs about $300 so
he should buy only a one-way ticket since he said that he couldn't
afford to buy his airline ticket but would borrow money. Mashaal
promised to give him another approximately $600 that would cover
the cost of a return ticket. He signed off suggesting that Martins
borrow the $300 if necessary and saying that he hoped that his own
medical condition would not oblige him to be hospitalized.

It appeared that messages crossed as shown by the time recorded
on them. It is also obvious that Martins thought Mashaal was flying
to Toronto as he asked Mashaal, *let me no when was you flight, i
will be waiting for you,now am staying in the hotel, very close to
the airport,you come to terminal 3 in the arriving gate, i have your
picture, i will have your name place on the board, so that when you
come you can meet with me, all you need to do is give me air line
name the time of arrive?*

In a follow-up message from Martins, Mashaal was informed
that he had refused the offer of a ticket and said, *i will borrow the*

*ticket fees by myself don't not pay, i will buy the ticket on my own, SO that when i come i will cor let the money for the ticket back from you. i which you soonest recovery. god bless you sir. James martins*
Martins phoned giving some information that Mashaal was unable to hear or understand, so Dr. Mashaal sent the following e-mail in which he also asked for a flight number and arrival time because to that point in time Martins had never mentioned any of those details.

```
Malaraexpert@aol.com wrote:

Dear Mr James Martins

Thank you for your phone. My hearing is not good.I did not
understood all what you said Kindly let me know arrival time
and number of the plane.
My Medical Physician is happy as I have no fever now but
still cough and I have painful throat
My Medical Physician asked me to visit him tomorrow at his
clinic. I shall not do that except few hours before your
arrival or soon after you leave Winnipeg.Please give me
details so that I inform my physician when I can visit him.

Please do not forget to bring official receipt of $ 7800 .

I thank you and Mr Kofi for your help
Best wishes

Dr.Hassan A.H.Mashaal
```

Then about 4:12 that Thursday afternoon, the long-awaited information arrived. See the following message. It is actually a copy of the original that Mashaal had forwarded to the detective. It would have been forwarded very shortly after being received by him. Notice that now the money would be collected during this visit by Martins and then he would return to Toronto and pay the costs of having the consignment released. A day later Martins would return to Winnipeg with the money and help Mashaal get it to the bank. Helping Mashaal to get the money to the bank had been promised earlier. The cost of that second return flight on the following day to transport the money to Winnipeg had never been mentioned.

From:   Malaraexpert@aol.com (Malaraexpert@aol.com)
To:     (the detective)@winnipeg.ca
Date:   Thursday, September 6, 2007 4:12:15 PM
Cc:     (e-mail address deleted)
Subject: Fwd: Arrival winnipeg on 7 Sept

rem member we need to make the payment before we can received
our receipt, i belive you no this when we pay there fees we
can now have receipt for you, i will very quick, so that i
can go back and pick up your package for you tomorrow.
if any problem with this please get back with me as soon as
possible, in not i should be with you tomorrow afternoon.

James martins.

Martins indicated in the above message that there would be no
receipt when he picked up the money, only when he returned the
following day having cleared the money. This message prompted
Mashaal to make contact with the detective telling him that at 2:10
p.m. Kofi had phoned from Accra, Ghana, with the message that
James Martins would be visiting him tomorrow, Friday, September 7.
Just ten minutes later, Martins phoned from Toronto. Mashaal asked
him for the airline and flight number and Martins replied that he would
send it by e-mail. The message below is from Mashaal to the detective.

From:   Malaraexpert@aol.com (Malaraexpert@aol.com)
To:     (the detective)@winnipeg.ca
Date:   Thursday, September 6, 2007 4:22:22 PM
Cc:     (e-mail address deleted)
Subject: James arrival Winnipeg tomorrow 11:45 am

Dear (detective)
Mr. James phoned to me at about 4.10 PM (few minutes ago) He
said he will arrive winnipeg at 12.00 noon
Also he sent e mail.I sent a copy to you.in the E mail he
said his arrival at 11.45
I asked flight number but he did not give

May be you can check the plane of tomorrow arrival at 11.45
to see his name in the list of passengers or not
I hope I do not get serious problem with him if he meets me
alone at my home and he realized I have no money for him

Thank you

Dr Mashaal

Dr. Agnes Chambers-Glenn

At 10 o'clock that morning, Mashaal phoned me and asked me again to get for him the arrival times of all flights from Toronto into Winnipeg for the following day, September 7. I was also to phone that information to the detective. In addition, he asked me to ask the detective if he could be at his home with backup the following day. So I went on the Internet, looked at, then I printed out the airline schedules for Friday for all relevant flights. We had not used the information of the past Saturday but Mashaal believed that he would have a visitor this time. I attached these airline schedules to an e-mail and sent it to him then phoned the detective and delivered Mashaal's message to him. We noticed that no flight agreed with the arrival at 11.15 a.m. as Martins had indicated as his arrival time for Friday. It did appear that the Air Canada flight #257, arriving at 14:32, leaving Toronto at 12:55, might be the best guess as Jazz and West Jet seemed to be out of the picture for any appropriate morning or afternoon flight for that day.

One could sense that Mashaal was becoming uneasy as he spoke with me. He said, *If Martins does not send the correct information but arrives and takes a taxi to my home, then there will be a problem.* This was what prompted him to send a message to the detective and ask him if he could check with the airlines for the names of all passengers arriving Winnipeg the following day. My search was not sufficient to satisfy his fears. With information on arrivals, he indicated that everybody—especially him—could take steps to be safe. In addition, he said, *If Martins can be taken into custody at the airport that will be great success,* but Mashaal had invited him to take a taxi to his home. The detective had told him that he expected that nobody would arrive on Friday just as no person had arrived the previous Saturday when Kofi had advised Mashaal that somebody would be calling by for more money.

Shortly after, Mashaal sent an e-mail to Martins thanking him for phoning and reminding him that his hearing was not good and asked him to please send an e-mail stating full details of his flight. He informed Martins that his health was improving but that he must visit his physician tomorrow either before his arrival or wait until after his departure, so it was most important that he had the correct arrival time for his visit. He also reminded Martins to bring an official receipt for the US$7,800 cash that he would give him for the cost of clearing the Ghana shipment.

Now there was another turn in events. A message from the detective informed Mashaal that he had finally received approval from the police station to travel with him to Toronto. So he had contacted the police in Toronto to assist them. However, since Mashaal had just spoken to Martins and it appeared that he was coming to Winnipeg, the detective would be available to give Mashaal support the following day in Winnipeg. If Martins did not come to Winnipeg, he would arrange flights to Toronto for Tuesday, September 11 or Wednesday, September 12, and he asked Mashaal not to make any other arrangements prior to speaking with him. He continued by saying *if Martins does not come to Winnipeg, tell him that you went to the doctor on Friday and he cleared you to fly next week. Then we will proceed with those plans. Once we have decided to go to Toronto we do not want you to offer him to come to Winnipeg again. We want them to commit to a meeting place so we can get our plans in place. Thank you and do not hesitate to call me if you have any questions.*

After about ten minutes, there was another message from the detective in which he informed Mashaal that *the police are able to check some flight manifests but not all airlines cooperate with us without search warrants. We also have a problem that in all likelihood Mr. Martin will travel under a different name. I think this is part of the reason he did not want you to book the flight for him. I will do what I can do to check the flights. I am working tomorrow and will be here to assist you.*

That evening, I was frightened for Dr. Mashaal. He had been very upset in the late afternoon when I saw him, and he asked me to contact the detective in his home and tell him that he really wanted the police in his home the following day as he believed that James Martins *was* coming from Toronto. I called the detective and he told me that he did not believe that Martins was any more likely to come as he was the previous Saturday that Mashaal had expected him—the day after he went to the police and told his story. Still that evening's messages and phone calls from Martins and Kofi continued arriving giving Mashaal the arrangements for the Friday visit. Should he arrive, the detective's advice was simply to phone 911 and give the Police Report Number as it contained all the details of the case. I stayed close to my phone to give Mashaal all the

Dr. Agnes Chambers-Glenn

assistance I could. However, the rest of the evening passed without incident.

Next morning, September 7 at 7 o'clock., I called Dr. Mashaal and asked if he was still concerned for his safety and, if so, would he like to leave his home and go to my home as I planned to go out for the day. He could avoid being home if Martins arrived. His reply was: *George and I have a plan. Will you sit in your car with cell phone and camera? When George or I phone you, you dial 911 and give the Police Report Number.* I preferred to sit in the foyer instead of in my car as I would be able to watch what buttons guests pushed as this could be seen from a certain angle of seating position in the reception area. Then I could phone 911 and the detective on my cell phone and inform them of Martins' arrival. Shortly after I had called Dr. Mashaal, the following message arrived in my inbox and a copy had been sent to the detective. (The sensitive information has been deleted.)

```
From:  Malaraexpert@aol.com (Malaraexpert@aol.com)
To:    (deleted)
Date:  Friday, September 7, 2007 7:23:53 AM
Subject: Arrival of Mr James today

7 September 2007

Mr James mentioned he will arrive at Airport Winnipeg Hour
11.45. The detective advised me not to go to air port.
I may see you any time but I think from Hour 11.30 you stay
in your car infront to observe taxis etc and to use your
camera. I was informed once he arrived when he call me from
down to open the door.I shall open the door and I have 2
minutes to phone 911 etc
But I am afraid 911 may be one minute occupied etc and then
I will be in difficulty
I suggest the following:
1-To phone to you and mentioned few words: (James arrived at
down door)
2-Then you phone at once to 911 and inform them Police
Report ROx-xyzz (changed, not real number)
3-This solution is better and very quick.Also if any one
phone to you ask them to close the phone and postpone so
that your phone is free all time at hour 12
4-Phone office (of detective) 988-xxxx: Direct phone
xxx-xxxx

Many thanks and regards

Mashaal
```

142

The above message was followed by the detective's message below. Martins must confirm his definite flight number and arrival time to Mashaal who was to return the information before nine o'clock to the detective. The Toronto departure time of 10:00 did not agree with the expected 11:15. arrival time that martins had given in an earlier message.

```
From:    (detective)@winnipeg.ca
To:      Malaraexpert@aol.com
Date:    Friday, September 7, 2007 8:29:29 AM
Cc:      (e-mail deleted)
Subject:
```

Dr. Mashaal,

Please phone James and tell him you will meet him at the airport and confirm his flight number and arrival time. Please phone prior to 9:00 as his flight is scheduled to leave at 10:00 Toronto time.

```
Cst. (detective)
Commercial Crime Unit
Winnipeg Police Service
PH: 204-xxx-xxxx  Fax:204-xxx-xxxx
```

From the above message we believed that the police knew that Martins planned to board the 10 o'clock flight. However, we had no proof. Within ten minutes, Mashaal received Kofi's message shown below and forwarded a copy to the detective.

```
From:    Malaraexpert@aol.com (Malaraexpert@aol.com)
To:      (detective)@winnipeg.ca
Date:    Friday, September 7, 2007 8:38:29 AM
Cc:      (e-mail address deleted)
Subject: Fwd: Arrival Winnipeg 7 September
```

Dear Sir,
Thanks ,please when james is with you,kindly call me to talk to both of you.
Regards,
Kofi

Shortly after the arrival of the above message, Mashaal phoned me with new instructions that he had just received from the detective. Prior to this, Mashaal had phoned Martins in Toronto who advised him that he was not arriving in Winnipeg at 11:30 a.m. as he had made a change in flight times and now he would be arriving at 2:30 p.m. Mashaal was to meet him at the airport so he made arrangements with his friend George to drive him there.

Then Mashaal sent a message to Kofi concerning the change in Martins' Winnipeg arrival and requested the flight number and the exact time of arrival as these were necessary for Mashaal now as he planned to go to the airport to meet Martins rather than having him come to his home. See message following which is actually a forwarded copy to the detective of Mashaal's message to Kofi.

```
From:  Malaraexpert@aol.com (Malaraexpert@aol.com)
To:    (detective)@winnipeg.ca
Date:  Friday, September 7, 2007 8:38:29 AM
Cc:    (e-mail address deleted)
Subject: Fwd: Arrival Winnipeg 7 September
```

Dear Mr Kofi

I phoned to Mr James in Toronto.He said his flight arrival Winnipeg 2.30 afternoon . Before it was 11.45 AM I told him my health now is greatly improved and I can come to air port to meet him He agreed.But I must know what airline and flight number because in Winnipeg Airport there are two arrivals.I must wait at one of them if I know the flight number

As soon as he arrives I shall take him to my Apt (15 minutes)and give him US\$ 7800.Also Can Dollar About 700 for his Ticket
At Airport we can book him flight back to Toronto.May be at 5 PM or an time suits him

Appreciate you contact Mr James and send to me Flight number.My hearing not good and my contact will not be efficient because of my poor hearing (old age)

I hope you get me urgently flight number to settle everything so that I can receive my 10.5 million Dollars.

Thanks and regards

Dr.Hassan A.H.Mashaal

It seemed that Martins did not want to meet in the airport and sent a message for Mashaal to remain in his home and he would take a taxi there. I had told the detective earlier that as George had decided not to drive Mashaal to the airport, I would drive him there at 1:30 so the police and Mashaal could get their plans coordinated before the flight arrived. George and his wife were making final preparations to leave the following day on a month's vacation and required the time, thus he had changed his mind about driving Mashaal to the airport.

Earlier that morning, the detective had told me that there would be police back up at the airport, but at 11:45 the message from the detective informed me that he and his police colleagues were on route to Mashaal's home. With Dr. Mashaal's difficulty in hearing on the phone, he asked me to relay the message to Mashaal immediately. He said that they, the police, would go to his home and set the plans to arrest Martins when he arrived. It was obvious at that time he had learned that Martins had purchased a ticket to Winnipeg and would soon board his flight. I hurriedly passed the message on to Dr. Mashaal. So now he could expect Martins' arrival shortly after 2:30 that afternoon. I also asked Mashaal if he had Kofi's phone number convenient as Kofi had asked him to phone when Martins arrived. Mashaal replied that he did have it but had misplaced it so would contact Kofi again by e-mail and ask for it. He did and Kofi replied that he could not reach Martins as he may be at the airport (Toronto) now but not to worry because as soon as he arrived in Winnipeg he would phone or come directly to his home. He told Mashaal again not to go to the airport to meet Martins. This change was very good as the police had their plans to make the arrest in Mashaal's home. Kofi gave his own phone number as 00233207715756 and reminded Mashaal that he was to phone him as soon as Martins arrived.

To get this latest information to Mashaal, I immediately sent an e-mail. However, to ensure that he did actually check his e-mail at that critical time, I phoned George in his home and asked him to please go to Mashaal's apartment and alert him to the important message that I had just received from the detective. Then I rushed to Mashaal's home, rang and was admitted. I entered the building, went up the elevator and knocked on Mashaal's door and was invited in. I found George in the apartment with Dr. Mashaal who gave me an entrance key to the exterior door of the building so I could enter quickly if he phoned for me as he wanted me to sit in my car and observe who was coming and leaving the building. As I was leaving the building, I recognized the detective and another person standing in the reception area. I greeted him and he introduced me to his colleague. I returned to Mashaal's apartment with them. After a few minutes, both George and I were asked to leave so I went to my car that I had parked in the visitors' parking space facing the main entrance of the building. Few people entered and some left but I particularly noted a pair of men of whom I felt looked suspicious. One man appeared to be young—in his early 20's and casually dressed with a backpack—while the other was older and dressed in a dark suit. The former appeared to me to be a student but the latter was not old enough to be his father. Friends, I thought. From my view, I was unable to see if they rang up or whether they passed through the security door by following other people entering the building. Often residents who gather in the reception area open the security door for people whether they know them or not. There is a sign against such action but that does not seem to deter this from occurring. About fifteen minutes later these two men left the building and to my surprise the older one headed straight in the direction of my car while the younger one veered off towards the exit to the street. I became very nervous as the older man approached my car.

When he reached my car, he tapped on my window. All my bravery had dissipated. Oh, I wondered what had I gotten myself into! I started the engine ready to take off then turned down the power window just a very little. He asked me to give him the key. I asked him how he knew I had a key. He then told me that he and his colleagues would need that key because Dr. Mashaal did not have any more extra keys and had directed him to get the key from me. Dr. Mashaal told him that I would be sitting in the visitors' parking. Without acknowledging that I had a key, I asked him who he was. He introduced himself and he told me that the key I had would be needed by the police officers who would be hiding somewhere outside the building and ready to enter as soon as they received a phone call from a colleague who would be hiding in Mashaal's home. He also told me what he believed was about to unfold with their plan. So I gave the key to him and prepared to drive out of the parking area as he had asked me to leave. He and his younger colleague continued together towards their unmarked police cruiser parked across the street. They drove away. They were going to pick up more officers and return to the condominium grounds. Meanwhile, the detective who was planning this entire scheme to arrest Martins was with Dr. Mashaal in his home and also the police officer whom I had met in the foyer.

When I drove from the grounds into the street, I was very excited, yet equally frightened. I decided I should keep busy, so I went shopping to pass this time of tension. I decided I needed a new camera to have for my upcoming planned tour of Europe. That would keep me very involved so I could forget what might happen in Sussex House on Roslyn Road.

About 2:35 pm, I was standing at a cash register paying for a purchase when I received a call on my cellular phone. It was from Dr. Mashaal who told me to come straight to his home. I wondered what could have happened as Martins was not expected at Dr. Mashaal's home until about 2:55 if his flight arrived as planned. I did not ask any questions. I simply completed the purchase and left in a hurry. I climbed into my car and within fifteen minutes I arrived at Dr. Mashaal's home.

# C𝐻𝒜𝒫𝒯𝐸𝑅 14

## James Martins' ARREST

Having arrived at Dr. Mashaal's building entrance, I rang up and he opened the entrance security door for me. As I walked through the reception area to the elevator, there was a group of about five or six ladies standing blocking the entrance to the elevators. I stopped for them to move over to allow me to pass. They seemed very excited. So, I asked what had happened. One lady spoke up and said that *a black man had just been taken out of here in handcuffs. I let him in a very short time ago but didn't realize it as he appeared to be accompanying a young man who had identified himself to me on my intercom camera. The young man was interested in seeing some of the furniture that I had advertised for sale in the local paper. I saw that he was accompanied by a big black man but when they knocked on my apartment door, I saw only the young man and then I saw the other big man knocking on the door across the hall, Dr. Mashaal's home. Then still with the security camera channel on my television, I witnessed him being taken out a few minutes later in handcuffs. Some other people must have also been watching the security camera at the entrance. I hurried downstairs as soon as the young man had finished looking at my furniture. That was only a few moments ago.*

I took the elevator up to Dr. Mashaal's apartment and knocked on his door. He had already called George and the two of them were sitting there on separate sofas looking dazed at each other. Both congratulated me for the criminal's arrest. I asked, *Why me?* George said that just convincing Dr. Mashaal to go to the police was step one in this arrest. You will recall that it took me about two months to convince him to go to the police and that was only accomplished during the previous week. I took a photo of Dr. Mashaal and George, and then George took a photo of the doctor and me. It was truly a very happy time, but we were oblivious to what might follow.

Dr. Mashaal described what had occurred in the setup and arrest within his apartment. His neighbour, the lady I met in the entrance, had told me how Martins entered the building. He had not rung up to Dr. Mashaal to be admitted. From inside the building he phoned Mashaal on his cell and asked for his suite number and arrived at his door and knocked. Mashaal unlocked the door and saw *a very dark, strong-looking, man standing there and welcomed him in.* As Martins entered, Mashaal saw him reach back slightly and turn the deadbolt in the door. Of course, his actions were supposed to go unnoticed. With door locked, he likely felt safe as he made his way into the livingroom only to see a man seated at the dining table at the far end of the large room. Mashaal introduced him as his nephew saying he had come to visit him for the day. His nephew, the detective, set there writing and pretending to be paying no attention to the conversation between the two men. Unknown to Martins, a second police officer was in the bedroom with the door closed and with his cellular phone programmed to quietly call to the other police waiting outside the building.

The doctor offered Martins a seat and he sat down on a sofa chair while Mashaal pulled up a chair facing his guest poised to count the money. Immediately the plan went into action. Small talk was about the flight arriving early as Martins' flight was expected to arrive at the Winnipeg Airport about the time he arrived at Mashaal home. Martins said that his flight had arrived early, at 2:10. Knowing that Martins was in a hurry to return to the airport to catch a return flight to Toronto, Mashaal suggested that they get down to business. Mashaal said to Martins, *Let's settle the cost of the ticket first in Canadian dollars then I shall pay you in US currency the $7,800 that Kofi insisted upon before the money from Ghana can be released to me. I have cash here for that also as I went to the bank yesterday.* Then Mashaal asked Martins for his airline ticket so he could reimburse him. Martins did not produce it but said that it cost him $1,000. Mashaal responded by saying that a return ticket to Toronto/Winnipeg usually costs about $600 when not on special. Martins claimed that since he purchased it at the last minute, the cost was $1,000 but he still did not produce a receipt. Dr. Mashaal pulled a pack of folded $100 Canadian bills from his shirt pocket. He counted them slowly from one hand to his lap in front of Martins: *100, 200, 300, 400, 500, 600, 700, 800, $900.* Then he said, *Oh, I guess I am $100 short.* To that Martins replied, *Oh that will do.* But Mashaal slyly put the $900 back into his shirt pocket and stood up and offered him something to drink saying that he never allowed a guest to leave his home without having something to drink, but he said that today since Martins was in a hurry to return to the airport and return to Toronto, there was not time to make coffee or tea. However, he did have orange juice if he would like that. Martins agreed and Mashaal left for the kitchen, poured a glass of orange juice and as he returned to the livingroom with the juice, he reached out and unseen by Martins, he unlocked the deadbolt on his entrance door. The small wall facing the livingroom has a closet on the entrance side, so this action was out of sight to Martins.

Having accomplished that feat, Mashaal entered the livingroom and handed Martins the juice. As Martins turned to set the glass of juice on the desk to the right of his chair, the three backup police officers who were waiting outside the building entered from his left. They had entered the exterior door with the key that one of them had taken from me earlier and had rushed up the elevator to the 15th floor. They arrived at the apartment door within a few minutes and according to their plan. The young man I had seen earlier leaving the parking area was the last officer to enter. All three had their guns drawn and aimed at Martins. The fourth officer who had made the call to those hiding outside rushed from the bedroom with his gun drawn also. James Martins did not have a chance and immediately threw up his hands. On went the handcuffs. This happened so quickly that all the while the detective who planned this arrest was still seated calmly at the dining table.

After only a few minutes, James Martins was lead from Dr. Mashaal's home, taken down the elevator from the fifteen floor and outside to the waiting unmarked police cruiser. What a short visit! And no money collected!—not the $1,000 Canadian for the air flight nor the US$7,800 to clear that large sum of money from

Ghana being held for clearance at the Toronto Airport. These fellows wanted US dollars but would that have been the currency required to clear the shipment from Canadian Customs in Toronto? Shortly after Martins was taken from the building, Kofi sent a message and asked, *I HAVE BEEN WAITING TO HEAR FROM YOU, HAVE YOU MEET WITH JAMES THANKS KOFI.* Remember Kofi had earlier asked Mashaal to phone him as soon as Martins arrived at his home. There were no incoming calls during the five minutes that Martins was actually in the house. After the arrest had been made, Kofi was sending one message after another and even phoning asking if Martins had arrived yet. Mashaal's response was always, *No, not yet.*

At 2:47 that afternoon, about the time Martins was expected to reach Mashaal's home, Kofi sent a message saying, *Please when james is with you,kindly call me to talk to both of you.* Another message two minutes later from him said, *I could not get him online again ,maybe he is at the airport but never mind,i believe as soon as he arrive he will call you or come directly to your home since he has the address with him. I can be reached at 00233207713756 Thanks Kofi* The first thing that the police did after handcuffing Martins was to take his cellular phone, so Kofi nor anybody else could make direct contact with Martins.

Now Vivian was back in the excitement again. At 3:51 p.m., a message arrived from her that said, *Thanks to almighty God, finally you receive the funds,i will vacate by end of this month so i cab come over to your end. Waiting to read from you.* I suspect this was a message from Kofi also only changing the sender's name.

Late in the afternoon in a telephone conversation, Mashaal said to Kofi, *No, James has not arrived. Do you know where he is?* Kofi was agitated, it seems during his numerous calls that followed, he was always wondering where James was. I even answered the phone once and changed my voice to sound somewhat like Dr. Mashaal. Immediately, Kofi called back. None of us, George, Mashaal or I, answered. He called again and again and finally Mashaal answered disguising his voice. Kofi sent a message late that night saying, *Dear Sir, I just call you and i heard your voice but you pretend not to be you and claim that is a wrong line,am not after your money but only want to ensure that you have safe delivery. However,if you wish to talk to me or reveal any details,you are free to do so but if not i have no option to be silence and wait.*

Still that evening, Mashaal sent a message to me saying that the detective had confirmed that Kofi's calls were coming from Accra, Ghana. He also told me that he had at least ten phone calls during the evening but refused to answer his phone. He had turned the ringer off but did not silence his fax machine beside his bed. He said that it kept him awake most of the night. He did not pull the electric power plug for his own reasons. He told me that he assumed these calls were coming from Ghana from Kofi hoping to find Martins.

Early the next morning, Dr. Mashaal called me to say that the calls had continued most of the night and he did answer only once with a disguised voice then he received an e-mail from Kofi saying he knew it was Mashaal playing a trick again. Dr. Mashaal invited me to meet him for lunch. As I had an appointment to meet friends, he asked me to bring them along as the four of us could celebrate the previous day's success and help him in an attempt to create normalcy in his life.

# CHAPTER 15

## MASHAAL TIDYING UP MATTERS
## & MEDIA REPORTS

Dr. Mashaal believed it was time to think about recovering his lost money, so two days after James' arrest he prepared a summary of the money sent to Ghana. He e-mailed this to the detective and a copy to me. He was hoping that the detective might be able to recover for him the US$37,500—or at least a portion of it. As usual, I removed some details before scanning his money summary. As for the bank account numbers, they were changed and protected against withdrawal without his written permission. He asked me to leave his name and the banking and residence particulars on all forms as his *business partners* in Ghana had all the information anyways and the credit bureaus' fraud departments had been contacted to protect his files. He had contacted his three banks, Swiss, German and Canadian and had alerted them to watch for anything that might look like fraud against his accounts. And by this time, he had also renewed his passport, so he already had a new number and photo. The form mentioned above is shown on the following page.

Later the same day, I received messages from Dr. Mashaal and a copy of a message from the detective. The detective wrote, *Thank you so much for your assistance in the matter. You did a wonderful job.* He also asked Dr. Mashaal to answer Kofi's calls now and to send him a message *to see if another criminal could be caught.* Victory was so sweet! From then on, Dr. Mashaal sent messages with copies to the detective and to me. I placed all the copies I received chronologically into a binder that became Binder Three. Dr. Mashaal passed to me his earlier correspondence a few days later. That was Binder One and Two.

Subj:   Total money sent
Date:   9/9/2007 9:53:49 A.M. Pacific Daylight Time
From:  Malaria expert
To:
CC:

Dear

I thank you sincerely for the great work done on 7 Sept with your collegues
This corrupted organization received from me Total US$ 35750
I wish to give you the tails, who received them ,Banks accounts adresses etc etc.May be helpful for you

US$ 5000 + 2000 =$ 7000
These were sent from my Swiss Bank UBS AG in Geneve
On May/June 2007

To.................................................Mr Good Rock Ventures
Account #.................................0510 2034 9216
Swift Code............................ BK TRUS 33
Bank received money ..... Cal Bank Limited
Address Bank...................... 23 Independence Avenue
                                          P.O.Box 14596 Accra-Ghana
Routing Number.................. 021 001 033
CAL SWIFT CODE ............... ACCCGHAC
cal'A/C No............................. 040 89719
The mioney for Lawyer Smith to obtain four documents
required by Swiss Bank

us$ 25000.00   on first July 2007
Sent from ...............................Bank Sparkasse in Bad-Lauterberg GERMANY
To etc   same as above
The Layer Smith received them but it was claimed he was killed in road
accident and the money disappeared (stolen)while he was transported
to the hospital

US $ 3750   ON 24 AUGUST 2007
Money was sent from Bank of Montreal Winnipeg
To................................... Mr ANNOR-KUMI RICHARD
Account No........................ 870 152 135 4300
Swift Code............................ SCBLGHAC
Bank received money...... Standard Chartered Bank.Ghana Ltd
Address Bank...................... P.O.Box 20 Tema-Ghana
                                      Tel & Fax:+233 21 7012205
                                      Telex 2671
Address Mr Annor-Kumi Richard:P.O.Box nt 12 community 20,Tema-Ghana
His Teleph No............................... 00233 242 977 878

Huis E Mail................................... sakimatti @ yahoo.com

I hope these data can be of use. Thank you

Dr.H.Mashaal

It was at this time that the detective advised him to be sure that he contacted the proper authorities with respect to having given out his banking information and passport number. He listed the credit bureaux fraud departments with telephone numbers and advised him to contact them. He also suggested that Dr. Mashaal notify the Passport Services of Canadian Government telling them that he had given out a copy of his passport to these people. The detective acknowledged having receiving Mashaal's most recent e-mails that had been forwarded and also asked Mashaal if Kofi was still contacting him. He finished by asking if he had yet told Kofi that Martins came to see him.

Vivian who was suppose to have been *out of the picture* long ago when Kofi took over her position at the bank sent a very short message that simply said, *Dear Sir, This is too bad,i mean your silence,you have betray the trust. Vivian.* Imagine such hypocrisy! Probably this message was really from Kofi. It did appear that Kofi and Vivian were really the same person - a bank employee who was falsely representing the bank. Mashaal had never spoken on the phone with Vivian. They had contacted each other only by e-mail, so he never heard her voice.

Early in the afternoon, Mashaal sent a message to the detective telling him that Kofi had phoned many times daily since Friday—about 15 to 20 times but he had not picked up the phone. He said that day alone Kofi had already phoned six times. Later in the afternoon, the detective sent a message to Mashaal saying: *We never thought that Kofi would continue to contact you. Perhaps we could make another arrest out of this. Please communicate with Kofi and tell him that James never showed up. You are very angry and this is why you did not answer his phone calls. Tell him you have taken the money back to the bank but you are still interested in sending it to him if he will come to Winnipeg. Maybe we will get lucky if they send another person.*

So after the detective sent him the above message, Mashaal sent an e-mail to Kofi telling him, *I am very sorry and deeply sad because Mr. James never showed up. I am deeply angry and this is why I did not answer your phone calls. If you treat me so badly like this I prefer not to communicate any more with you.*

Shortly after sending the above message, Mashaal sent another to Kofi.

Dr. Agnes Chambers-Glenn

```
From:    Malaraexpert@aol.com (Malaraexpert@aol.com)
To:      (the detective)@winnipeg.ca
Date:    Monday, September 10. 2007 5:46:26 PM
Cc:      (omitted)
Subject: Fwd: (no subject)
```

Mr Kofi

I had taken $ 7800 back to my bank
I am still interested in sending the money to him
if he will come to Winnipeg.

Dr Mashaal

Then he sent a message to the Assistant-Director of the Swiss
Bank. In it he thanked him for his advice that he had not heeded, but
now wished he had.

```
From:    Malaraexert@aol.com
To:      (Detective) winnipeg.ca
Date:    Monday, September 10, 2007 6:08:55 PM
Cc:
Subject: Fwd: Documents from Ghana
```

10 September 2007

Mr. Xxxxx
Assistant Director
UBS AG
Chemin Louis Geneve
Switzerland

Dear Mr.Xxxxx

On 12 June you wrote to me the following
(I WANT TO WARN YOU ABOUT THIS SITUEATION AND PLEASE DON'T
SEND ANY FURTHER FUNDS TO GET THESE DOCUMENTS)

I realized that you was 100% correct but I did mistakes and
followed them.Now I cut relations with them but was informed
they may imitate my signature or even my passport and
requeste funds from my account in Geneve.That is why I write
to you today so that the bank to be very careful to avoid
any further problems

Thank you again for your outstanding advices

Dr.H.A.H.Mashaal
P.O.Box xxxx
Winnipeg
MB.Canada R3C 4B5
```
```

Messages were exchanged between Kofi and Mashaal the following day. In Kofi's e-mail, he suggested that Mashaal would have to travel to Ghana to collect the money if he ordered the consignment to be returned from Toronto to Ghana.

```
From:   Malaraexpert@aol.com (Malaraexpert@aol.com)
To:     (the detective)@winnipeg.ca
Date:   Tuesday, September 11. 2007 9:50:10 AM
Cc:     (omitted)
Subject: Fwd: (no subject)

Dear Sir,
If that should be the case,i will write and order the
consignment to come back to Ghana if i did not hear from him
today,i try to reach but couldn't get him via email,please
send me his phone number if you have it but if not i shall
call back the consignment which memas you will have to come
down to ghana to pick it up.

Thanks
Kofi
```

Probably Dr. Mashaal would be in very great danger if he were to travel to Ghana? Still Mashaal replied to Kofi denying that Martins had ever come from Toronto to his home in Winnipeg to collect the money. This was four days after Martins had been arrested. Mashaal was up to tricks again with guidance from the detective.

```
From:   Malaraexpert@aol.com (Malaraexpert@aol.com)
To:     (the detective)@winnipeg.ca
Date:   Tuesday, September 11. 2007 10:06:58 AM
Cc:     (omitted)
Subject: Fwd: ref e mail 11 Sept 2007

Dear Mr Kofi

Mr James never came to visit me.The cash I had US$ 7800 were
deposited back to my bank account
Before you order the consignment to come back to Ghana I
suggest the following
Send anyone from Toronto To Winnipeg. He can meet me in my
apartment in Road Roslyn Winnipeg or I can go to meet him at
the Airport Winnipeg.I shall pay fully the price of ticket
```

Dr. Agnes Chambers-Glenn

Toronto-Winnipeg-Toronto.Also once I hear from you in detail
,I can draw again $ 7800 from my account in Winnipeg.

In case you cannot send anyone to receive $ 7800 to Winnipeg
,give me detail address in Toronto to send the money from my
bank to the address in Toronto
Your detail early answer is appreciated in order to take
action on time

Dr.Hassan A.H.Mashaal

The detective contacted Dr. Mashaal with the message that
follows. Mashaal now knew that Kofi would be aware of Martins'
visit to his home. Martins, after being held in custody for the
specified time, had been allowed a phone call according to Canadian
law. In Martins' case, he was allowed a collect call with good
reason. The police wanted to learn who his contacts were. As we see
from the detective's message, he made his call to Toronto, perhaps
to his wife. You will recall there was a Mrs. James who was to
receive part of the $7,800 that Mashaal had once been asked to split
and send to the two ladies at 1400 Dixie Road, Toronto. Certainly in
time, the Toronto party would relay the message of James Martins'
arrest to Kofi in Ghana.

From:  (the detective)@winnipeg.ca
To:    Malaraexpert@aol.com)
Date:  Tuesday, September 11. 2007 4:52:44 PM

Dr. Mashaal,
Judging from the last email I am guessing that they are
getting wise to the fact that we made an arrest. Have you
received any more phone calls?

If you have not received anything further that looks like
they might meet again then you can disregard any further
emails or telephone calls. The accused has telephoned to
Toronto so I am afraid that they are well aware of his
arrest.

Thank you for your continued assistance.

Cst. (name deleted)
Commercial Crime Unit
Winnipeg Police Service
PH: 204-(deleted) FAX:204-(deleted)

As mentioned earlier, the detective had directed Dr. Mashaal to notify the three Canadian credit offices concerning putting a notice on their file for his protection. He asked for my help due to his hearing problem. So on Tuesday, I went to his home and spent the entire morning making the phone calls. You know how phone calls are made today: press this button; press that button. It was easy to kill one hour on each call placed. Then, as directed also, I phoned the Passport Office and was told that it was necessary for Dr. Mashaal to cancel his passport and to order a new one. He had put himself into such a big mess by befriending these people. The following credit agencies were contacted by phone: Equifax Credit, Transunion, and Experience Credit. These are stated here so as to give assistance should any reader find himself innocently in a similar scam. A request was made to each company to place a fraud warning on Dr. Mashaal's credit file. Some agencies protect the file for five years while others are for six.

After lunch, I drove Mashaal to the neighborhood police station where I had taken him ten days earlier to report the extortion. He wanted to pay the constable a visit to thank him for his part in making the arrest possible. A very happy looking constable greeted Dr. Mashaal who thanked him for his part in the capture of Martins on the previous Friday. In gratitude, Dr. Mashaal presented the constable with a set of his recently published books containing anecdotes of happenings while working worldwide as a WHO medical officer. Then the constable proudly showed the letter he had received earlier that morning. It was a copy of a letter that the detective's superior had sent to his superior to be passed along to him, a message of commendation for his part in the arrest. After all, it was he who finally after hearing the story from Mashaal had made the arrangements for him to meet with the detective at the Crime Unit. We were told by the detective that the arrest of James Martins from the West African fraud letter scam was the first in Canada outside the Toronto area where an arrest had been made approximately two years earlier. From the Police Station, we drove to the Passport Office to apply for a new passport. However, after more than an hour waiting in the queue, he was told that he should not cancel his current passport to apply for a new one but that he was to wait for the current one to expire as that date was only a few months away.

That evening, another message arrived from Kofi. In it was a list of countries where Mashaal would probably have to go now if he still wished to receive his inheritance. This message was forwarded to the detective as most messages had been recently.

```
From:    Malaraexpert@aol.com (Malaraexpert@aol.com)
To:      (the detective)@winnipeg.ca
Date:    Tuesday, September 11, 2007 6:07:56 PM
Cc:      (omitted)
Subject: Fwd: ref e mail 11 Sept 2007

Dear Sir
Very pity that James could not come to your hom,however we
do not understand your silence since he left Toronto and
till now we could not be able to reach him either,however i
request you to send me his phone number as the management
were deciding to send the consignment out of Canada to this
different country for you to go and collect it

THIS ARE THE COUNTRY THAT THE CONSIGNMENT WILL BE SEND FOR
YOU TO GO THERE SINCE WE ARE FINDING IT DIVVICULT TO CLEAR
IT FROM THE HOMELAND SECURITY IN CANADA.

1:UNITED KINGDOM
2:SPAIN
3:ARMSTERDAM
4:GHANA

PLEASE REPLY TO THIS BECAUSE WE TOUGHT YOU COULD GO TO
TORONTO WHEN THEY ARRIVE BUT DUE TO YOUR FEVER WE DO
UNDERSTAND YOUR MOTIVE.

PLEASE THIS ACTION WILL BE TAKEN EFFECT WITHIN 5 WORKING
DAYS.
HOPE TO READ FROM YOU

Regards,
KOFI
```

The following message from the detective referred to a phone call that Dr. Mashaal had received the evening before. He said that a man called and asked him to come at once to treat a patient who was very ill. Unable to hear well on the phone, Dr. Mashaal did not hear the address if it were given. At any rate, he was not interested as he retired nearly 25 years ago. He told the man so and that he no longer had a licence to practise. When he told me about this phone call, I asked him how he thought the man had gotten his name. He had not given that any thought. I reminded him that he was not listed in the phone book under any clinic so why would he think the call to be an honest one. Why would some person he did not know call him to treat a patient? Without a doubt, it was most probably a ploy to get him to a home unknown to anybody and one could only conjure that perhaps he would never have been seen or heard from again. A mystery would no doubt have resulted in his whereabouts especially if somebody had come and driven him to the location where he was supposedly to have treated a patient. This event occurred during the same evening that Martins was allowed to make a collect call from his confinement, the Winnipeg Remand Centre. Most probably Martins' gang had connections in Winnipeg and they were contacted by his Toronto colleagues-in-crime. This was likely an attempt to force Mashaal to have Martins set free or wanted to get even with the doctor.

```
TO:     Malaraexpert@aol.com (Malaraexpert@aol.com)
From:   (detective's e-mail)
DATE:   Tuesday, September 11, 2007 7:24:07 PM
SUBJECT: Fwd: (no subject)

Dr. Mashaal,

No you certainly do not need to answer the email or phone
calls. I would like you to start tracing your phone calls.
You do this by pressing *57 after you receive a call.

How do you know the phone call you received yesterday was
from Winnipeg? Where did they ask you to go to treat a
patient?

(name deleted)
Commercial Crime Unit
Winnipeg Police Service
```

Later that evening, the detective sent a follow-up message with further instructions how to use caller tracer and why. Then he said, *Please respond to Kofi that you have the $7,800 and can get the other $15,000 that you originally needed to send. The only way you can transfer this money to them is if they come to Winnipeg.*

*You want to get your $1.5 million that is owing to you and you are willing to provide them with the funds they need. Have they been phoning today?* I believe that he intended to write $10.5 million or $1 million as I do not recall any mention ever of the sum $1.5 million. Earlier because the detective said that Martins had been allowed a collect phone call and he called Toronto, Kofi probably knew the evening before of James' arrest. He finished his message by saying: *Please notify me immediately if you receive any threats, and if any strangers come to your door certainly call 911.*

I wrote a message to the detective thanking him for the assistance and the protection given to Dr. Mashaal in the sting. I mentioned that I had driven Dr. Mashaal to the Tuxedo Police Station to thank the constable that had directed Dr. Mashaal to him on August 31. And I mentioned how proud the constable was of the letter of commendation for having made this arrest possible. It appeared that the letter was worth a million dollars to him. I told the detective in that message that I had advised Mashaal not to meet strangers unless he authorized Mashaal to do so in which case the police would give him a backup for protection. I was very concerned that the elderly doctor's ego and naivety would lead him into more trouble as he is too trusting and believes in the good in people while ignoring the possible evil.

When communicating with Dr. Mashaal, he was showing signs of fear for his safety. He wrote to the detective telling him that Kofi had phoned earlier that day and had mentioned many things but again he said he had told Kofi that he did not hear well and it was necessary for them to communicate through e-mail. Shortly after Kofi e-mailed and accused him of *playing games with him.* Depending very much on direction from the detective, Mashaal asked if he should respond to that letter. He repeated the information about receiving the phone call the previous evening asking him to come and attend to an ill patient. He repeated to me that he had told the caller that he was on pension, thus no longer had his medical licence and, therefore, he could not visit any patient, and *closed the phone.* He finished his message by saying: *I understand that Mr James the accused has telephoned to Toronto. The Canadian law to allow the accused to phone certainly is extremely wrong. Many countries never allow this. Now Kofi will realize that all my male to him was not correct. Also by his phone to Toronto my life now is in great danger.*

I sent a message to Dr. Mashaal and asked him if the criminals had his German address, and I suggested if they did not that he should change his October flight ticket after his medical appointment with his heart specialist and fly to Germany to his other home. However, in the meantime, he should be extra careful both in his home and when he goes out. This suggestion to leave Canada, of course, was only if he had not given the Ghana people his German address. However, he had. They knew where to find him in Germany. I cited a story of what happened to an elderly gentleman whom I knew in Mexico. He left town fast after he had been attacked, glasses broken, attempted to be strangled holding his cane to his throat and dumped from a taxi into the street. His wife and friends found him there around the corner from his home. The driver was arrested 45 minutes later picking up another passenger. The next morning two Mexican men knocked on the door of my friends and demanded that the victim withdraw his charge or they would *fix him.*

These men identified themselves as the brother and the lawyer of the arrested man. His Mexican neighbor advised him and his wife to leave town immediately. They did but not without leaving a message with the housekeeper and gardener to tell any callers that they had returned to Canada. Actually, they caught a bus that day to Puerto Vallarta and spent two weeks there believing the situation would quiet down during that time. I suggested to Dr. Mashaal that the people he was dealing with might be able to travel around the world because they had stolen plenty of money and they had access to passports. For example, they had all the details of his passport as he had sent a copy of it to them.

A week after James Martins' arrest, a message arrived from Kofi asking Mashaal why he had not replied to his message of the previous day. Mashaal wrote to the detective asking if he should reply. He also said that at exactly 10 a.m., Kofi phoned wondering about his not replying. Mashaal told him that he was not feeling well then pressed *57 to trace the call.

That evening, September 12, about 7 o'clock, Dr. Mashaal phoned me and told me that somebody had come to visit him for an interview. I inquired as to where the person was at that moment and was told that she was in his apartment and that he would like me to speak with her. I agreed and the lady took the phone. She asked about interviewing Dr. Mashaal. This was after he had already called the detective who told him that he could not say no, but he preferred Mashaal did not take any interviews. I asked a few questions to the journalist then my cellular phone began to ring. It was the detective calling me about the call he had received from the newspaper journalist who was on my other line at that time. While I spoke with the detective, the journalist hung up as the line was dead when I returned to it. Mashaal later told me that she had bid him goodbye and left his home. I am sure that she knew it was the detective calling me as she probably heard my conversation with him on my other phone. I called Mashaal and asked him how the lady had entered. He had been advised by the detective and I had asked him not to allow any persons into his home if he did not recognize who it was at his door. Why had he given her permission to enter when he did not recognize the visitor through the security peep hole? He told me that there was a knock on his door and through the peep hole in his door, he *saw a pretty young lady with a book in her hand standing there,* so he opened the door and invited her in. She had not rung up from the entrance; she had passed through the security at the main entrance just like Martins had the previous week—by following another person. She had told Dr. Mashaal that the reason that she had not rung from the main entrance was that she had learned of his case and gotten his address from the police report at the Police Station. However, she had not been given his name so was unable to ring up from the entrance and had followed somebody else through the security area into the building. I asked him how he knew that this young lady trying to gain entrance was not one of the characters, such as Vivian or Susan or James' wife, or somebody that belonged to the gang. He had forgotten about the detective's advice re not allowing unknown visitors to enter his home.

The detective sent a message to Dr. Mashaal with a copy to me after his phone call asking what our opinions were about granting an interview. In the message he said that *certainly we did not give the media your name or suggest that they contact you. I trust that she left without any further incident.* Then in the message, the detective asked to visit his home again the week of September 17 in order to print out more earlier e-mails to prepare for Martins' court upcoming hearing.

Still that same day, Vivian sent a very short message in which she said to Mashaal, *You must respond before they call the package back.* Another message dated September 12 from the detective advised Dr. Mashaal to *ignore all further e-mails from Kofi.* He continued by saying: *We have made a media release and I think if they haven't heard about the arrest yet, they will know about it by the News time tonight. Please continue to do the call trace on any suspicious calls and let me know how many calls you are still receiving.*

Shortly after his previous message that day, Kofi sent another message with the Subject Line in all capital letters: *IT SEEMS YOU ARE NOT FAITHFUL.* This was followed by a couple of messages the following day. One contained the photo of the money in cases in the vault. It makes one wonder if and how all these cases had been transported to Toronto and soon to be brought to Winnipeg after the $7,800 was paid for their release. Kofi had followed up the photo of the shipment with a phone call. Dr. Mashaal, although he picked up the phone, he did not speak but pushed *57 to trace the call. Kofi's message below was forwarded to the detective. As for the photo, it is difficult to believe that it was taken in the Toronto Airport. Dr. Mashaal thought from the messages that the trunks were still in Africa at the bank. However, Kofi had said that they were in the Toronto Airport.

```
From:  Malaraexpert@aol.com (Malaraexpert@aol.com)
To:    (the detective)@winnipeg.ca
Date:  Wednesday, September 12, 2007 6:27:02 PM
Cc:    (omitted)
Subject: Fwd: IT SEEMS YOU ARE NOT FAITHFULL

Sir
I WILL SHOW YOU THE TRUNK BOX TOMORROW WHEN WE FINALLY CLEAR
OUT,WE HAVE APPOINTED CARRIER TO ASSIST BUT THEY THINK
THEY CAN GET ROD OF OUR CLIENT SO THAT THE BANK WILL BE
RESPONSIBLE FOR THE LOST: NEVER OT WILL NOT HAPPEN,I WAIT
FOR YOUR REPLY TO MY PREVIOUS EMAIL IF NOT THE CONSIGNMENT
WILL BE FULLY SCAN AND COPY WILL BE SEND TO YOU AND WE SHALL
DELIVER TO MOTHERLESS HOME
```

Dr. Agnes Chambers-Glenn

```
THANKS, KOFI
Sent: Thursday, September 13, 2007 8:50:01 AM
Subject: Fwd: PACKAGE WILL BE SEND BACK TOMORROW

DEAR SIR,
THE PACKAGE WILL BE SEND BACK TOMORROW SINCE YOU ARE NOT
READY TO RECEIVE IT,ATTACH IS THE CONSIGNMENT /PACKAGE FOR
YOU TO KNOW THE TYPE OF TRUNK THAT WAS USE TO FREIGHT YOUR
FUNDS TO TORONTO.

I WILL NOT REPLY YOU AS FROM TOMORROW IF I HEAR NOTHING FROM
YOU.

REGARDS,
KOFI
```

That evening on the 6 o'clock news, a local Winnipeg TV station, CBC 2, broadcasted the story about the elderly Winnipeg man who was bilked out of thousands of dollars by a group involved in an Internet scam. It also reported the arrest of a person involved in the Nigerian scam. It said that he had come to the elderly man's home for more money. No name or address for the victim was reported at that time. Later that evening, a similar news report was given at 10:45 p.m. on CTV 5 news. However, nothing had appeared in the paper that day.

Dr. Mashaal phoned me the following morning and told me that somebody was knocking on his door and that he was frightened. He asked me to phone the detective. I asked him what he saw as he peeked through the security hole. He replied that he could see a man and a woman but didn't know who they were. They had not rung up from the main entrance. I suggested that he not answer his door and they would leave. He decided to view the TV in-house security channel to watch them leave the main entrance. As he watched, the couple stopped at the entrance and rang up. This time he was able to identify them on the TV and opened the security door for them to enter and return to his apartment where he greeted his relatively new German friends. He had forgotten that they planned to pay him a visit that day.

Dr. Mashaal forwarded more e-mails from Kofi to me and to the detective that day. That was the day that an article did appear in the Winnipeg Free Press. Dr. Mashaal's identification still was not revealed, but the person that we knew as James Martins was introduced as Toluwalade Alonge Owolabi, his legal Nigerian name. The facts as they were reported in the article were not entirely accurate especially related to the money amounts and the time taken for the arrest.

The first public mention of this arrest appeared in the Thursday, September 13, 2007, *Winnipeg Free Press*. The article entitled *Elderly Victim Turns Tables on Con Man: Cops* reported the event as follows: It claimed that an 84 year-old man was allegedly swindled out of $30,000 in a Nigerian e-mail scam. This retired elderly doctor after telling police earlier what had happened to him allowed the police into his home and a person connected to the Nigerian scam group was arrested in his home when he flew in from Toronto to collect another US$7,800 plus more in Canadian to cover the airfare return Toronto. Also stated was that this suspect was a Nigerian refugee who had been living in Canada for one year and used a false name to conduct his collections.

Police believe he was an agent for a fraud ring, and they took him into custody and were holding him in the Winnipeg Remand Centre until his court appearance on the following Friday. The article further stated that this arrest was the first one in Canada outside of Toronto where police had caught someone in connection with a world wide fraud ring that had scammed thousands of people for more than ten years.

The police newspaper article said further that this case was an example of how the Nigerian e-mail scam works outlining how in April when the doctor was asked to wire money to Ghana to finance an inheritance of $1.5 million, he started his contact with the hope of eventually gaining some of that money. He was continuously asked to send more and more money. Eventually agreeing with friends that he was being duped, the retired doctor went to the police. He did not want his photo taken or name released fearing he would be targeted by members of that gang.

Advice given by the police in the event of receiving such e-mails was to contact Phonebusters at www.phonebusters.com and to report any losses to the police. Finally, the legal name of the perpetrator was given as Toluwalade Alonge Owolabi who was charged with numerous offences including fraud over $5,000, fraud under $5,000, and two counts of possession of a credit obtained by fraud.

You, the reader, have learned thus far that the plan to attempt to arrest James Martins was engineered and supervised by a very clever detective with four of his Winnipeg Police colleagues in Dr. Mashaal's home and outside on the property. Working with Dr. Mashaal for one week in an attempt to guarantee success, the detective appeared relaxed sitting at the dining table writing when Dr. Mashaal entertained James for the length of time needed for the police officers to enter the building after they received the crucial phone call from a closet behind the closed bedroom door. Until arrested, the visitor was known as James Martins and all negotiations occurred under that name. The actual inheritance was $10.5 million; however, this amount fluctuated during the negotiations over the previous week prior to Martins' visit to the Roslyn Road residence.

# CHAPTER 16

## KOFI, MATHEW & MASHAAL

Among the e-mails from Kofi that Mashaal forwarded to the detective and to me was a photo as shown below.

**From:** Malaraexpert@aol.com (Malaraexpert@aol.com)
**To:**         @winnipeg.ca
**Date:** Thursday, September 13, 2007 8:56:11 AM
**Cc:**
**Subject:** (no subject)

One or more of these trunks were to contain the money that had supposedly been freighted to Toronto. The content of the trunks was US$10.5 million, or was it $1 million—whatever was being sent via Toronto to Mashaal? That was never really clear. It seemed that the amount fluctuated at the will of Kofi, Vivian and others. Kofi mentioned that this photo was taken in the securities vault with the caretaker of all that gold. Was this at the Ghana bank? Earlier he had informed Mashaal that the money had been freighted to Toronto and on its way to Winnipeg. At one point, Kofi also told Mashaal that the money had been sent to the USA.

The day after the arrival of the photo of these trunks, Mashaal received several messages from Kofi. In one of the messages, Kofi talked about needing an urgent reply from him as they were not able to return the consignment to Ghana and they would be sending another team to Toronto to make the delivery to him in Winnipeg. He said that he would update Mashaal as soon as the replacement team arrived in Toronto. Mashaal would be asked to give the $7,800 to this new team as soon as Kofi informed him how and where so they could clear the package in Toronto and deliver it to his home in Winnipeg. In another message, Kofi said that Mathew (a new person to enter the delivery of Dr. Mashaal's inheritance) would be coming to visit him in Winnipeg and pick up the money and take it to Toronto where Mathew would clear the consignment then take it to Winnipeg. No mention had yet been made about Martins or his whereabouts; however, in another e-mail, it was not difficult to understand that Kofi was angry when he said that the wrong person had been arrested. It is not entirely certain whom he meant by that statement but most probably he thought for some reason that the arrested person should have been Mashaal. Mashaal would have been very happy if Kofi could have been arrested also as he appeared to be leading the pack of thieves.

Kofi sent a message saying *they will contact you very soon, hopefully tomorrow and deliver to you.* Then a conflicting message told Mashaal that the money had been returned to Ghana and wonders *what to do with it as Susan Smith is still coming to the bank requesting it.* Then the following message arrived from Kofi. Was he confused? Was there more than one Kofi?

From:   Malaraexpert@aol.com (Malaraexpert@aol.com)
To:     (the detective)@winnipeg.ca
Date:   Friday, September 14, 2007 10:38:08 AM
Cc:     (omitted)
Subject: Fwd: URGENT REPLY NEEDED


DEAR SIR,
WE CANNOT BE ABLE TO SEND THE CONSIGNMENT BACK TO GHANA
,THEREFORE WE AREWORKING TO SEND ANOTHER TEAM TO TORONTO TO
COEM AND MAKE THE DELIVERY TO YOU. I WILL UPDATE YOU AS SOON
AS THEY ARRIVE AND THEY SHALL CALL YOU FOR YOU TO SEND THE
FUNDS TO THEM SO THAT THEY CAN START COMING TO DELIVER TO
YOU AT HOME.

THANKS
KOFI

In the message below, Kofi said that the money was back in Ghana. In the message above that was sent only six hours earlier on the same day, he said: *We cannot be able to send the consignment back to Ghana.* Kofi suggested that Mashaal was *required to come here and retrieve the funds or come and clarify yourself.* Can you imagine what might have happened to Mashaal if he were to have gone to Ghana with Martins arrested and in jail in Winnipeg? If you read some of the articles in the Internet in Google, *Ghana Corruption*, you could easily imagine his fate. One of the most gruesome stories in that website concerned the young Greek man who was challenged to meet the Nigerian mafia in Durban, South Africa. All that remained of him when found was a dismembered body. That was similar to the fate that Dr. Mashaal might have met that Monday night after Martins' made a phone call from the Winnipeg Remand Centre. It is probably very fortunate for Dr. Mashaal that he did not go to that home to administer medical help to that unknown person. His innocence paid off to his advantage that time; it likely saved his life.

Dr. Mashaal told me that he had told Kofi on the phone that due to the deterioration of his health, he was leaving for three months to Australia and New Zealand in an attempt to recover. He had hoped this would get Kofi *off his back.* Then he finally sent the message below after many attempts from Kofi to hear from him. In this message, he gifted the $10.5 million.

Dr. Agnes Chambers-Glenn

From:   Malaraexpert@aol.com (Malaraexpert@aol.com)
To:     (the detective)@winnipeg.ca
Date:   Friday, September 14, 2007 4:30:47 PM
Cc:     (omitted)
Subject: Fwd: ref your e mails dated 14 Sept 2007

Dear Nr Kofi

Many thanks for your two E Mails .I was out to visit my
physician and just now I received your two E mails.
As you know the lady who gave the 10.5 Million dollars to me
was aiming to use the money to help children and poor people
. But as my health is not so good,therefore I cannot use the
money to help people as this requires great efforts

Therefore I decided to give you the 10.5 Million Dollars and I
hope you can use a good part to help children and poor people.
Therefore you pay $ 7800 at the air port Toronto and do not
send the parcel to me.I authorize you to take it on my behalf
The team you are sending to Toronto can receive the the
money and send it to you and not to Winnipeg.

Also within few days I shall go on a holiday trip to
Australia and NewZealand for few months in order to improve
my health.Very soon my both Computor and telephone will not
be in use

I wish to thank you for your help
Dr.Hassan A.H.Mashaal

Following is a message from Kofi finally revealing that he is
aware of Martins' arrest.

TO: Malaraexpert@aol.com (Malaraexpert@aol.com
Subject: Fwd: ref your e mails dated 14 Sept 2007

Dear Sir,
You have arrested wrong person,please is better for you
leave him or you face more problem,you told me that you have
not seen james but why do you arrest innocent person,do you
know him or ever seen him before,please don run away to
australia ,make sure you tell the police to release wrong
person because even here late smith wife has file a motion
against the bank that yoou have stolen their money so why do
you go ahead and arrest wrong person,the funds is back in
ghana so you are require to come her and retrieve the funds
or come and clarify yourself
Thanks
KOFI

172

When a message arrived announcing a visit on Saturday, September 15, by another representative of Kofi's, named Mathew, Mashaal contacted the detective by e-mail and also placed a call to him via cellular phone, but he had left his office for the weekend and did not respond that evening. Mashaal was very uneasy about a visit on behalf of Kofi's representative the following day, so I invited him to come to my home on the following morning where he would be free from the ringing of his phone and any visit that Mathew might pay him. However, he declined my invitation. I sent him a message again later that evening and repeated the offer saying I would leave my home for most of the day and he could have it to himself, but still his reply was *No*. I was very worried about him as the stress from his involvement in this scam was really showing.

However, the next morning at 9 o'clock Dr. Mashaal phoned me and said he had changed his mind and was ready to leave his home and wanted to come to mine for the day. So within ten minutes I was at his home to pick him up and drive him to my house, and I left him as I had promised and went to help a friend. When I returned after 5 p.m., he told me that he thought he would return home around 7 p.m., so at that time I drove him home. He said that on the following day he would remain in his own home and would ignore all phone calls, faxes and e-mails. He did that for even I could not reach him the following day. Around noon I rang up from the entrance of his building but there was no reply. Knowing the prognosis of his heart condition was a concern for Dr. Mashaal and his friends, and with no reply, I was worried. The heart specialist said that his condition could cause him to drop dead from a heart attack without warning. His heart condition was most likely created by all the stress, frustration and fear from Kofi's money game, but his doctor was not aware of his involvement in the Nigerian money scam. With no response, I left his building and decided to check back around 2 p.m. Again at the later time there was no response to the ringing bell. I tried every two hours receiving no response with each visit. He had not replied even to my earlier e-mail. Dr. Mashaal told me later that he simply rested on his bed the entire day and only checked his e-mail after 9 p.m. Upon seeing my message, he phoned me knowing that I was concerned about his health. Had I not received that phone call or an e-mail from him, I planned to go to his home before bedtime and ask the site manager if she would allow me to accompany her to his apartment with her master key and check on him. His late phone call was very welcomed and made that visit unnecessary.

On Monday morning, the detective phoned and apologized for not having answered Dr. Mashaal's message late Friday afternoon about Mathew's announced visit to his house for Saturday. We do not know if Mathew did visit or not. At this time, the detective asked again to access his e-mail as he wanted to print more of the messages. We agreed that I would drive Mashaal to the police station where he could open his e-mail for the detective and the detective could print at his leisure those he wanted among the near 400 available. So, I drove him there at 10 a.m. and waited for him while a video was taped also. In the video, he gave a statement of the offence. However, when the video was checked, the camera had not been operating well so the taping had to be repeated and that was another 20 minutes' wait for me. In the afternoon of the following day, I drove him to a Hearing Center appointment. His health was really deteriorating as until he got himself involved with this Nigeria scam, he enjoyed excellent health with no prescription medication.

Following is one example of what the detective retrieved from Dr. Mashaal's inbox. This information was used by the police to trace the origins of the messages.

```
X-Apparently-To: vkamara77@yahoo.com via 209.191.125.56; Sun, 19 Aug 2007 10:33:07 -0700
X-YahooFilteredBulk: 207.183.238.112
X-Originating-IP: [207.183.238.112]
Authentication-Results: mta256.mail.re4.yahoo.com from=icbb.zzn.com; domainkeys=neutral (no sig)
Received: from 207.183.238.112 (EHLO c2mailgwalt.mailcentro.com) (207.183.238.112)
  by mta256.mail.re4.yahoo.com with SMTP; Sun, 19 Aug 2007 10:33:07 -0700
Received: from c2web203 (c2mailgwalt.mailcentro.com [207.183.238.112] (may be forged))
  by c2mailgwalt.mailcentro.com (8.12.8/8.12.0-c2mailgw03) with SMTP id I7JHWtOa031799
  for <vkamara77@yahoo.com>; Sun, 19 Aug 2007 10:32:55 -0700
X-Version: Mailcentro(english)
X-SenderIP: 41.210.20.213
X-SenderID: 11763400
X-RealDate: 8/19/2007 10:32:57 AM
From: "kofi banson" <kofi@icbb.zzn.com>
Date: Sun, 19 Aug 2007 18:32:54 +0100
X-Priority: 3
Priority: Normal
X-MSMail-Priority: Normal
To: vkamara77@yahoo.com
Subject: Fwd: NON INSPECTION CERTIFICATE NEEDED
X-Mailer: Web Based Pronto
Mime-Version: 1.0
Content-Type: multipart/mixed ;boundary=Interpart.Boundary.11.22.33.M2Y27094
X-Virus-Scanned: by Mailcentro using amavisd-milter wirh reject option
Content-Length: 140120
```

During Dr. Mashaal's visit to the Police Station, he was given a Manitoba Victim Impact Statement to complete and submit to the Winnipeg Crown Office on Broadway Avenue. Some of the pages of the completed Victim Impact Statement appear below.

## The Manitoba Victim Impact Statement Program

# Personal Information

Manitoba 🐂

Because we may need to contact you again about your Victim Impact Statement, please provide us with the following personal information. The Prosecutions Branch of Manitoba Justice is collecting this information from you under the authority of the Victim Impact Statement Program. It will be used to carry out and administer the provisions of the *Criminal Code* (Canada) respecting Victim Impact Statements, The Manitoba Victim Impact Statement Program and *The Victims' Bill of Rights* of Manitoba.

Your personal information is protected by *The Freedom of Information and Protection of Privacy Act* (FIPPA) of Manitoba. We cannot use your information for any other purpose without your consent, unless the law permits it or requires it. We cannot share your information outside Manitoba Justice without your consent, unless the law permits or requires this. If you have any questions about the collection of this information, please contact your local Crown's office at one of the numbers listed below.

**Note:** This information will not be submitted with your Victim Impact Statement to the court. It is not intended to be accessed by the offender and/or their lawyer.

NAME: Dr. HASSAN ABDEL-HADI MASHAAL

ADDRESS: Apt. 1502 Sussex House, 230 Roslyn Rd
WINNIPEG MB R3L 0H1

BIRTH DATE: 02 / 05 / 1923
DAY MONTH YEAR

*By providing us with your date of birth, we can ensure that your statement is attached to the right court file.*

TELEPHONE NUMBER(S):
(204) 284-2448
HOME            WORK

Keep us informed about your address and telephone number. This information is necessary so we can contact you about your statement and your case. Please report any changes by calling your local Crown's office or **1-866-4VICTIM (1-866-484-2846)**

**CROWN OFFICES:**

| WINNIPEG CROWN OFFICE | THOMPSON CROWN OFFICE | DAUPHIN CROWN OFFICE |
|---|---|---|
| 5th Floor – 405 Broadway Winnipeg, MB R3C 3L6 Ph: (204) 945-2852 Fax: (204) 945-1260 | 59 Elizabeth Drive, Room 81 Thompson, MB R8N 1X4 Ph: (204) 677-6766 Fax: (204) 677-6516 | 114 River Avenue Dauphin, MB R7N 0J7 Ph: (204) 622-2081 Fax: (204) 638-4004 |
| **BRANDON CROWN OFFICE** 204 – 1104, Princess Avenue Brandon, MB R7A 0P9 Ph: (204) 726-6013 Fax: (204) 726-6501 | **THE PAS CROWN OFFICE** 300 – 3rd Street The Pas, MB R9A 1M5 Ph: (204) 627-8444 Fax: (204) 623-5256 | **PORTAGE LA PRAIRIE CROWN OFFICE** 200 – 25 Tupper Street N. Portage La Prairie, MB R1N 3K1 Ph: (204) 239-3343 Fax: (204) 239-3136 |

Ces renseignements sont également offerts en français.          MG-0106

**Victim Impact Statement – Page 1**

Dr. Agnes Chambers-Glenn

**PLEASE COMPLETE THE FOLLOWING SECTIONS**
(Please print or write clearly. If you need more space, please attach additional pages.)

1. **Emotional Impact:** Please describe how the crime has affected you emotionally.
Consider the effect of the crime on your life. For example:
   - emotions, feelings and reactions
   - spiritual feelings
   - lifestyle and activities
   - relationship with your partner, spouse, friends, family or colleagues
   - ability to work, study or attend school
   - counselling or therapy provided

AS A RESULT OF BEING SCAMMED FOR $35,750, I
Am VERY SAD + VERY ANGRY. Now I Am AFRAID TO
GO OUT IN CASE SOME OF HIS GANG, LIKE MATTHEW
MAY SEE ME AND HARIM FOR NOT GIVING JAMES
more MONEY + HAVING JAMES ARRESTED. I DO NOT
ANSWER MY PHONE NOR DOOR. I AM AFRAID. MY
HEART SPECIALIST, DR John Rabson, SAID MY heart is
racing at 100 instead of the usual 60. He said I could
drop dead without warning by a massive heart attack.

2. **Physical Impact:** Please describe any physical injuries or disabilities that you suffered
because of the crime. For example:
   - pain, hospitalization, surgery you have experienced because of the crime
   - treatment, physiotherapy and/or medication you have received
   - ongoing physical pain, discomfort, illness, scarring, disfigurement or
   physical restriction
   - need for further treatment, or expectation that you will receive further treatment
   - permanent or long-term disability

On Sept 18, 2007, I had to go to the Health Sciences
Centre and I had a heart monitor put on for
24 hours, then I must visit my heart
Specialist Cardiologist Dr. John Rabson, on
Sept 24. I do have some chest discomfort
from the tension caused by fear of Matthew
coming to my apartment for more money.
The physical pain causes some physical
restrictions.

**Victim Impact Statement – Page 3**

176

3. **Financial Impact:** Please describe any financial or property losses that resulted from the crime. For example:
   * the value of any property that was lost or destroyed and the cost of repairs or replacement
   * insurance coverage and the amount of the deductible you paid
   * financial loss due to missed time from work
   * the cost of medical expenses, therapy or counselling
   * any costs not covered by insurance

*I lost #35,750 to this gang and they were requesting more. I am on pension settlement a loss. They never sent me any of the money they promised to me. They continued to ask for more and more. I asked them to stop contacting me but they continue to but I don't pick up the phone now.*

This is not an application for financial compensation or restitution. If you wish to inquire about compensation, contact the Compensation for Victims of Crime Program at 204-945-0899 (Winnipeg) or toll free: 1-800-262-9344. If you wish to inquire about restitution contact the Victim/Witness Assistance Program at 204-945-3594 (Winnipeg) or toll free: 1-866-635-1111.

4. **Other Comments or Concerns:** Please describe any other concerns that have arisen as a result of the crime. For example:
   * other ways your life has changed because of the crime
   * how you feel about contact with the offender

*My telephone continues to ring day and night and disturbs me. I need it to call out and for the Internet. I shall cancel it on Oct 9, when I leave for several months in Europe. The calls are coming from Kofi in Africa and likely the gang in Toronto. I have traced them. I do NOT want any contact with James (in prison) nor any of his gang.*

**Victim Impact Statement—Page 4**

A couple of days later, I received a forwarded copy from Mashaal of Kofi's latest e-mail. In my diary, I wrote: *Not good! Frightening!* As I was leaving the following day for a two-week holiday, I believed I should inform the detective so I sent him a message telling him about my planned absence and my dread of leaving Dr. Mashaal alone in the city. Dr. Mashaal had few people whom he could depend on as his friend George had also gone on vacation the day after James Martins was arrested. So Dr. Mashaal had since George's departure relied heavily on my help, especially since the arrest.

In late September, having recently arrived in Europe, I recorded in my journal that I had sent a message to Dr. Mashaal from Prague, Czech Republic. That day I had spoken with an Australian couple who were on the same tour, and they told me that about six months earlier an African had been caught in London, England, involved in a similar money scam. Enough information was obtained from the arrested thief that the authorities were able to locate others involved in the extortion and recovered $80,000 for the elderly Australian victim. In the message I sent that evening, I asked Dr. Mashaal if I were to help him recover his money would he give me half of that recovered. In his reply the following day, he acknowledged that he would. I had in my mind a strategy for proceeding with a recovery plan. However, after more thought, search and reading in Google, I decided that I certainly wanted nothing to do with these people. Some stories were very brutal including the one about the Greek man of whom I made mention earlier. These people meant business and they were not to be fooled with. I read many experiences given on the website www.419eater.com, and I also Googled *Ghana Corruption*. That was enough for me!

In the message mentioned above, Dr. Mashaal also told me that he had received no further word from Kofi as of that date. Then on September 27, Mashaal forwarded a message from Kofi. It read as follows:

*DEAR SIR,*

*CONSIGNMENT HAS BEE SEND BACK TO GHANA SO HOW IS YOUR HEALTH AND YOUR FAMILY. JAMES IS ALSO HERE IN GHANA.*

*UPDATE ME*
*THANKS*
*KOFI*

Mashaal knew the above message was not true as he was aware that James Martins who was now known as Toluwalade Alonge Owolabi was in Winnipeg in the Remand Centre. By this time, Dr. Mashaal had started the perhaps useless and dangerous duty of trying to recover his lost money.

# CHAPTER 17

## ATTEMPTS TO RECOVER THE MONEY

The process of attempting to recover his money began in late September. First, he drafted letters to send to the three Accra, Ghana banks. Then he sent the drafts for approval to the detective. After learning the name of the managers of one of the banks, the following e-mail was sent to inform the bank that it had some very corrupt people in its employ—if they did not already know—and he wanted his money back!

```
From:  Malaraexpert@aol.com (Malaraexpert@aol.com)

Date:  Tuesday, September 25, 2007 2:48:18 PM

Subject: Fwd: STRICTLY CONFIDENTIAL

The Trust Bank Ltd
Reinsurance House
68 Kwame Nkrumah Ave.
P.O.Box 1862
Accra-Ghana-West Africa
Tel:233-21-222407 , 230403 , 230416 , 240049-52
Fax: +233-21-240056 / 9
E.Mail : trust@ttbgh.com

STRICTLY CONFIDENTIAL

Mr.Isaac Owusu Hemeng
Managing Director / Chairman

Dear Mr.Hemeng

Since few months ,a lady nemed Dr. Mrs Vivian Kamara Her E
Mail:vkamara77@yahoo.com . Iam sure this is not her or his
```

name but was put to hide the personality. She sent letters to me on printed forms of The Trust Bank Ltd.signed by her as management.She indicated that Linda Morgan before her death deposited US$ 10 ½ million US Dollars on my name in your bank.

It is possible one of your junior staff is corrupt and put his name as Dr.Mrs Vivian Kamara.Recently Vivian said another person will continue to correspond with me His name Mr. Kofi His phone:00233 2077 137 756.His Fax: 00448 709 382.His e Mail Address: Kofi@jobb.zzn.com
I hope you can investigate how these corrupt people managed to send official letters printed on your bank forms

May be they are some of your junior staff ,hiding their names.They requested US$25000as 2 ½ % fees of the bank totransfer to my account abroad one million Dollar.On their request the $ 25000.00 was sent to another Bank in Accra.At Last The Lawyer Adam Smith receivd the money but on his way to your bank to deposit $ 25000 he died in an accident and the money was stolen as Dr.Mrs Vivian reported.It is 100% sure they are thieves and stole many funds from different people.

These thieves managed to put your bank under unfavorable reputation . They must be caught and put in prison.
I hope you can manage to detect them who committed these irregularities. Your detail answer is more than appreciated.
Thank you
Best wishes


Yours sincerely
Dr.H.A.H.MASHAAL
United Nations Expert (WHO Pen.)
P.O.Box 2968 Winnipeg.MB
CANADA R3C 4B5

E.Mail : malaraexpert@aol.com

After approval from the detective, he sent the following letter to the CAL Bank addressing it to its Director.

From:  Malaraexpert@aol.com (Malariaxpert@aol.com)

Date:  Tuesday. October 2, 2007 8:11:31 PM

Subject: Fwd: Immediate answer

Dr. Agnes Chambers-Glenn

CAL BANK LTD
23 Independence Avenue
P.O.Box 14506 Accra
Ghana - West Africa

This letter was sent to E.Mail tdibranch@calbank.net but was
returned.Another E Mail is used today

Dear Director Cal Bank Ltd

In your bank an employee or client who has account
number 05102034926 Name: GOOD ROCK VFENTURES .He is an
international thief and stole money from many persons. At
the beginning I thought wrongly that Mr Good and his people
working with him are honest but now I am 100% sure they are
very dangerous international thieves

I transferred to GOOD ROCK VENTURES US$25000.00 in order
to deliver to Mr..Adam Smith (Another thief) in order to
deposit this sum to the Trust Bank Ltd in Accra. The Trust
Bank Ltd informed me once it receives US$ 25000.00 the bank
will transfer to my account in Germany One Million US$.When
Mr Adam Smith received the money from GOOD ROCK VENTURES and
he proceeded to pay it to The Trust Bank Ltd.On his way he
was killed by road accident and the US$25000.00 was stolen.
Of course all these stories were fabricated in order to
steal the US$25000.00
In your bank Mr GOOD ROCK VENTURES is very dangerous
international thief and must be punished
Your bank got very bad reputation , because of the acts of
Mr. FOOD ROCK VENTURES.It is appreciated to let me know the
following:
(1)Is Mr GOOD ROCK VENTURES an employee or client in you bank
(2)Account No: 05102034926 in your bank on name GOOD ROCK
VENTURES.Is it still working ? Is it possible to block the
deposits in this account ?In this case let me know what you
require to block this account.

Mr.GOOD ROCK VENTURES is an agent for a dangerous
international thieves.These are as follows:

(A)-Dr.Mrs.Vivian Kamara E.Mail:vkamara 77@yahoo.com
(B)-Mr Kofi Tel: 00233 2077 137 756 Fax; 00448 70382 E Mail:
Kofi@icbb.zzn.com
(C)-Adam Smith. Fax;00233-21-2382960. Mobile; 00233 243-403
E.Mail: adam-smith @lawyer.com and associate law firm@yahoo.
com
(D)-Susan Smith E.Mail: susansmith 233@yahoo.com

182

These are very dangerous group who destroyed the reputation
of your bank in Accra Ghana.They ought to be punished.
Your early answer will assist us to catch them. Thank you

Dr.H.A.H.MASHAAL
United Nations Expert (WHO Pen.)
P.O.Box 2968 Winnipeg. MB
CANADA R3C 4B5

E.Mail: malarexpert @aol.com

The following letter was sent to the Director of the Standard
Chartered Bank of Ghana.

From: Malaraexpert@aol.com (Malaraexpert@aol.com)
To:
Date: Sunday, October 7, 2007 9:02:15 AM
Cc:
Subject: Fwd: Urgent answer is required

The Director
Standard Chartered Bank,Ghana Ltd
P.O.Box 20 Tema-Ghana
Tel & Fax +233 21 7012205
Telex 2671

Dear Sir,
An employee or client to your bank MR.ANNOR-KUM RICHARD
His account number 870 152 135 4300
Swift Code SCBLGHAC
His personal addres :P.O.Box nt 12 community 20,tema-Ghana
His Telephone No:00233 242 977 878
His E.Mail: sakimatti@yahoo.com

I transferred to him from my bank in Winnipeg Canada a total
of US$ 3750
Later I realized he is an international thief and he stole
my money.His account ought to be blocked
Til policecomplete the investigation
He is cooperating with the following dangerous international
thieves:

(A)-Mr.Kofi : Phone.00233 2077 137 756
Fax: 0043 709 382
E.Mail:Kofi@icbb.zzn.com
(B)-Dr Mrs Vivian Kamara E.Mail : vkamara 77@yahyoo.com

This group+others are highly specialized international
thieves and ruined the reputation of Ghana

Dr. Agnes Chambers-Glenn

You are kindly requested to take the following actions:

1-Inform me wether Mr Annor-KUMI RICHARD is employee in your
bank or client.
His account number in your bank 870 152 135 4300
2-Can you block his account till the police complete
the investigation if required anything to block the
account,Please inform me

In case you answer early , this will prove that your bank is
not involved in the theft and corruption. However in case I
receive no answer this swill confirm that Standard Chartered
Bank,Ghana Ltd is heavily involved in corruption and theft.
I appreciate an early answer in order to reach to practical
solutions.

Thank you
Dr.H.A.H.MASHAAL
United Ntions Consultant (WHO Pen.)
P.O.Box 2968 Winnipeg.MB
CANADA R3C 4B5
E.Mail: malaraexpert@aol.com

Meanwhile, having waited for a week and no reply from his first
letter to the Trust Bank, Dr. Mashaal e-mailed a follow-up letter.
He demanded a reply from the authorities at the bank. This letter
follows.

From:  Malaraexpert@aol.com (Malaraexpert@aol.com)
To:    @Winnipeg.ca
Date:  Tuesday, October2, 2007 8:12:15PM
Subject: Fwd: Letter of 25 Sept 2007 NOT ANSWERED

The Trust Bank Ltd
Reinsurance House
68 Kwame Nkrumah Ave.
P.O.Box 1862
Accra . Ghanna.West Africa

Managing Director /chairman

Dear Mr. Isaac Owusu Hemeng

I wrote to you a detail letter dated 25 Sept 2007.I expected
to receive from you an answer as a Managing Director but you
never answered.

```
Within few days if I do not receive an answer; this will
confirm that some of the staff of the The Trust Bank Ltd are
involved in severe corruption and theft from me and other
clients and therefore one ought to report to the authorities
The Trust Bank Ltd is considered the worse bank in the
world because some of its staff took illegal money from
foreigners.I had detail forms to proove the
corruption.In case you do not answer necessary actions will
be taken.Therefore it is appreciated to answer before it is
too late

Thank you.

Dr.H.A.H.Mashaal
United Nations Consultant (WHO Pen.)
P.O.box 2968 Winnipeg
MB.CANADA R3C 4B5

E.Mail:malaraexpert@aol.com
```

While still in Europe, I received another e-mail from Dr. Mashaal in which he made reference to Kofi's message that stated that both James Martins and the consignment were back in Ghana. Mashaal declared that Kofi's message was *a big lie* as he knew that James was being held in the Remand Centre in Winnipeg at that time. Most probably Kofi thought that this message would get a response from Mashaal. Kofi had tried several tricks to date in an attempt to get a response from him, but as yet he was not successful.

One day while I was still on the tour in Europe, a fellow tourist cut an article from the October 4, 2007, International Herald Tribune, an American international newspaper, and gave it to me. It reported that more than $2.1 billion in counterfeit cheques had been seized and that 77 people arrested in an international crackdown on scams in the U.S. Postal Service. Officials of the United States, Canada, Nigeria, the United Kingdom and the Netherlands were involved. It stated that most of the cons started with an e-mail that told of an inheritance of a lottery win and asked victims to help bring the money to the United States.

A few days after I returned home from the European tour, I drove Dr. Mashaal to the airport for his flight to Germany where he would stay for the next six months. He mentioned that he hoped he would be free from harassment. Only time would tell.

Once settled into his home in Germany, he forwarded messages to me that he had received from different characters in his African ordeal. He also told me about telephone conversations he was still having with Kofi and Vivian. However, eventually with a change of telephone/fax number in his home in Germany, the phone calls ceased, but a few e-mails continued to arrive as he refused to change his e-mail address. He had an extensive list of people in his e-mail address book—friends from around the world—and he feared that he might lose the list if he cancelled that e-mail box. He said he just would not reply to any e-mails from Ghana with the hope that soon all messages would cease. Eventually, he did change his e-mail address also. Following are most of the e-mails that were received after he arrived in Europe. These he forwarded to me to update the material he had given me in September as he wanted his story recorded. As the detective had advised him to no longer reply to any messages, he did not send copies to him. The detective had told Mashaal in a message that he could not help him recover any of his money and advised him to cease all correspondence with the gang.

On October 14, the following message arrived after many days of no messages. Notice it was from the UK from a Michael Raymond who identified himself as the uncle to the late Linda Morgan. Although Michael Raymond sent this message three times, Mashaal ignored each copy giving no reply and hoping that the thieves would leave him alone. Notice the tremendous improvement in typing and in the English used by Michael. You will recall that at the time dying Linda Morgan offered her inheritance to Dr. Mashaal she said she had no living relatives. Well, one had surfaced.

```
Date:   Sun, 14 Oct 2007 02:36:35 +0100 (BST)
From:   "Michael Raymond" micraymond202@yahoo.co.uk
Subject: Attn Mashaal, Hassan Abdel-Hadi
To:     malaraexpert@aol.com
HTML ATTACHMENT { Scan and Save to the Computer }
Attn:Mashaal, Hassan Abdel-Hadi

Dear Sir,

I want to use this medium to extend my greetings to you,
I know that you will be surprise to receive this message,
because we have not had any previous correspondence in the
past.
```

I am Micheal Raymond, the uncle of Ms.Linda Morgan who
passed away in Ghana about some months ago. I want you to
kindly assist me in an investigation that is going on,
because I would like to know what is the present development
with the fund that suppose to be released to you. I contact
Ms. Susan Smith the wife of Late Adam Smith to know were the
fund is currently deposited, I was informed that the fund
has been taken to Canada for the delivery to you.

I want you to get in touch with me immediately, because I
would like to know what is happening to my niece fund that
is in your custody.

I will be expecting your prompt response.

Thanks,
Michael....

The message that follows was received by Dr. Mashaal from
Kofi who was pleading with him to correct matters with the bank.
It would appear that Mashaal's letters reached the banks; however,
there were *no* replies from any of the bank officials. It appears that
so-called Kofi may well have been an employee at one of the banks
since he knew about Dr. Mashaal's most recent letter sent to the
bank. It would appear that some bank employees may have been
involved in this money scam, and perhaps Kofi—whatever his real
name, but an employee at the bank—was very frightened that his
participation in these illegal and corrupt banking acts had been
discovered by his bank superiors. I found that this message was
received on November 8.

Dear Sir,

I have try to reach you but proof vain,However the parcel
has been at Amsterdam's since all this whiles since it was
your name that is the receiver but the most issue that
happen here is that the late dam smith wife come to our
office with the a relative that claim that you send letter
to the CAL BANK where you send to the late smith's but it
may interest you to know that the bank account does not
belong to late smieh,it was only use to receive the funds to
do the job for you,so i am pleading with you to kindly write
back to the CAL BANK to apologies that you did not mean what
you write to the them because the bank is creating problem
with the owner of the account that say he suppose to send

```
you $1m usd but the CAL'S BANK has nothing to do with this
transaction so please try and amend this problem with the
bank.

Also,let me know your final decision on the parcel since you
are back in Germany.

Waiting to read from you,
Regards,
Kofi
```

Three days later another message arrived from Kofi. In it he said that he did not work in the CAL BANK, but Vivian had introduced Mashaal to Kofi some time ago as the person who assumed her position to tend to his account at that bank. Kofi had assumed the responsibility of getting the late Linda Morgan's money out of Ghana to Mashaal in Switzerland, Germany or Canada. It would still appear that there was a problem now at the bank with the employees and the illegal accounts they had established. See e-mail below.

```
From: Malaraexpert@aol.com (Malaraexpert@aol.com)
To:    (deleted)
Date: Saturday, November 10, 2007 9:51;20 AM
Subject: Fwd: (no subject)

---Inline Message Follows---

Dear Sir,
As you know that i do not work at CAL BANK but i have
contact late adam smith wife to get the details for me so
that i can send to you to correct the letter ,its really
affect the owner of the account as the account doesn't
belongs to the late adam smith ,i guess he only use it to
receive the documentation require by your swiss bank?

Will update you soonest and since you will be going to
london then why dont we send the consignment to london for
you to pick it up?

Regards,
Kofi
```

From the above message, Mashaal learned that Kofi suggested sending the money from the Toronto International Airport to London for Mashaal to pick it up there. Or was it that they had a plan to silence him? Can you imagine the problem of clearing the money through London Customs whether it was $1 million or $10.5 million and then having to forward it to one of his bank accounts—in Switzerland, Germany or in Canada?

Next day there was another plea from Kofi to Mashaal begging him to send a message to jschriever@alumnidirector.com and ask the receiver to disregard his earlier letters to the bank in which he had asked the bank to investigate its employees. It was obvious this *gang of thieves* had their contacts in London as they did in Amsterdam, Australian, the USA, Toronto and Durban, South Africa. The message follows:

```
From:  malaraexpert@aol.com (Malaraexpert@aol.com)
To:     (detective)@Winnipeg.ca
Date:  Sunday, November 11, 2007 2:15:24 AM
Subject: Fwd: (no subject)

---Inline Message Follows---

Dear Sir,
This is the email contact that i got for now: jschriever@
alumnidirector.com

if you can kindly write them that they should disregards
your letter dated on ......... and so on.

please,send copy of what you send to me,also you did not
reply regards to the consignment if to be freight to london
for you to pick up .
Regards,
Kofi
```

This message only encouraged Dr. Mashaal to send another e-mail letter a few hours later confirming his complaints to the CAL BANK LTD. It was addressed to Kofi as well as to the Director of the bank as shown below. Perhaps this might put Kofi deeper into trouble with his bank. Why would Kofi have suggested a pick up of the money in London when in a previous message he had mentioned that the money was waiting in Amsterdam as was Susan Smith? Other locations that he had suggested for the money pickup were Ghana, New York, Winnipeg, and Toronto. Do you recall that Kofi had said on at least two occasions that it was not possible to return the consignment to Ghana? However, on at least two occasions since, he suggested that Mashaal go to Ghana to claim the money. Was Kofi confused since Dr. Mashaal had complained about him and others to the managers of the Ghanaian banks?

It was on November 11 that Dr. Mashaal sent me the message in which he said that his heart condition had worsened and he was looking for medication. He asked me to contact a Chinese doctor friend of mine in China and ask for herbs for helping to cure *atria fibrillation*. So, I spent hours on the Internet searching for two drugs that he had mentioned and asked if I could find them in Canada. I found only sites that offered people suffering from this problem to enter hospital experiments in several countries including Canada. The drugs were not yet approved to go on the market. You will recall that Dr. Mashaal had developed this heart condition in the days leading up to James' arrest—waiting for James' visit in Winnipeg.

That same day, Dr. Mashaal also sent to the CAL Bank a follow-up letter in which he demanded his money to be returned. Notice it was directed to Mr. Kofi *and* the Bank Director. He had a few matters to clear up with the Director. It was *Good Rock Ventures* that he believed had his money and that organization certainly included Adams Smith and others who were benefiting from his money. A copy of the following message was sent to the detective.

```
From:  Nalaraexpert@aol.com (Malaraexpert@aol.com)
To:    (detective)@winnipeg.ca
Date:  Sunday, November 11, 2007 7:42:35 AM
Cc:    (deleted)
Subject: Fwd: Analysis
To Mr.Kofi
and
To Director CAL BANK LIMITED
       23 Independence Avenue
       14596 Accra Ghana

The claim of existing 10.5 million Us Dollars is not true.
It is mentioned only to clients in order to steal money
from them.It was said this millions of dollars were sent to
Toronto and now it is said it was sent to Amesterdaym.This
100% was not correct
```

Also all the names mentioned as Linda Morgan,Adam
Smith,Vivian Kamara etc etc are not their real names. their
Ghana names is well known to us now

The name of GOOD ROCK VENTURES is correct Ghana name
My Swiss Bank in May 2007 transferred US 5000$ to Cal Bank
on name Good Rock Ventures.Adam Smith requested that so he
will not state his Ghana name.
Also another transfer To Cal Bank to Good Rock Ventures of
US $ 2000 was made in June. Similarly my German Bank in June
2007 transferred US$ 25000 to Cal Bank ,also on name of Good
Rock Ventures.
Mr Adam Smith never died in accident.This was said in order
to take the 25000$ illegally between Adam Smith And his
friend Good Rock Ventures

Cal Bank Ltd never answer my letter wether Good Rock
Ventures is emplpyee in the bank or client His account
Number 051 020 349 216.No answer because the Cal Bank is
also involved in this corruption.

To cut the story short.I request the payment of $5000
+2000+25000 US$ to be returned to me by Good Rock Ventures
and his collegues involved.If this takes place.The subject
is closed for ever but in case not Mr Good Rock Ventures ,
Adam Smith (not his real name) and others including Cal Bank
will be subjected to very serious trouble by the Government
and the court because they spoiled badly the reputation of
Ghana.

I advice Good Rock Ventures and his group to manage
to return my money back to close the subject without
complications.

Dr. Hassan A.H.Mashaal

On November 11, the same day as the above e-mail was
sent—and only a few hours later—Mashaal received a message from
Susan Smith. It appeared that she too was very concerned about the
letters that he had sent to the CAL BANK. She claimed she was
in Amsterdam and would like to meet him there. What she meant
by her final statement keeps one wondering what she intended: *I
believe you are an elderly man, choice is your's.* Following is the
copy he forwarded to the detective.

Dr. Agnes Chambers-Glenn

From:    Nalaraexpert@aol.com (Malaraexpert@aol.com)
To:      (detective)@winnipeg.ca
Date:    Sunday, November 11, 2007 2:42:50 PM
Cc:      (deleted)
Subject: Fwd: ref email 18 August 2007

Since you do not believe and you think my late husband is
still alive then go ahead and do what ever pleases you, the
GOOD ROCK VENTURES and CAL BANK has no business with this
transaction which i am ready to testify if matter arise,
i read all your communication with my late husband,you
are the one first contact him in the first place, i am
presently at Amsterdam's and if you ready to see me i am
here for now, your letter to CAL BANK AND GOOD ROCK will
not solve anything because the issue of sending the money
to my husband is totally different issue which you ask him
to do a job for you so why now asking CAL BANK or GOOD ROCK
question.

I believe you are elderly man, choice is your's
Susan

You will recall that before Dr. Mashaal had left to spend the
winter in Europe, the detective had advised him not to respond to
any more messages because he realized his health was failing due
to his frustrating involvement in this event of paying out money
and receiving nothing. At this time, Dr. Mashaal told me that his
misfortune would make a great book to warn others not to get
involved. He said to me, "*Please commit my story to paper.*"

Below you will find his reply to Susan's above message. Why
would he give her his bank information now? The money and Susan
Smith are supposed to be in Amsterdam. It appeared that perhaps
Mashaal was confused by the latest message as she had told him that
she and the money were in Amsterdam. (Note: The bank account
given in the message below has been closed.)

Dear Mrs Susan

Many thanks for your letter
The bank in your country send the money to UNITED STATES
TRESURY VAULT if you give me the address in USA of Tresury
Vault where the money was transferred I am able to see you
in USA

My bank account in Canada as follows

Dr.Hassan A.H.Mashaal
Account # 5703 4058 8759
Bank of Montreal
330 Portage Avenue
Winnipeg, Manitoba
CANADA R3C 0C4

Thank you.Best wishes

Dr.Hassan A.H.Mashaal

In the following message to Kofi, Mashaal again uttered threats of exposing the *corrupt gang of thieves* in the hope that his money would be returned. No doubt Kofi has had such threats many times during his corrupt career of extracting money under false pretences.

From: Malaraexpert@aol.com <Malaraexpert@aol.com>
To:    (detective)@winnipeg.ca
Cc:    (deleted)
Sent:  Monday, November 12, 2007 12:52:08 PM
Subject: Fwd: ref your maul of 12 Nov 2007

Dear Mr Kofi
You know very well Mr Adam Smith knew that the 10.5 'Million Dollars never existed.It was a method to steal people.Highly professional theif..He never mentioned his Ghana name.
Mr. GOOD ROCK VENTURE knew very well that his name was not Adam Smith but accepted to get my US$ 5000+2000+25000 to him inspite his name was not Adam Smith except in our correspondences
Mr GOOD ROICK VENTURE Knew very well that Mr Adam is a thief but because he share some benefit with him he accepted to get the money on his name.Also Cal Bank supported him and responsible too

I have detail information which I cannot mention to you which proove beyond doubt That both GOOD ROCK VENTURE and CAL Bank are involved
In order to consider that GOOD ROCK VENTURE AND CAL Bank are not guilty,They must get the money back and send it to me otherwise they will be charged heavily

Also you knew very well that no money parcel of 10.5 Million Dollars were sent to Toronto or Amesterdam. You belong to

193

Dr. Agnes Chambers-Glenn

the group and one day you will be responsible for your
actions

Dr.Hassan A.H.Mashaal

Kofi replied to the above message perhaps attempting to clear
the name of *Good Rock Ventures*. Before any money had been sent
starting in May/June from Switzerland to Ghana, Mashaal had
wondered about the name of that bank account to which he had been
asked to send the money. However, he still sent money expecting
to gain much more money. That money he sent was to be used to
purchase the necessary documents to legally get his inheritance out
of Ghana and into his bank account in Switzerland. The deceased
lawyer Adams Smith and Ms Vivian both had directed him to send
money to that specific account. No doubt it was set up only to
collect the illegal money for the *gang of thieves* who operated this
scam. The message below was from Kofi but he did not sign it. It
was forwarded to the detective.

From: Malaraexpert@aol.com (Malaraexpert@aol.com)
To:    (detective)@winnipeg.ca
Cc:    (deleted)
Sent: Monday, November 12, 2007 12:52:08 PM
Subject: Fwd: Analysis

---Inline Message Follows---

Dear Sir,
Let be realistic,GOODROCK VENTURE never know you or have any
dealing with you so its imperative that trying to involve
GOOD ROCK VENTURE which might result to court issue because
the director of GOODROCK makes us to understand that its
not a crime to receive funds on behalf of somebody since he
doesnt know the kind of business both of you are dealing
into,which all of us knows that for in ghana law you can
assist someone to receive the funds and give to the receiver
so when you are sending the funds to adam smith,did you
ask or have agreement the good rock director that if the
transaction that you are dealing with adam smith is not
favourable you will hold him responsible for it?or did you
contact cal bank that you are sending money to goodrock
account?

Good rock is only an account holder in cal bank not a staff
and i never see where the good rock is been involved in
this tansaction,if you are not interested or claim that
the transaction is false then go ahead and sue the late
adam smith or contact her wife susan smith that is now at
amsterdam has you claim the deal those not exist.

I wish you good luck in your findings because GOOD ROCK
VENTURE has never in anyway ask you to send money to their
account,what you do is on your own risk.

Regards

Get your Free E-mail at http://icbb.zzn.com
Get your own email service at ZZN.COM.

On November 13, 2007, the detective wrote to Dr. Mashaal
and acknowledged that he was receiving his forwarded messages.
He included very wise advice for Mashaal as shown in the letter
below. It was after receiving this message that Dr. Mashaal ceased
forwarding messages to the detective but continued contact with the
African scammers and continued to forward incoming and outgoing
messages to me for his mentioned future book.

Good Morning Dr. Mashaal,

I have been receiving the copies of emails you have sent to
Kofi and Susan. I understand that this is a very frustrating
situation. Unfortunately I don't think there is any chance
of recovering any money that you have sent to individuals.
They are corrupt and as such use false names and you may be
receiving email responses from different people pretending
to be "Kofi" etc. In the past they have been known to take
turns taking on the identity of different persons.
I understand that your health is not well. I would advise
you to stop corresponding with these people and attempt to
reduce the stress in your life.
When "James" has his day in court we will try to recover
some of your money in the form of restitution.
I hope that you are enjoying your time in Germany and please
take care of yourself. These people have taken your money,
don't let them take your health as well.

(signed by the detective)

On November 15, Dr. Mashaal received a message from a Mr. Michael Godfred who introduced himself as the Branch Manager of the Standard Chartered Bank. He made no reference to the message that Dr. Mashaal had sent to his bank on October 7. What an inviting offer he had for Mashaal! Does this not make you wonder about the honesty of this bank director and employees? Michael Godfred was most probably just another character, or a recycled one, in the money game. He probably hoped to extract more money from what he believed to be a rich, elderly person. His English and typing did, however, show a vast improvement over Kofi's and others. It was, however, very similar to another Michael, the uncle of the late Linda Morgan who e-mailed Dr. Mashaal from the UK and to whom Mashaal never replied.

Sent: Thursday, November 15, 2007 10:37:43 AM
Subject: Fwd: Attn: Dear Dr. Hassan A.H.Mashaal

Attn: Dear Dr. Hassan A.H.Mashaal

I am Mr.Michael Godfred, the branch manager of Standard Chartered Bank Ltd(SCB).You might not know me very well but by the end of this transaction you shall be thankful knowing somebody like me. During the end of our auditing of accounts at my Branch Bank last year ending, I came across a ghost account, in which the account reads the sum of $21,550. ooo.oo (USD) (Twenty-One Million, Five Hundred and Fifty Thousand United States Dollars).

I continued in my search and discovered that this said account was owned by one of our deceased customers. And there was no next of kin affixed at the time of the deposit. Although personally I kept this informatio's secret within myself to enable the whole plan and idea be profitable and successful during execution. And it's my obligations to send my financial reports to our headquarters' in Accra. Before then i decided to place this money in what we call SUSPENSE ACCOUNT without any beneficiary.

As a Senior Officer in the Bank I cannot directly claim this money here in Accra, on this ground I contact you for us to work together, so that you can assist and receive this money at any of your nominated Bank account for us to share. I have so placed this fund for the sharing 30% for you 50% for me and the remaining 20% for any miscellaneous expenses in the course of the transaction.

I will also want you to understand that it is 100% risk
free and legally blinded. It will strictly be bank to bank
transfer: all I need from you is to represent the real
depositor of this fund in our bank, so that my head office
can order the transfer to your designated bank account.

However, if my offer is granted by you,please do furnish me
with the following information's: Your Full name,Occupation/
Position, Contact Address, Date of Birth,Place of Birth,
Marital Status,Edcuational Status, Tel/Fax Numbers,
Nationality, Name of Your Next of Kin and Tel/Address,To
enable me fix your information in our account data file, so
that you will be recognized in our bank as a customer before
the onward transfer will be made.

I will appreciate it very much, if this proposal is accepted
by you.

Best regards,

Mr.Michael Godfred,

Branch Manager

What would be the rationale for the Branch Manager requesting
all the information that Mashaal had given to the bank on more
than one occasion already during the process of trying to move
those funds? Mashaal replied to Godfred only to show him that he
would not be tricked again by deceit. He was also hoping that the
correspondence from the corrupt gang would cease so he would be
left in peace to restore his health as that was more important now
than his lost money. True to Mashaal's character, he closed uttering
his usual threat.

Sent: Thursday, November 15, 2007 4:50:43 PM
Subject: Fwd: ref e mail dated 15 Nov 2007

Malaraexpert@aol.com wrote:

Mr.Michael Godfred

What you mentioned in your letter 100% not true
This is a system by corrupt organization to take money from
people illegally

```
In case I receive any letter from you I shall inform the
Police in Accra about this corrupt organization so that the
staff of this organization out to be in prison

Dr.H.Mashaal
```

Still messages continued to arrive in Mashaal's inbox. Godfred professed to Mashaal that he was not a person with fraud intent. Would his guarantee entice Mashaal to accept his offer? The message that is shown below appears to be Kofi's writing and style. You will notice that the English is not as good as in Godfred's previous message.

```
Dear Dr.H.Mashaal,

Thank you so much for your reply.

I am not among of those people fraud by using the Internet.I
am calling you for the great opportunity between you and
I.I am giving you that you will not regret,if I read from
you that you have ready to join with me to complete this
transaction and I also stated this is 100% genuine and
authentic.

Once again,I am thanking you for your reply.

Regards,
Mr.Michael Godfred,
Branch Manager.
```

The above is the final message that Dr. Mashaal forwarded to me from his Ghana scammers. He was $35,750 poorer than when he began his involvement with Ms Linda Morgan eight months earlier. Much more important, his health was of deep concern to his Canadian friends.

On December 28, I received a message from him from Germany where he had gone for the winter months. In that message, he said that he was no longer being harassed by Kofi and his Ghana *corrupt gang of thieves*. He had finally changed his e-mail address and that cut off all contact. You will recall that he had much earlier changed his phone and fax numbers both in Canada and in Germany.

Dr. Mashaal's involvement in this Nigerian money scams from April 2007 to November 2008 had left him in very poor health.

# CHAPTER 18

## THE DETECTIVE &
## RESOLUTION OF THE CASE

In mid-October 2007, the detective informed Dr. Mashaal by e-mail that the trial had not yet been scheduled. He thought *it might be a long time in coming*. And he said that he would keep Dr. Mashaal updated concerning the date for trial. In April 2008, Dr. Mashaal was informed by the detective that Toluwalade Alonge Owolabi, a.k.a. James Martins, still remained in custody awaiting his day in court. He said that his case was scheduled for hearings on June 5 or 6, 2008, and that his sentencing would be announced shortly after. At that time, it would be necessary to have a subpoena served on Dr. Mashaal to testify in court. The tape that was made in September at the police station would be used as would selected messages from the computer disk of e-mails and forms and the information that he had gathered from Dr. Mashaal's computer. Then the following message arrived later in April.

```
Date:   Tuesday, April 29, 2008 3:19:11 PM
Cc:     Malaraexpert@aol.com
Subject: Trial June 5-6, 2008

Good Afternoon,

I have just been notified by the Crown Attorneys Office that
Toluwalade Owolabi is pleading guilty to the charges. The
details of his sentence are still being worked out. When I
get the details I will be sure to let you know.

As such you will not be required to testify in court and I
will not need to meet with you to serve you the subpoena.
```

Dr. Agnes Chambers-Glenn

```
Thank you for all your help. I will be in touch with the
details of his sentence.

(detective)
Commercial Crime Unit
Winnipeg Police Service
Phone: 204-xxx-xxxx
```

What great news for Dr. Mashaal who recently had just returned to Canada after spending the winter in Germany. He appeared really upset over having to go to court. One could see his health deteriorating further from the stress and fear from all that had gone on and was likely yet to come. The detective also shared with Dr. Mashaal the possible charges against Owolabi as shown in the following e-mail.

Date: Wednesday, April 30, 2008 8:27:46 AM
Subject: Charges

Fraud Over $5000 Section 380(1)(a) Criminal Code
Fraud Under $5000 Section 380(1)(b) Criminal Code
Conspiracy to Commit Indictable Offence Section 465(1)(c) Criminal Code
Possess Property Obtained by Crime Section 354(1)(a) Criminal Code
Possess Credit Card Data Section 342(1)(c)(i) Criminal Code  ( 2 counts)
Personation with intent to gain advantage Section 403(a) Criminal Code

When I find out I will let you know which of these charges he has pled guilty to and what the sentence is.

Thank you for all you help.  Take care,

Commercial Crime Unit
Winnipeg Police Service
Ph: 204-986-

The May 8, 2008's edition of the Winnipeg Free Press contained an article that yielded very good news for Dr. Mashaal and his friends. Owolabi had pleaded guilty to conspiracy to commit fraud for his role in the international con, which was uncovered last fall following an undercover Winnipeg Police operation. The article summarized the facts leading up to the arrest of Owolabi. It mentioned that an 84-year old retired Winnipeg doctor—a victim of a Nigerian e-mail scam—had given more than $35,000 thinking that he was to inherit more than $1 million. This inheritance the doctor planned to donate to Third World countries to be used to fight malaria. The doctor, a world-renown malariologist who had worked many years for the World Health Organization, had been contacted in early 2007 with the offer. The article named the perpetrator as 37-year old Toluwalade Alonge Owolabi, and said that he had pleaded guilty to conspiracy to commit fraud for his role in the international con that had been uncovered last fall by a Winnipeg Police operation. It continued that the Crown was seeking a 30-month sentence for Olwalabi and after release from prison would deport him back to Nigerian. However, his lawyer was seeking a penalty of less than two years. The judge would not give her decision until May 29. A sentence of more than two years meant that Owolabi would automatically be deported. A lesser sentence would allow him to fight to remain in Canada. The Crown Attorney added that *this was only the second case of its kind ever prosecuted in Canada despite the fact thousands have been duped by this scam.* The jail sentence followed by immediate deportation was the verdict that everybody was hoping for.

Then Dr. Mashaal received the long awaited message: Owolabi's sentence as shown in the message below.

```
To:    Malaraexpert@aol.com
Sent:  Thursday, May 29, 2008 12:37:38 PM
Subject: Sentencing

Mr. Owolabi was sentenced today. He received the 30 month
sentence that the Crown was asking for. This will also mean
that after he serves this sentence he will be deported.

Thank you for your assistance in this matter.

I wish you well.

(the detective)
Commercial Crime Unit
Winnipeg Police Services
```

The sentence handed down by the judge was greeted with immense joy by Dr. Mashaal and the friends who supported him during his dreadful ordeal with the Nigerian scammers who used Ghanaian banks to move their money. Dr. Mashaal learned that Owolabi had entered Canada as a refugee barely one year before his

Winnipeg arrest; and that during that first year, Owolabi had been arrested by the Toronto Police four or five times.

It was in August 2008 in Dr. Mashaal's residence that the domestic while cleaning found a cellular phone down behind the cushion of the sofa chair where Owolabi had sat that day almost a year earlier. He asked a friend to take it and buy the appropriate charger for the unit so he might determine to whom the phone belonged. Dr. Mashaal was very surprised when a series of African names and Ghana telephone numbers appeared in the address file. He asked me to contact the detective and ask if he would like to have this phone. The detective said that he always believed that there was another phone besides the one the police confiscated from Owolabi at the time of his arrest. That cell phone had only a few Canadian names and telephone numbers recorded in it. He said that he would be very happy to receive this *treasure*. A few days later, I drove Dr. Mashaal to the police station where he learned that the detective was working evenings that week. The doctor left the phone with one of the detective's colleagues—one of the four other police that took part in the arrest of James Martins eleven months earlier.

Further information was e-mailed in February 2009 to Dr. Mashaal from the detective. In this message he updated him on Owolabi's case saying *Mr. Owolabi is still in custody and will not be deported for some time yet.*

Certainly this event changed Dr. Mashaal's health and life. Today, his life was much slower than it normally was due to his serious heart problem. He tried to put this dreadful ordeal behind him and at 86 years of age he was making every attempt to enjoy life at its fullest. His wishes were that others would not be lead to believe in these Internet scams. That is the purpose of giving his correspondence to me, so his story would be told. He continued to forward to me other scam offers that he received before deleting them so some could be included in his book as examples of Nigerian scams like the one that deeply affected the quality of his life. He was determined that he would not be tricked again as one of these events are enough, even one too many in one's life.

# OBITUARY

Dr. Hassan Mashaal passed away in Germany in November 2009 in his 87th year. Upon returning to Germany for the winter, he visited his doctor and was diagnosed with liver cancer and had very little time to live. He flew immediately to the USA for treatment – the same clinic* that he believed cured his sister-in-law of her cancer. He was unable to complete the three-month treatment. After only one month at the clinic, he left Texas and returned to his home in Germany. He died one week later. He is buried beside Monika, his only child, on a hillside overlooking the German city. Monika died a tragic death in 2004 in her 43rd year in a motorcycle accident. Dr. Mashaal left no living descendants.

*Do you recall that very early in this scam story Dr. Mashaal had recommended this cancer clinic to Linda Morgan, the lady who had offered him her inheritance? Rather ironic!

From: Detective . . . . @winnipeg.ca
To: (name deleted)
Sent: Fri, September 3, 2010 1:48:31 PM
Subject: RE: Wondering if the deportation took place.

Hi, (name of Dr. Mashaal's friend)

I apologize for my extremely delayed response to your earlier e-mail. Yes, I have confirmed that Toluwalade Owolabi was deported in March 2009. He left Headingly Jail and was deported out of Toronto.

Sorry to hear about Dr. Mashaal's death. Thank you for letting me know.

Take care of yourself.
Winnipeg Police Service

# ℰ𝒫𝒥ℒ𝒪𝒢𝒰ℰ

## BE AWARE OF SCAMS

Newspapers and television constantly warn readers and listeners about the most recent scams. In the *Kingston Whig Standard* people were told to be aware *of the Nigerian princes asking for your money*. The article went on to say that *common sense provides the best protection from scams*. I have to highly disagree as I knew Dr. Mashaal as a person with the highest degree of common sense but with deep trust and naivety.

Scams at the time of completing the writing of *Double Deceit* were the federal income tax scam occurring in Canada and the grandparents' scam in Canada and the USA. Newspaper articles and television were warning people about these scams in which innocent people were becoming victims. By reading Dr. Mashaal's story and the examples that follow, it is my hope that readers will gain information about the great variety of scams into which people are being tricked. Everybody should be knowledgeable in making a decision whether an offer is bona fide or a scam. Most scams originate in Nigeria where it is a way of life for people to compete against one another in an effort to devise an idea to gain more money than a friend. Most of these *vultures* use e-mail today; however, some fantastic offers are received through telephone messages, while a few others arrive in the mail, especially for the elderly who are not computer literate. By exposing this information concerning scams, many people may be saved much money and heartache.

If you are told that you have won a large sum of money in a sweepstakes or by other means and it sounds *too good to be true*, it most probably is. Furthermore, if you have to pay some money to get your *winnings*, **it is a scam**!

As well as making wise decisions yourself, it may be necessary to watch your spouse and/or elderly parents carefully as thousands of dollars can disappear in just a matter of days. This can happen to anyone, anywhere, if one is not careful. It happened to Dr. Mashaal and continues to happen to unsuspecting and trusting people like the grandparents' stories recently told in the local newspaper. That story goes like this: The grandparents receive a phone call from a young person who poses as their grandchild asking for help by sending money to him, but they must not reveal this request to his parents. Grandpa or Grandma goes to the bank and withdraws the money and sends or prepares to send the money, usually by Western Union. In one quoted case Grandpa sent the money and found out later that he had been scammed. In the second case, a grandmother in the same town withdrew and prepared to send the money but had not done so because the employee in the money transfer office advised her not to. The employee said that she had just completed another similar case and this seemed very suspicious to her. She advised the grandmother to check with her daughter first. The grandmother phoned the grandson's home and was told by her daughter that her son was not in Quebec with an arrest problem but was at home.

The following pages contain several examples of different types of e-mail scam offers. These were selected from the many samples sent to me by Dr. Mashaal, family members and friends who knew that I was writing about a major money-losing scam.

www.419eater.com is a computer site where one can find recipients of scam letters interacting in a game of cat-and-mouse with the scammers. These people are very knowledgeable with the many tricks played by the Nigerian scammers and can make their responses hilarious. However, this would not be the outcome if the scam were for real.

*4-1-9 Schemes* frequently use the following tactics:

- Offices in legitimate banks and government buildings appear to have been used by impostors posing as real occupants or officials.

- An individual or company receives a letter or fax from an alleged official representing a foreign government or agency or a family. Most of the interaction between the parties is then handled by e-mail, fax, through money transfer offices, the post office or banks.
- Personal information along with banking particulars is requested from the victim.
- The confidential nature of the transaction is emphasized.
- Usually an offer is made to transfer millions of dollars into your personal bank account with a large amount paid to you for your involvement.
- You are often encouraged to travel overseas to complete the transaction—to Nigeria or another country such as the Netherlands, United Kingdom, South Africa, USA, etc.
- You receive numerous official-looking documents with stamps, seals and logo testifying to the authenticity of the proposal. These really convince people, like the doctor.
- Eventually you must provide up-front or advance fees for payment of various forms, taxes, attorney fees, transaction fees or bribes. Each fee is claimed to be the last one.

Other forms of scam schemes include: c.o.d. of goods or services, real estate ventures, purchases of crude oil or gold dust at reduced prices, beneficiary of a will, or recipient of an award or lottery.

The perpetrators of these fraud schemes are often very creative and innovative. Unfortunately, there is a perception that no one would enter into such an obviously suspicious relationship. However, a large number of victims are enticed into believing that they have been singled out to share in a multi-million dollar windfall for doing absolutely nothing to start the relationship. Money demands come later. In almost every case there is a sense of urgency and secrecy. This was stressed several times in correspondence between Dr. Mashaal and his Ghanaian contacts.

Dr. Mashaal's scam was the so-called Advance Fee Fraud. This is the most prevalent and successful type. In this scheme, a company or individual receives an unsolicited letter—in the doctor's case, by e-mail—from Accra, Ghana, claiming the sender is looking for a reputable foreign individual or company to assist in moving money out of Nigeria or another nearby western or southern African country. In the doctor's case it was out of Ghana. The recipient's bank information is necessary for a destination for the large amount of money to be transferred. In compensation, the sender will share the wealth for assisting in moving his/her funds. The criminals obtain the e-mail addresses from various sources but usually they send unsolicited mailings en masse. The sender claims that rather than give the money to the government, they have decided to transfer it to a foreign account and the recipient has been chosen for this movement and will be compensated for offering his/her services.

Early in the episode after going on the Internet and visiting 419eaters.com, I copied and sent information to the doctor that was similar to his situation with hopes that he would realize that he was involved in a scam. The message was about a brother and sister in Africa who were desperate to have a taker for their offer, but with no name available they simple addressed their offer to Sir (for example, Dr. Mashaal) and asked for help to get custody of their father's wealth upon his death.

A rather hilarious cat-and-mouse game between scammer (the brother) and the recipient (the non-believing e-mail recipient), was told on the website. The would-be scammed had questions. He wondered why this person's e-mail was registered in Californian when he said he was living in South Africa, so he decided to look into this further, but he decided to answer the e-mail anyways.

Although believing from the beginning that it was a hoax, the recipient decided to play along, but first he did an Internet search and found that these characters were sometimes referred to as the *Lads from Lagos*. Nevertheless, everything indicated that they were genuine con-men and the recipient wondered how they could actually manage to make a full-time living out of scamming people. On another website, he found a list of characters that these people had created. The sender was listed on that site as a *Prince*. However, he found no mention of the sister.

The recipient found another website that gave a brief outline of the *Nigerian Sting* and still another that gave an explanation of where the name *419 scam* originated. He found still a further explanation why it was not confined to Nigeria. In fact, the Nigerian *gang of thieves* had operatives in the USA. The recipient was determined to shut down this scamming site. That process he found was extremely difficult. He complained to the registered owner of the net block, but with no success.

Sending out such spam material is a criminal act as it is mailed out en masse to various addresses with a clearly criminal intent. Also the Exodus website carries an unequivocal policy statement which states that use of their network for spam or criminal behavior is expressly forbidden, and offenders will have their service terminated. An anti-spam policy should have placed some form of obligation on the new or temporary owners of the network believed to be *Cable & Wireless*. Nothing was returned to the recipient from the Exodus abuse mailbox. Apparently Exodus had been slow to take action even when they were solvent, preferring to let the abuse notifications die. With no reply, the recipient still attempting to have the e-mail of the sender shut down, contacted the abuse.net database and sent an abuse notification to the mailcentro's abuse mailbox. Almost immediately he received an e-mail.

He reported that he waited about 24 hours and then sent another e-mail to *Prince* to see if he was still able to contact him. The message appeared to be delivered meaning that the mailbox had not been de-activated. So he sent a notification of the incident to the *US Law Enforcement Agencies*. Their website claimed that they would not acknowledge receipt of reports that involved *No financial loss*. It was a week later that the recipient again decided to check the delivery status for *Prince* by sending another message and this time he received a notification indicating that the message could not be delivered: ***bad destination mailbox address***. However it was most probable that *Prince* had several other e-mail addresses.

When I went to *419 eater*, I found warnings to ignore the Nigerian scammers saying that *they are thieves, liars, and generally very nasty*. It also said that *most scams come from Western and Southern Africa; however, scams also come from other countries such as England, Spain, Ireland, USA, Canada, the Netherlands, Australia and many others*. The site also says that *these criminals are not poor people trying to scratch a living, but are very prosperous compared to their law-abiding countrymen, and many operate in highly organized and highly successful criminal gangs. Millions of dollars are stolen on a daily basis with absolutely no thought given to victims who are losing vast amounts of money, homes, relatives, jobs and even worse. And contrary to popular belief, it is not just greedy and stupid people that fall for these scams.* Perhaps you will recall from much earlier in this book that while reading about Ghana corruption, it said that the entire country is corrupt including the highest government officials. Dr. Mashaal was going to write a complaint letter to the President until he learned about the corruption that prevails in the entire country of Ghana. A complaint would most probably bring no results, he was certain.

Following are a variety of types of scams. I am scanning in some and re-typing others *as is* with the intention that those who read this book will never find themselves in any Nigerian scam. That's my hope and Dr. Mashaal's purpose of getting his story to the public.

The following example is of the type of a person asking for assistance to move money to a supposedly safe bank in another country, usually on another continent. This is similar to the scam that Dr. Mashaal found himself involved in except the money to be moved in this offer is in Hong Kong.

```
Date: Saturday, January 31, 2008 9:27 PM
Subject: Dear Sir/Madam: Endeavor To Read
Very profitable business for you...!!!
31/01/2008

Dear Prospective Partner,

I am writing to you on behalf of Mr.Kim Woo-Choong. My
name is Mr.Daniel Wu and I am a Managing Director at the
chinatrust Commercial Bank in Hong Kong. Our bank website is
www.chinatrust.com.

My friend Mr.Kim Woo-Choong has presented a delicate
transaction which will need the collaboration of a partner
like yourself to complete successfully. This is the
proposition. Mr. Kim Woo-Choong is in a diffucult situation
and he must immediately relocate certain sums fo money out
of the Chinatrust Commercial Bank in Hong Kong. Moreso,
```

this must be done in such a way that it must not be tied to Mr.Kin himself. I assure you that this is a legal transaction and the sum in question is currently deposited in the name of an existing legal entity in chinatrust Commercial Bank in Hong Kong. Your role will be to act as a business trustee and end-title holder to funds which are in excess of US$19 million. Everything will be done legally to ensure the rights to the funds are transferred to you and you will be duly compensated with a very good percentage of the total money. Please, you must have a viable legal company and a verifiable equity line of credit. For Mr.Kim Woo-Choong's current profile visit these sites:

http://www.newser.com/article/1A1-D8TS71900.html
www.news8.net/news/stories/1207/483974 share.html

You can call me for further details, terms and agreement.

Mr.Daniel Wu
Managing Director, Investment Banking Group
Chinatrust Commercial Bank

Another example of the same type follows. Perhaps, the reason that most money movement requests are made from western and southern Africa countries is the fact that they usually involve requests from families who have accumulated great wealth from transactions in oil, diamonds or gold. The letters generally request help to move their funds from an African bank to a safe haven and will compensate the foreign partner for allowing them to use their bank account.

What a ludicrous offer follows!

Sent Monday, December 10. 2007 7:16:13 AM
Subject: Fwd: FROM :EDEMA FAMILY.

FROM :EDEMA FAMILY.
ABIDJAN, COTE D'IVOIRE.
WEST AFRICA.
BUSINESS RELIONSHIP.

MY NAME IS RAPHAEL EDEMA. NATIONALITY OF SIERRA LEONE. I AM 25 YEARS OLD, STUDIED MARKETING IN BUSINESS ADMINISTRATION IN THE UNIVERSITY. I LOST MY FATHER YEAER BACK. MY FATHER WAS POISONED TO DEATH BY HIS BUSINESS ASSOCIATES ON ONE OF THEIR OUTING ON A BUSINESS TRIP. MY LATE FATHER WAS ONE OF THE DIRECTORS OF GOLD AND DIAMOND UNDER TIJAN KABBAH

211

Dr. Agnes Chambers-Glenn

GOVERNMENT. MY MOTHER IS AGED SHE IS 62 YEARS NOW AN OLD WOMAN. I HAVE THREE YOUNGER ONES WE ARE ALL LEAVING IN COTE D'IVOIRE SINCE PAST FOUR MONTH.

IT IS MY DESIRE TO WRITE FROM MY HEART HOPING THAT YOU WILL NOT BETRAY US. MY FATHER DIVERTED SOME HUGE SOME OF MONEY WHICH HE DEPOSITED WITH ONE GOOD BANK CALLED BICICI WHEN HE WAS ALIFE, IN FACT IN A BRIFE IINTODUTION. ALL THE INFORMATION WILL BE GIVEN TO YOU WHEN I HEAR FROM YOU. THIS MONEY TOTALING US$6,000,000.00 (SIX MILLION UNITED STATES DOLLAR ) NOW WE ARE SEEKING FOR A TRUSTED PERSON WHO WILL RECEIVE THIS MONEY INTO HIS/HER ACCOUNT FOR ONWARD INVESTMENT.

HOWEVER, WHAT WE NEEDED FROM YOU IS YOUR GOOD ASSISTANCE IN HELPING US TRANSFERRING THE SAID SUM TO YOUR ACCOUNT SINCE WE ARE INEXPERENCED IN THE WORLD OF BUSINESS, THAT'S THE REASON WHY WE ARE ASKING FOR YOUR SUPPORT. ALL DOCUMENTS CONCERNING THE DEPOSIT MAY BE GIVEN TO YOU FOR YOUR VERIFICATION. WE REALLY NEED TO MOVE THE FUND OUT OF AFRICA TO ABROAD.

I AND THE REST OF MY FAMILY HAVE DECIEDED TO GIVE YOU 10% OF THE TOTAL SUM FOR YOUR KIND ASSISTANCE. THE WORLD IS FULL OF BAD PEOPLE PLEASE CAN YOU PROVE YOUR GUNUITY TO US FOR US TO HAVE YOU AS PARTNER. SORRY I AM NOT SAYING YOU ARE BAD PERSON BUT CONSIDER THAT THIS IS MONEY AND HOW THE MONEY WAS GOTTEN. IT IS INHERITACE AND LAST HOPE.

ALSO EXPLAINED TO ME BEFORE THAT IT WAS BECAUSE OF THIS WEALTH THAT HE WAS POISONED BY HIS BUSNESS ASSOCIATES. THAT I SHOULD SEEK FOR A FOREIGN PARTNER IN A COUNTRY OF MY CHOICE WHERE I WILL TRANSFER THIS MONEY AND USE IT FOR INVESTMENT PURPOSE SUCH AS REAL ESTATE MANAGEMENT, HOTEL MANAGEMENT OR ANY OTHER INVESTMENT WICH YOU KNOW THAT MAY GIVE US A GOOD PROFFIT IN YOUR COUNTRY.

SHOW YOUR INTEREST AND WE PROCEED ON THE NEXT STEP OF ACTION. AFRICA IS NO LONGER CONDUSIVE FOR US TO STAY. YOU CAN CALL US ON TEL NUMBER ABOVE.

OUR BEST REGARDS.

RAPHAEL ON BEHALF OF THE FAMILY.

In March 2008, six months after Owolabi's arrest, a message arrived addressed to Dr. Mashaal's e-mail address from Vincent Quattara who had a fantastic offer for him. By that time, Dr. Mashaal's personal e-mail address must have been well-known by the Nigerian *gang of thieves* because only one day later, another offer arrived—again addressed to Dr. Mashaal personally. The messages are shown below. Notice that a French-language form was used for the first one while an English form was used for the second one. Perhaps the two e-mails were sent by the same person except the source of the second e-mail appears that it may have been sent from Egypt.

```
Subj:  READCAREFULLY
Date:  3/18/2008 4:56 P.M. Pacific Daylight Time
From:  vincentquattara2008@yahoo.fr
To:    malaraexpert@aol.com


Vous etes READCAREFULLY
        Invite:
Par votre Vincent Quattara
        hote:
Message:
Greetings,
My name is Mr. Vincent Quattara, Auditor and head of the
computing department here in our bank. I have only written
to seek your indulgence and assistance. I wish to make a
transfer involving a huge amount of $28,500,000USD (TWENTY
EIGHT MILLION FIVE HUNDRED THOUSAND UNITED STATES DOLLARS)
30% of the total sum will be your loyalty if you accept my
offer.

PLEASE INDICATE YOUR INTEREST, BY WRITING VIA MY PRIVATE
EMAIL (vincentquattara2008@yahoo.fr) TO ENABLE ME FURNISH
YOU WITH FU

Date: mardi, 18 mars 2008
Heure: 18 h 00 - 19 h 00 (GMT+00:00)
Viendrez-vous? Repondre a cette invation
```

Then another fantastic offer arrived from Aziz Kone who identified himself as Auditor and Head of the Computing Department in *our* bank. *Our* bank was identified as BOA Ouagadougou, Burkina Faso. It appears that Aziz Kone has two e-mail addresses as shown in his message below.

```
Subject:    URGENT RESPONS
Date:  3/19/2008 5:41 A.M. Pacific Daylight Tme
From:  aziz_kone107@yahoo.com
To:    malaraexpert@aol.com


You are invited to: URGENT RESPONS
By the host: Aziz Kone
```

Dr. Agnes Chambers-Glenn

Message:
Dear Friend,
I am Dr. aziz kone, I work in the foreign remittance
department bank of Africa (BOA Quagadougou Burkina_Faso.
I have a business which will be feneficial for both of us.
The amount of money involved is ($12.5 million us Dollars)
which I want to transfer from abandoned account to your
account. All to our financial benefit and our families.
This is 100% risk free.
Please do not hesitate to contact me Via: (azizkone2@aim.
com)
Best Regard,
Dr. Aziz kone

Date: Wednesday March 19, 2008
Time: 1:00pm - 2:00 pm (GMT +2:00 Egypt)

Will you attend? RSVP to this invitation

Be wary of those who come bearing gifts. There is a new and clever credit card scam that a friend recently told me about. It works like this:

Carol had a phone call from someone who said that he was from some outfit called *Express Couriers* asking if she was going to be home because there was a package for her, and the caller said that the delivery would arrive at her home in roughly an hour. And sure enough, about an hour later, a delivery man turned up with a beautiful basket of flowers and a bottle of wine. Carol was very surprised since it did not involve any special occasion or holiday, and certainly she didn't expect anything like it. Intrigued about who would send her such a gift, she inquired. The delivery man's reply was, he was only delivering the gift package, but allegedly a card was being sent separately. (The card never arrived!) However, there was also a consignment note with the gift.

The delivery man went on to explain that because the gift contained alcohol, there was a $3.50 delivery charge as proof that he had actually delivered the package to an adult and not just left it on the doorstep to be stolen or taken by anyone.

Since it sounded logical, Carol offered to pay cash, but the delivery person said that the company required the payment to be by credit or debit card only so that everything was properly accounted for.

Carol's husband, who, by this time, was standing beside her, pulled his wallet out with the credit card, and the delivery man asked her husband to swipe the card on the small mobile card machine which had a small screen and keypad and he was also asked to enter the card's PIN and give the security number. A receipt was printed and given.

To their horrible surprise, within the next four days $4,000 had been withdrawn from their account at various ATM machines around the city.

It appeared that somehow the *mobile credit card machine* that the deliveryman carried had all the information necessary to create a *dummy* card with all their card details.

Upon finding out the illegal transactions on their card, of course, they immediately notified the bank which had issued their card and their account was closed. They also went to the Police where it was confirmed that it was definitely a scam because several households had been similarly hit.

**WARNING:** Be wary of accepting any surprise gift or package which you neither expected nor personally ordered, especially if it involves any kind of payment as a condition of receiving the gift or package. Also, never accept anything if you do not personally know of, or there is no proper identification of who the sender is.

There are also the lottery-type scams that I received from friends. There were six different letters informing recipients of the large sum of money that they had won. I have shown here the one that arrived personally addressed to Dr. Mashaal. I received others—slightly different and originating from other e-mail addresses—sent to me by friends and family. One came from a Mexican friend living in San Antonio, Texas. She asked me if this was genuine as she believed that I was a specialist in detecting scams after preparing for the writing of this book. Of course, I told her immediately to forget about it as it was surely a scam. Another appeared to be from Denmark and sent to my friend in South Africa. A friend in British Columbia sent a copy of the scam that she had received. She was told that if she replied with the requested information, she would receive US$4.6 million although it had been sent from the

UK Lottery Organization (uklotterywinnings0201@yahoo.es). With the '*es*' designation, perhaps it was sent from Spain (The Spanish word for Spain starts with *es*.) or Estonia. And a friend in Manitoba was told in an e-mail addressed personally to her business that her business had won in cash $3 million British pounds Sterling. Amongst those received by Dr. Mashaal was another from SuperEna Lotto 2009 congratulating him on winning 7,947,183.69 Euros or US$10,185,110.62. Certainly the distribution of lottery scams is near world-wide. Following is an e-mail sample of a lottery scam.

```
From: euroepelots [mailto:euroepelots@mynet.com]
Sent: 13 September 2007 01:57 AM
Subject: Personal

SELECTED.Million Lottery EMAIL AWARD PRIZE

This is to inform you that your Email Address attached to
a Ticket Number: TL754/22/76 has won the prize Sum of:
2,000,000.00 )Two Million Euro),in an Email Sweepstakes
program held on the 11th of Sept 2007.

Do contact the Details below for your claim:
Attention: Mr. Fred Van
E-mail:pbankplc_1@yahoo.de
Phone: +316-272-351-41
Fax: +31-847-185-133
ReferenceNumber: 421/613/580-EB Serial Number: 176087,
Lucky Number:TL 22/15406 Batch Number: 42100546-934-VE

Furnish them with the following:
Names:
Phone/Fax number:
\Nationality:
Ref Number:
Batch Number:
Occupation:
Yours Faithfully,
Vjertis Von Adrian (Ms.) CPA.
```

Some scams are so ridiculous that one wonders who could fall for them. The scam that follows was found on Yahoo in the daily Canadian news. It was reported on May 10, 2008, that a Vietnamese man in Norway lost $35,000 to a 32-year old Frenchman after he was led to believe that by putting cash into a special liquid and leaving overnight that it would double its value. The Vietnamese man did so. He left a mixture of cash and blank bills in the liquid to marinate overnight expecting his cash would be doubled by morning. However, the following morning both cash and the Frenchman were missing. Days later, the Frenchman was arrested while trying to leave the country with nearly 200,000 kroner. The Frenchman said that he had come to Norway to find cars in mint condition to sell in Africa and was very surprised at being charged for cheating a gullible man out of 180,000 kroner.

Another site on the Internet reported that vacation scams and travel-related fraud are on the rise. It reported that the travel industry is in the top 25 industries for fraud despite warnings. The article said individuals fall prey to scams regardless of age, education or financial situation. It continued giving advice to people, so hopefully they would not be deceived and lose their money and their vacation. (Website: 50plus.com)

Friends also sent scams of the job offer types. A letter would inform the recipient that s/he had been selected for a position to work at home and to act as the representative of the company in a foreign land; for example, the United Kingdom now required help in the recipient's country due to the expansion of the British company overseas.

```
From:    "Scott Young" pnasca@pnapr.com
To:      <undisclosed-recipients:>
Sent:  Wednesday, November 21,2007 4:15 PM
Subject ******Online Job Vacancy******

Payments Managers Needed For New quarter 2007
United Asia Trading Company Ltd Group
Imports and Exports, General Merchants.
Unit 5, Wharram Street
Hull, HU2 0JB Humberside
United Kingdom
+44 703 194 7374

EMPLOYMENT JOB OFFER:

WE HAVE A JOB OFFER AVAILABLE FOR YOU IN RESPONSE TO YOUR
INITIAL REQUESTING THE JOB SEARCH DIRECTORY IS FOR USA/
CANADA ONLY WE ARE BASED IN UK, BUT WE HAVE BEEN RECEIVING
ORDERS FROM NORTHERN AMERICA, WHICH WE HAVE NOT BEEN ABLE
TO PROCESS COMPLETELY SINCE WE DO HAVE A PAYMENT RECEIVING
PERSONNEL IN THESE AREAS.WE HAVE DECIDED TO RECRUIT PAYMENT
```

Dr. Agnes Chambers-Glenn

```
OFFICERS ONLINE HENCE WE WILL NEED A REPRESENTATIVE TO
PROCESS OUR PAYMENTS IN THESE AREAS. IF YOU ARE INTERESTED.
KINDLY GET BACK TO ME WITH THE BELOW INFORMATION. AND I
SHALL SEND YOU MORE DETAILS WELCOMING YOU TO THE COMPANY.

FULL NAME::::::
FULL ADDRESS (STATE, CITY, ZIP CODE)::::::
PHONE NUMBER CELL/HOME::::::
OCCUPATION::::::
AGE ABOVE 21::::::

WARM REGARDS,

Name: Scott Young
Position: Payments Officer
Email:scottyoungcompany1@yahoo.dk
Time 24Hrs Daily
```

From the e-mail described below and sent from *yahoo.dk*, it would appear that the sender is registered in Denmark but his phone number, if valid, is in the UK. This employment offer was received by a friend who forwarded it along with other scams.

A Mark Anderssson—yes, three *s*'s here in his family name, but later there are only two—sent her an e-mail with the subject *Employment!* The offer started with *Congratulations to you.* Mark also offered a work online from home position. The person selected would be *paid weekly by RAC COMPANY.* Required was *a Representative/Book keeper in USA (and its ENVIRONS) and in EUROPE.* Mark described his company as *an integrated yarn and fabric manufacturing operations using the state-of-the-art textile equipment from the world's leading suppliers.* Andersson continued by saying that *Order processing,production monitoring and process flow are seamlessly integrated through a company-wide computer network.* Salary would be about $4,000 USD on the average per month, and *no form of investments were required* from the chosen employee. Best of all, the person would be *required to work only 1 to 3 hours per day* and could retain their current position as well. The tasks were listed which included that money would be moved by *either Money Gram or western Union Money Transfer or any Local Money transfers that take barely hours* so that Mark's *company would receive the customers payment almost*

218

*immediately*. Mark describes how the money payments would be divided and contradicts himself by saying that *the job takes only 3-7 hours per week*. He continues by saying that he *wants the worker who satisfies his company's requirements* after having begun with *congratulations*. So *if the recipient is a serious and earnest worker and wants to work for RAC COMPANY, s/he is to email and inform me what their interest is and are to send the following requirements below to get started with this job offer:-*
*APPLICATION FORM*
*FIRST NAME-*
*LAST NAME-*
*ADDRESS-*
*CITY*
*STATE-*
*ZIP CODE-*
*COUNTRY-*
*PHONE NUMBER (S)*
*GENDER*
*MARITAL STATUS*
*AGE*
*NATIONALITY-*

*ATTESTATION*
*According to how you have been briefed earlier by a qualified representative of this establishment. Your are required and mandated to receive payment on behalf of the above mentioned firm. You are to deduct 10% of all funds processed on a particular order and forward the balance payment via Western Union Money Transfer to any of RAC COMPANY regional warehouses that will be given to you later. You will notify the company a week ahead if eventually you want to discontinue this job so as to terminate all payment coming you way to avoid conflict.*
*In agreement to this kindly append signature below.*

*Mark Andersson*
*RAC COMPANY*
*+44-70111-41155*

Below is a message that was sent to me from friends in Winnipeg concerning another type of scam that is out there—advertising, selling or purchasing on the Internet. In an e-mail message John described his and his wife's ordeal as follows:

```
Hello,

Here is our story:
Last year we advertised our antique dining table and chairs
in the local Free Ads for Winnipeg. We were surprised to
receive an email the next day from an email address ending
in yahoo.uk. The fellow was really interested and since we
wanted $1200, he said he would send a local guy around to
pick it up.

He wanted to pay with a cheque for $3000 US, and we should
give his man the difference. After several emails and delays
of his man, we finally received a cheque in the mail for
$3000. When I took it to the bank to cash it, I asked them
to call the bank and verify the funds. What a surprise! They
found the bank account had been closed and had no money in it.

We started to get suspicious early on, and had some serious
doubts when the man with the .uk e-mail address sent us an
envelope postmarked in California, with a cheque drawn on a
South Dakota bank. ??????

We were lucky that we did not lose anything, but it just
goes to show, you have to be so very careful dealing over
the Net.

That's our story,
John
```

A story that involved purchasing on the Internet was reported by CBC news in December 2007. It said that a Canadian man lost $20K after an eBay bid. That article reported that this fellow was among the 1,000 Canadians who have been scammed on eBay through a tactic known as hijacking, and that the RCMP said that the online auction service is not co-operating with criminal investigations.

It seems that the fellow won an eBay auction for a car. He believed he was dealing with a reputable seller with a 98% customer satisfaction rating. He had purchased costly items from eBay before. With the car deal, still after six months there was no sign of the car or the $20,000 he had wired to the alleged seller. When he complained to eBay, the company replied telling him that someone had temporarily taken over, or hijacked, the seller's page, and that he would have to contact police and the FBI. The Anti-Fraud Call Centre spokesperson said that about 1,000 Canadians since 2000 had been victims of similar scams. They also said that eBay has never returned any phone calls to the RCMP. That article said that it appears that eBay is trying to hide the problem as it doesn't want people to know criminals have figured out how to abuse the site.

The RCMP spokesperson added that *there needs to be tougher laws so internet companies will act more responsibly.* CBC also said that *eBay did not respond to several phone calls and an e-mail* from them.

Then there was the article on the Internet about two 16-year old British girls being arrested for drug smuggling in Ghana. They were caught carrying several kilos of cocaine as they passed through airport security on their return trip home to Britain. Sentence had not been given yet, but it was stated that they could receive as many as 10 years in prison.

One of the students said that they *were given the two bags by two boys to deliver to another male at the airport in London.* The girls said they *did not know what was in the parcels.* A fellow called Jay in Britain paid for their airfares and told them to meet two people at the airport in Accra. Jay promised them $3,000 each to bring him from Ghana two laptop bags. These bags had cocaine concealed in false compartments. The two fellows at the Accra Airport who gave the laptop bags to the young British girls had not been caught.

One of my very religious friends was deeply offended by the scam from a Mrs Marie Jones (mrs.mariejones05@hotmail.com) as Mrs Jones *used the Lord Jesus Christ's name.* The message was addressed personally to my friend. She told me that *our Lord would not want this to continue,* and she asked if I could advise her with whom she should get in touch.

The greeting was *Dearest in Christ,* and the message concerned this woman recently becoming a convert to Christianity in the Federal Republic Benin. At 62 years of age, in addition to being a recent widow, she also was suffering from cancer of the breast with six months to live. Since she was doomed to die soon, and with no children, she wanted *all the wealth her husband left to her to be used to contribute to the development of the churches in the world.* She said, A*fter praying to our father in heaven, I opened my laptop and browsed to the chamber of commerce where I found you and selected you after visiting web site and I prayed over it. I am willing to donate the sum of $6.700.000.00 us dollars, to the less privileged. Please I want you to note that fund is lying in a bank.* (Does the Chamber of Commerce list individual personal names? My friend is retired and certainly has no business.) She was offered 30% of the funds for her help and the remaining *70% was to be used to fund philanthropic organization, orphanages* as the widow *did not want the money to be used in an ungodly manner.*

Mrs Marie Jones continued with her request/offer by saying that she would *have her lawyer change all legal documentation to the recipient's name to ensure that she would have the funds transferred into her name,* and she signed off by saying *I honestly pray that this money when transferred will be used for the said purpose, because I have come to find out that wealth acquisition without Christ is vanity. May the grace of our Lord Jesus the love of God and the fellowship of God is with you and your family.* And she stated, A*ll correspondence must be by strictly by email due to the condition of my health, but if you want to speak with my Attorney, that is fine and okay by me. His chambers will be representing my interest with you.* She awaited an urgent reply, and signed off: *Yours in Christ. Mrs. Marie Jones.*

You will notice that the following e-mail offer was sent directed personally to Dr. Mashaal almost three months after Owolabi's arrest. Dr. Mashaal was by then spending the winter in his home in Germany.

```
To:     malaraexpert@aol.com
Date:   Saturday, November 24, 2007 2:53:08 PM
Subject: Re: Buy Gold Dust

Dear Mashaal,

We have some quantities of 22+ carat alluvial gold dust
which we have decided to put on sale for sometimes now. We
```

are also capable to supply you more than 600kgs on monthly basis after a workable agreement with you/your buyer.

If you are interested to work with me, kindly get in touch with me immediately.

(FULL CORPORATE OFFER)
PRODUCT:.............................. -Alluvial gold dust(AU)
ORIGIN:.............................. Ghana Gold
QUALITY:.............................. 22+carat.
PURITY;.............................. :999.9/1000 (99.999)
PRICE PER KILOGRAM:...... $12,000USD(Negotiable).

Best regard,
John Poku
Skype:johnpoku
Tel:+233246049617

Again, prior to the income tax filing deadline, Canada Revenue Agency put out a warning to alert Canadians of a mail scam where a letter with pretense of coming from their office requested personal information claiming that they had insufficient information for the individual's tax return. CRA notified the proper enforcement authorities of that scam and advised readers to report deceptive telemarketing activity by visiting www.phonebusters.com or sending e-mail to info@phonebusters.com or call 1-888-495-8501.

A friend of mine in Hamilton who is very active in her church received the following request addressed to her personally. Do you suppose that there is a person in her church congregation connected to these scams? Perhaps, as some parishioners are of African origin. It does appear that this e-mail's owner is registered in France (hotmail.fr).

From: Brenda vandesie <brendamark@hotmail.fr>
To: D......
Sent: Thursday, October 25, 2012 1:36:24 PM
Subject: My beloved.

My beloved.
Greetings in the name of our lord Jesus Christ. I am Mrs Brenda Vandesie from Holland, a widow to late Mark Vandesie I am 69 years old, i am now a new Christian convert, suffering from long time cancer of the breast, from all

indication my condition is really deteriorating and it
is quite obvious that I won't live more than 2 months,
according to my doctors, this is because the cancer stage
has gotten to a very worst stage.

My late husband and my only child died last years, his death
was politically motivated. My late husband was a very rich
and wealthy business man who was running his cocoa business
in Cote d'Ivoire and after his death; I inherited all his
business and wealth. my doctors has advised me that i may
not live for more than 2 months, so i now decided to divide
the part of this wealth, to contribute to the development
of the church in Africa, America, Asia, and Europe. i
collected your email address during my desperate search on
the internet and i prayed over it.

I decided to donate the sum of $2,500,000.00 usd( Two
million five hundred thousand united states dollars) to the
less privileged because i cannot take this money to the
grave. Please i want you to note that this fund is lodged in
a bank in Ivory Coast in West Africa.
Once i hear from you i will forward you my late husband's
lawyer in ivory coast who will work the transfer legally to
you.I honestly pray that this money when transferred to you,
will be sure for the said purpose, because i have come to
find out that wealth acquisition without Christ is vanity.
may the grace of our lord Jesus the love of god and the
fellowship of god be with you and your family.

Please contact me in this my private e-mail id aranyite7@
yahoo.co.jp so that I will give you all the details
Your beloved sister in Christ.
Mrs Brenda Vandesie

The following e-mail was supposedly sent by Kofi Annan,
former Secretary General of the United Nations. I received a copy
from someone who had not lost any money to a scam. It has not
been checked for authenticity as it is assumed it was nothing more
than another type of scam to procure people's names and e-mail
addresses.

# Double Deceit

—Original Message—
From: un001n_17@peoplepc.com
Sent: Sunday, December 09, 2007 11:11 PM
Subject: Re SCAMMED VICTIM/US$ 250.000.00 BENEFICIARY.REF/PAYMENTS CODE 06654

 ZENITH BANK COMPENSATION UNIT, IN AFFILIATION WITH THE UNITED NATION. Send acopy of your response to official email: zenithbankplc117@yahoo.fr

ATTN:Sir/Madam,

How are you today? Hope all is well with you and family?,You may not understand why this mail came to you.

We have been having a meeting for the passed 7 months which ended 2 days ago with the then secretary to the UNITED NATIONS.

This email is to all the people that have been scammed in any part of the world, the UNITED NATIONS have agreed to compensate them with the sum of US$ 250,000.00 (Two Hundred and Fifty Thousand United States Dollars)This includes every foreign contractors that may have not received their contract sum, and people that have had an unfinished transaction or international business that failed due to Government problems etc.
Your name and email was in the list submitted by our Monitoring Team of Economic and Financial Crime Commission observers and this is why we are contacting you, this have been agreed upon and have been signed.

You are advised to contact Mr. Jim Ovia of ZENITH BANK NIGERIA PLC, as he is our representative in Nigerian, contact him immediately for your Cheque/International Bank Draft of USD$ 250,000.00 (Two Hundred and Fifty Thousand United States Dollars) This funds are in a Bank Draft for security purpose ok? So he will send it to you and you can clear it in any bank of your choice.

Therefore, you should send him your full Name and telephone number/your correct mailing address where you want him to send the Draft to you.

Conatct Mr. Jim Ovia immediately for your Cheque:

Person to Contact Mr. Jim Ovia
Email: zenithbankplc117@yahoo.fr

Goodluck and kind regards,

Mr. Kof Annan.
Former Secretary (UNITED NATIONS).
Making the world a better place

---

PeoplePC Online
A better way to Internet
http://www.peoplepc.com

A recent real estate scam follows. Friends of mine, Paul and Margaret have lived a nightmare for several months. This is for me one of the most troublesome scams that I have included in this section because to date they have been scammed out of a great deal of money, and health is now an issue.

We set one morning over coffee as they told me of their nightmare—a never-ending useless effort to sell their timeshare in Mexico. I thought of Sisyphus, the ancient King of Corinth, Greece. You may recall that he was punished in the Underworld for his trickery by being made to roll a huge boulder up a steep hill, and before he could reach the top, the massive stone would always roll back down forcing him to begin again. Sisyphus was consigned to an eternity of this useless effort and unending frustration. Frustrated and with little hope remaining and resigned to acceptance, Paul described their interminable activities of trying to find a sale this past year to end up disposing only of sums of money after being convinced that fees had to be paid to the Mexican government to discharge the ownership of the property. These fees were given by the Masons to a lawyer in California who had contact with the Mexican authorities, so that CA lawyer told them. Having shared Dr. Mashaal's frustration during his scam, I empathized deeply with Paul and Margaret.

Since purchasing the timeshare while on a vacation to Puerto Vallarta in 2004, Paul and Margaret have never returned to the timeshare as they always found an all-inclusive vacation package to Puerto Vallarta cheaper than airfare only. On one occasion only, Paul's brother and family spent a vacation at the timeshare celebrating a family festivity. Having initially paid US$23,000 and the first annual maintenance fee of US$350, those fees have steadily increased reaching US$750 this year. In addition, to date there has been one-maintenance fee. This property being expensive to keep, a decision was made to sell when on February 6, 2012, they received their first phone contact asking for Mr. or Mrs. Mason and offering them US$43,740 for their Mexican timeshare. Sounded great! So the process began. The caller sent in the mail an *Offer to Purchase*, and Paul and Margaret signed it *in good faith* and returned it by mail.

For the next four months, information was exchanged between the seller and the attorney for the buyer. It seemed that during this period it was not unusual for a change in the buyer to occur along with changes in legal offices and lawyers and that necessitated the sales process to start all over again. Still Paul tried to satisfy the requests as they so badly wanted to rid themselves of the foreign property as to date he calculated that he was indebted to about US$50,000 considering the initial cost, annual fees, a one-time renovation cost to date, and all the sums of money sent in the legal sales transactions between February 6 and May 31. Apparently, when the property was purchased in 2004, included in the deed was a clause stating that the annual maintenance fee would continue for 99 years. Perhaps this 99-year clause is a huge problem in a sales transaction. To date, apparently none of these offers to purchase have been legitimate. It was on May 31 that Paul sent a message and asked, *Is this truly a scam!!!*

Consideration was given to just forgetting about the property and *let happen what may*. However, with a perpetual annual fee, it would only accumulate and my friends would be approached later to pay up. I was asked if I wanted the timeshare at no cost. No thank you with that 99-year clause. Is this not a nightmare?

Besides all these examples of scam invitations that friends sent to me, I have one of my very own. I personally got caught. Who? Me? I was considered by my friends to be an expert in recognizing scams! Yes, in January while I visited an office in my city, a receptionist had told me about a letter she had received from Hotmail telling her to send information or her mailbox would be closed. But her Hotmail box was closed although she had sent the requested information. I thought, *Oh well she was late in sending the requested information.* Then a month later I received a message from *Windows Live Team*. I believed it best that I send the information on time. I did not notice that the reply was directed to turtlebaby@hotmail.com because it came to my inbox on what appeared to be a Hotmail business form. I replied sending all the information asked for **except** my password saying that Hotmail would have that on file, so there was no need for me to give it. Immediately, I received a reply saying that it would be best if I also included my password, so I replied with my password believing that it was Hotmail/Microsoft who would receive that message. Little

Dr. Agnes Chambers-Glenn

did I realize that my mailbox would be hijacked. That e-mail from *windowslivesteam* has been scanned below. This is a very popular e-mail that I have received at least five times in my Hotmail box. It appears that Hotmail had done nothing to warn their users about this scam. And as for help after being hijacked, I found it necessary to pressure them for help in recovering my mailbox.

Doesn't the message that follows appear to be sent by Hotmail through Windows Live Hotmail Team? It did to me! I did panic somewhat as I did not wish for my account to be closed as it was my only e-mail account, and I used it almost daily.

**Verify Your Account Now to Avoid It Closed 9VX2G99AAJ)**
From: windowslives team (turtlebaby79@hotmail.com)
Sent: 13 February 2009 09: 45M
To: (Unknown)

Dear Account User

This Email is from Hotmail Customer Care and we are sending it to every Hotmail Email User Accounts Owner for safety. We are having congestions due to the anonymous registration of Hotmail accounts so we are shutting down some Hotmail accounts and your account was among those to be deleted. We are sending this email to you so that you can verify and let us know if you still want to use this account. If you are still interested please confirm your account by filling the space below.Your User name, password, date of birth and your country information would be needed to verify your account.

Due to the congestion in all Hotmail users and removal of all unused Hotmail Accounts, Hotmail would be shutting down all unused Accounts, Your will have to confirm your E-mail by filling out your Login Information below after clicking the reply button, or account will be suspended within 24 hours for security reasons.

**\*Username:** . . . . . . . . . . . . . . . . .
**\*Password:** . . . . . . . . . . . . . . . . . .
**\*Date of Birth:** . . . . . . . . . . . . . . .
**\*Country Or Territory:** . . . . . . . .

After following the instructions in the sheet, your account will not be interrupted and will continue as normal. Thanks for your attention to this request. We apologize for any inconveniences.

Warning!!! Account owner that refuses to update his/her account after two weeks of receiving this warning will lose his or her account permanently.

Sincerely,
The Windows Live Hotmail Team

Three days later, around 8 a.m., a friend phoned me to see if I was at home as she had just opened her mailbox and found a message sent by me the previous day saying that I was stranded in Malaysia having been robbed of my small leather bag containing my money and documents and needed money to pay my hotel bills and to buy food until I left for home. We had seen each other only a few days earlier and she wondered why I had not mentioned that I was on my way to Malaysia. Below is the letter that was sent out by the hijackers with my name after the final *Sincerely*.

From: (me)
Subject: Please I need your help
To: (receiver—my friend)
Date: Monday, February 16, 2009, 8:33 AM

I am in a hurry writing you this message. I don't have much time on the pc here, so I have to brief you my present situation which requires your urgent response. Actually, I had a trip to Malaysia for a program called "Empowering Youth to Fight Racism, HIV/AIDS, Poverty and Lack of Education, the program is taking place in three major countries in Asia which are Taiwan, Singapore and Malaysia. But unfortunately for me, my little bag where my money, passport document's and other valuable things got stolen at the hotel where I lodged due to a robbery incident that happened in the hotel. I have been so restless since last night, the present condition that I found myself is very hard for me to explain, I am really stranded here because I have been without any money, I am even owing the hotel here as well, moreover the Hotel's telephone lines here got disconnected by the robbers and they are trying to get them fixed back. I have access to only emails at the library because they also took my cell phone which I have all my contacts. I am now owing a hotel bill of $1,200 and they wanted me to pay the bill soon. I need this help from you urgently to help me back home, I need you to help me with the hotel bill and I will also need $1,000 to feed and help myself back home. So please can you help m with a sum of $2,200 USD to sort out my problems here. I am sending you this email from the city Library, I will appreciate what so ever you can afford to send me for now and I promise to pay back your money as soon as I return home. So please use the details of one of the hotel managers below to send the money to me through Western Union money transfer because that is the only way I could be able to get it fast and leave since he has a valid ID to pick up the money for me from the western union office here. These are the details below . . . .

Dr. Agnes Chambers-Glenn

Name: Jerry Kingson
Address: 298 Jalan Loke Yew, Bandar Melaka, Malaysia
Test question: To whom
Answer:

After you have send the money, email to me the western union money transfer control
number or you can attach and forward to me the western union money transfer receipt so
that I can pick up the money fast and leave.

Thanks and get back to me soon.

Sincerely,

(signed with my name)

Shocked and angry, frantically, I tried to open my Hotmail
but had been denied access. Somebody had obviously changed
my password and had possession of my hotmail. My mailbox
had been hijacked! Having a mailbox in Yahoo, I went into it
and although most of my contacts were different in it, there were
some duplications, so I simply sent out a message to all listed and
apologized to them for the letter scam and asked them to please
ignore it as I was at home and not short of money. However, in the
meantime I did receive messages from friends who were only in my
Hotmail Contact list and had not received my message to ignore. A
friend in my Hotmail who had received one of my requests knew
me well and my financial state. He suggested that I call my son
and ask him to go to my bank and send money from my account.
Messages from two other letter recipients wondered if I was really
in Malaysia and out of money. I had my Visa so would not have
requested help from the people whose email addresses were in my
Hotmail Contacts. Later some told me that they were considering
helping me out if my request was true. A friend in Hong Kong who
had received one of my requests knew me well and my financial
state. He said that he had been hijacked also and that is probably
where the scammers had gotten my e-mail address. A Chinese friend
whose e-mail address was in my Hotmail Contact list later told me
that he was working with his cousin in Singapore to send the money
on his behalf but had not yet sent any money by the time I finally
made contact with him. Later in the day of the hijacking of my
Hotmail account, I received the scam letter in my Yahoo mailbox

as that address was among my contacts in my Hotmail as I used it for forwarding messages from that box to the other. It was from that request for Hotmail upgrading information that allowed my mailbox to be hijacked. What an error! I should have realized that one gives their password to nobody!

When I found myself in this dreadful situation, I sent an e-mail to the detective who had prepared the plan to arrest Owolabi and asked him what else I could do to prevent my friends from possibly losing money since lacking addresses I had not been able to reach all of them who lived outside of Canada. He replied advising me to contact Phone Busters at 1-888-495-8501. I did so and was given a file number. I learned that Phone Busters are a group consisting of officers from the RCMP and the local provincial or city police force. One of their duties is to investigate Internet fraud. Then I found an address and sent a message to Hotmail but was told that I must contact Microsoft Customer Support which I did only to be told to contact Windows Live Technical Support—a runaround in attempting to reclaim my Hotmail account. These messages in an attempt to reach Hotmail were being executed from my Yahoo mailbox while I desperately tried to regain access and ownership to my Hotmail box.

Microsoft replied asking me to identify mail and contacts that I had in my Hotmail. I explained that I had opened it in 1999 when e-mail first came available in China where I was living at that time. I said that it might be difficult for me to recall names and addresses and e-mail messages saved. However, I was able to recall three messages that I had not erased from my inbox—one being an electronic airline ticket which would certainly have my name on it—and as well, the names of some people in my contacts list if the hijackers had not deleted these. I also told Microsoft how I believe that the Nigerian scammers had gained ownership of my box—from my Hong Kong friend and from my stupidity of replying to that scam message supposedly from Hotmail and finally giving them my password.

I was devastated when I received Microsoft's reply saying that I had not given them sufficient evidence that the box belonged to me. Desperate to regain control of my e-mail as I could not imagine what the scammers might do next, I returned a message to Microsoft Customer Support and offered to go to the police or a Commissioner of Oaths and swear an affidavit that I was who I said I was and that this Hotmail box did belong to me. It was a relief when the message came back that Microsoft had reviewed my information and sent the instructions as to how I was to go about regaining ownership. Immediately I followed the instructions and there I was back in my Hotmail e-mail box!

However, I was not entirely finished with the scam-letter problem. For the eight days that I had been locked out, I found three letters from a friend in China to the scammers and their two replies coaching him how to send money. All the while, he had been making arrangements with his cousin in Singapore to get the $2,200 US to the fellow at the hotel in Malaysia who was to pass it on to me. My friend's cousin was slowed down in the delivery as he was seeking the most effective means to transfer the money as he was not familiar with the process of moving money internationally. It seems that I had also been locked out of my Chinese friend's box as he had never received any of my desperate messages, only those messages from the scammers in their pathetically poor English language. I thought my friend would have known from the language that the messages he was receiving were not mine. Now after many days having no access to my Hotmail box or able to reach him, I finally got a message through to him and the next morning—two weeks after losing my mailbox—I received his message telling me how relieved he was that his cousin in Singapore had not yet sent the money on his behalf. Today, I have no Hotmail e-mail as my box was hijacked again and I gave up trying to convince Hotmail that it was mine, not the current owners. Since then, I lost my Yahoo e-mail after making a purchase on-line and having to give my 3 secret numbers on the back of the card. This recover was not as difficult to recover ownership as Hotmail had been.

Very recently, there was report in the newspaper of a person in my city who was tricked into the same scam as I had been caught in. It was determined that the hackers were sending their messages from Nigeria. In the article, it said that the hijacked person had abandoned her Hotmail account after a failed attempt to interest the company (Hotmail) in what was occurring. However, she had informed the police. I decided to phone the reporter and offer my help with the information of how to regain ownership of the lady's mailbox. So I phoned and left a message in the reporter's box and asked him to pass on my name, phone number and e-mail to the person who had lost her mailbox. However, I received no response. In that news report, it was mentioned that hackers a few months earlier had taken over the personal e-mail accounts of such high profile persons as Sarah Palin, Britney Spears, Barack Obama and the Fox News channel.

The Internet and e-mail communication have made it all too easy for scams to exist. The scams vary but usually an unsolicited victim will receive a letter asking them to partner with the sender and both will be richer after the transaction has been completed. In the examples that I have given in this section, it can be observed that there are several types of scams in which people get hooked. There are other types not described here such as the telephone call about your automobile warranty expiring or insurance scams as well as others. And one of the latest at this time is the phone call from some person posing as an official of your telephone company who tells you that the telephone company is carrying out a test and asks you to touch 90# and hang up. If carried through, it is reported that the caller then has control of your line and when your bill comes in, it could show thousands of dollars as your telephone number is used by the caller and gang to make calls all over the world. It is said that the telephone company is not forgiving when you are scammed. You pay up or lose your telephone service.

There are warnings that dealing with these scam criminals can be deadly. For example, the Australian government reported that fourteen people had been murdered trying to get their money back. Learning this, Dr. Mashaal gave up his attempts to recover his loss. It is not known what his fate may have been had he kept his scam to himself. We can only wonder what might have happened had he gone to Amsterdam to meet Susan Smith or to Nigeria to claim his inheritance. Or what might have happened if he had gone with the caller that evening to tend to the sick person in Winnipeg.

The information in this section was offered with the intention that readers will be better informed and thus better equipped to make wiser decisions when a scam letter comes their way—resulting in no loss of money and in retaining their good health.

Common sense may help to protect one from getting involved in a scam, but I know from my experience that it does not protect one entirely from it. Dr. Mashaal was a person with the most common sense of anybody I know or have known yet he trusted those scammers.

If you are contacted by a person or company making you a fantastic offer, check to see if they are registered by going to **www. osc.gov.on.ca,** or telephone **1-877-789-1555**. By doing so, your action also helps the OSC agency keep track of the current scams.

Following are some very helpful information and numbers should you need them. Another agency you can contact is the Anti-Fraud Centre (CAFC) @ 1-888-495-8501, formerly known as Phone-Busters.

Convenient numbers to keep handy if you live in Canada should you need to place an alert or fraud warning on your credit file:
- Equifax Canada 1-800.465-7166
- Trans Union Canada 1-800-663-9980, or 1-877-525-3823
- Experian 1-888-397-3742

To cancel a Credit Card or a Debit Card:
- For *VISA*: Contact the issuing financial institution.
- For *MasterCard* and *Amex*: Call the card company directly.

# Remember:

## *Never pay money to get money!*

### *And*

## *If it sounds too good to be true, It probably is a scam!*